Britain in the
European Union today

MANCHESTER
UNIVERSITY PRESS

Politics Today

series editor: Bill Jones

Britain in the
European Union today

Second edition

Colin Pilkington

Manchester University Press

Manchester and New York
distributed exclusively in the USA by Palgrave

First edition published 1995 by Manchester University Press

This edition published 2001 by
Manchester University Press
Oxford Road, Manchester M13 9NR, UK
and Room 400, 175 Fifth Avenue, New York, NY 10010, USA
http://www.manchesteruniversitypress.co.uk

Distributed exclusively in the USA by
Palgrave, 175 Fifth Avenue, New York,
NY 10010, USA

Distributed exclusively in Canada by
UBC Press, University of British Columbia, 2029 West Mall
Vancouver, BC, Canada V6T 1Z2

British Library Cataloguing-in-Publication Data
A catalogue record for this book is available from the British Library

Library of Congress Cataloging-in-Publication Data applied for

ISBN   0 7190 5790 6   *hardback*
          0 7190 5791 4   *paperback*

First published 2001

08 07 06 05 04 03 02 01   10 9 8 7 6 5 4 3 2 1

Typeset
by Helen Skelton, London
Printed in Great Britain
by Biddles Ltd, Guildford and King's Lynn

Contents

Preface to the
second edition

When I wrote the preface to the first edition of this book in November 1994 I stated quite categorically that British involvement in the European Union was one of that handful of subjects, present in all political science syllabi, that are inadequately dealt with, in that it is an area about which students are mostly ill informed. Apathy and ignorance of European issues on the part of both students and teachers are two important factors, but of even greater importance is the lack of correctly targeted information, for the teacher as much as for the student.

At that time there were a number of text books dealing with the European Community itself, but for the most part they either concentrated on the history and institutions of the Community or they discussed the economic or constitutional aspects of the Community in a very technical sense, and without any specific British dimension. That situation has changed to a certain extent in that there is an increasing number of resources available to those seeking basic information about the European Communities, not least the availability now of the massive Europa website on the Internet. On the other hand, it still remains difficult to keep up to date on European issues if the intention is to retain a clear, objective picture of what is involved. Too many of the words that have been written about Europe take the form of polemic argument, with a partisan agenda either for or against (but mostly against) the idea of European integration. As for the British press, it is so eurosceptic in its outlook that most newspapers only publish as many negative aspects of the European Union as they can find, while totally ignoring anything that might be held to be positive.

The European dimension is of increasing importance in British politics, affecting all the many different aspects of British legislation and decision making. There is also no doubt that the long debate over economic and monetary union has raised the profile of European issues considerably, especially over the question of sovereignty. Nor can we ignore the impact Europe is having on the political parties, a divisive issue comparable with the effects of the Corn Laws or Home Rule in the past.

A knowledge of the relations between the UK and Europe has been useful to candidates for some time, but now, with the increased emphasis on European issues in recent years, examiners are likely to lay even more stress and importance on this aspect of a candidate's answer. This is applicable to all students who are following a course in government or politics at school, college or university – which makes my point about the paucity of basic, objective source material even more relevant than it was in 1994. Hence this second and almost completely re-written edition of a book in which my aim has been to write a clear, concise and accessible account to cater for all politics students, as well as to members of the general public looking for clarification over British membership of the European Union.

At this point I feel I should make a disclaimer about my own personal position. I have tried, throughout my writing of this book, to retain a detached and unbiased view of Europe and of issues such as sovereignty. Readers, however, may detect a slight leaning towards pro-Europeanism on my part. I have to say that this is less because of a strong ideological belief than it is the result of the overwhelming euroscepticism of most British commentators, especially in the tabloid press, that have forced me to argue the pro-European position as a sort of devil's advocate in order to overcome their vicious and often inaccurate anti-European arguments.

I should like to thank Dr Bill Jones, the series editor, and Richard Purslow, then the commissioning editor for Manchester University Press, both for the trust and confidence they showed when they commissioned me to write the first edition of this work and for the help and encouragement they provided during the writing process. For later assistance at MUP, leading up to this second edition, I am indebted to Nicola Viinikka, who took over from Richard Purslow, and to Pippa Kenyon who kept me on the straight and narrow. As always, I owe a great deal to the team involved in examining politics at AQA-NEAB, in particular Dennis Harrigan and Cliff Jones, for making suggestions that were mostly useful. A relatively tame headteacher of my acquaintance, Dr Rob Gibson, spurred me on to greater efforts by showing, through his questions to me on behalf of his sixth form, just which areas most needed to be covered. A grateful acknowledgment is also due to many members of the Politics Association, but I am particularly indebted to Glynnis Sandwith of PARC.

I also have to say that I received much useful guidance as to what students actually need from those candidates whose work was submitted to me as examiner. Indeed, I should like to pay tribute to one student in particular. For his highly competent and merciless evaluation of the worth, usefulness and readability of resource material about the European Community I salute the work of Matthew Forrester, then a student at Leftwich County High School in Northwich, Cheshire. Matthew was only sixteen and a year eleven student when he wrote his critique, but his conclusions were very logical, incisive and mature, such as to give this academic writer considerable pause for thought as to how far what he had to say had any relevance or meaning for the average student for whom he was supposed to be writing.

We are in the midst of a period of major changes to the European Union and the next few years will see us plunged into a fresh round of growth and development. I trust that this book might help students to understand just what is happening in Europe and what impact that is having on the British political scene.

Colin Pilkington

Abbreviations

The European Union is littered with the acronyms which exist for the various institutions, treaties, agencies, political groupings, etc. The following is a glossary of the acronyms used in the text of this book. Readers may be puzzled when the initials of a supposed acronym do not agree with the meaning given, but as an explanatory example I give the meaning European Free Alliance to the ALE, although the acronym actually stands for *l'Alliance libre européenne*.

ACP	African, Caribbean and Pacific countries associated with the EC
ALE	European Free Alliance
BBQ	British Budgetary Question (1979–84) *aka* the Bloody British Question
BEUC	European Bureau of Consumers Organisations
CAP	Common Agricultural Policy
CCC	Consumers' Consultative Council
CECG	Consumers in the European Community Group (UK organisation)
CEDEFOP	European Centre for the Development of Vocational Training
CEEP	European Centre of Public Enterprises
CEN	European Standardisation Committee (not EU body)
CFP	Common Fisheries Policy
CFSP	Common Foreign and Security Policy (one pillar of the TEU)
Coface	Confederation of Family Organisations in the EC
COPA	Committee of Professional Agricultural Organisations
COR	Committee of the Regions
COREPER	Committee of Permanent Representatives
COSAC	Conference of European Affairs Committees of National Parliaments.
DG	Directorate-General of the Commission (there are twenty-three, differentiated by Roman numerals, e.g. DGVI, Directorate-General for agriculture)

DTI	Department of Trade and Industry (UK)
EC	European Community, merger of EEC + ECSC + Euratom (1967)
ECB	European Central Bank
ECHR	European Convention on Human Rights
ECJ	European Court of Justice
Ecofin	Economics and finance (Council of Ministers)
ECSC	European Coal and Steel Community (Treaty of Paris 1951)
ECU	European Currency Unit, used as a currency of account
EDC	European Defence Community, aborted in 1954
EDD	Europe of Democracies and Diversities (group in the EP)
EEA (1)	European Economic Area – applicant members of EFTA
EEA (2)	European Environmental Agency
EEC	European Economic Community – the original Common Market 1957
EFTA	European Free Trade Area, rival to EEC founded 1959
EIB	European Investment Bank
EIF	European Investment Fund
EIICA	European Inter-regional Institute for Consumer Affairs
ELDR	European Liberal, Democrat and Reform Party
EMCDDA	European Monitoring Centre for Drugs and Drug Addiction
EMEA	European Agency for the Evaluation of Medical Products
EMFC	European Monetary Cooperation Fund
EMI	European Monetary Institute
EMS	European Monetary System
EMU	Economic and Monetary Union
ENEL	Italian nationalised electricity industry
EP	European Parliament
ERM	Exchange Rate Mechanism, within the EMS
ERP	European Recovery Program, part of the Marshall Aid Plan, 1947
ESC	Economic and Social Committee
ESCB	European System of Central Banks
ETUC	European Trade Union Confederation
EU	European Union, made up of EC plus defence and security pillars
Euratom	European Atomic Energy Community (Treaty of Rome 1957)
Eurocoop	EC Consumer Co-operatives
Europol	European Police Office
FCO	Foreign and Commonwealth Office (UK)
GATT	General Agreement on Tariffs and Trade
GUE/NLG	Group of the European United Left/Nordic Green Left
I-EdN	Independents for a Europe of the Nations
IGC	Intergovernmental Conference

IMF	International Monetary Fund (of the United Nations)
MEP	Member of the European Parliament
NATO	North Atlantic Treaty Organisation
OECD	Organisation for Economic Co-operation and Development
OEEC	Organisation for European Economic Co-operation
OHIM	Office for Harmonisation in the Internal Market
PPE/ED	European People's Party (Christian Democrat) and European Democrats
PSE	Party of European Socialists
QMV	Qualified Majority Voting (in the Council of Ministers)
SCA	Special Committee on Agriculture (like COREPER but for agriculture)
SEA	Single European Act of 1987
TEN	trans-European network
TEU	Treaty for European Union (Maastricht)
TGI	Technical Group of Independent Members
TREVI	anti-terrorism group within the Council of Ministers
UEdN	Group for a Europe of Nations
UKREP	United Kingdom Permanent Representation
UNICE	Union of Industries of the European Community (employers group).
UPE	Union for Europe
VERTS/ALE	Group of the Greens/European Free Alliance
WCED	World Commission on Environment and Development
WEU	Western European Union, defence arm of the Council of Europe
WTO	World Trade Organisation

Introduction

Early in the nineteenth century the great Austrian statesmen, Metternich, faced with rampant Italian nationalism, stated contemptuously, *'Italien ist ein geographischer Begrift'* – that is to say, 'Italy is no more than a geographical expression'. And yet the term 'Italian' was always rather more than merely geographical. The concept of being Italian may not have been a statement of nationality, but it did make a statement about an entire people's culture, language and way of life, even though there was no cohesive political entity called Italy at that time.

What was true for Italy in the first half of the nineteenth century was equally true of Europe in the first half of the twentieth – 'European' meant an indication of geographical origin and could also be a statement of cultural identity, but had very little meaning other than that. The result has been that there have always been latter-day sceptics who dismiss the idea of European integration with as much contempt as Metternich showed for Italian nationalism. Nevertheless, despite Metternich's dismissal of the idea, Italians overcame their internal differences and did achieve political union. Similarly, throughout the twentieth century, there have been those who ignored the sceptics and, through their personal vision of a European identity, have sought ways in which Europe might be encouraged to develop its own political and economic union, just as the fragmented states of Italy and Germany had achieved unification in the late nineteenth century. As Hallstein, first president of the European Commission, said in his memoirs:

> Europe shares a sense of values: of what is good and bad; of what a man's rights should be and what are his duties; of how society should be ordered; of what is happiness and what disaster. Europe shares many things such as its memories that we call history ... (Hallstein, 1972)

It should be noted that while this book is about Europe and is about politics, it is not necessarily about European politics. Aimed at the student of British government and politics, the intention is to study the impact which the movement towards European integration as it has developed since 1945 has had upon the British peoples, on the British political system and on the constitution of the United Kingdom.

One factor emerges very clearly from any consideration of the European Union's history and present structure – that the debate over Europe has not been primarily about membership or non-membership, but about just what it is that politicians of the component states hope to gain from membership. Over the years there have been at least two perspectives governing attitudes towards what is seen as European co-operation and these two – often diametrically opposed – perspectives thread themselves through the historical development, lay constraints upon the function of European institutions and determine the degree of British commitment to the European ideal. To the casual and uninformed onlooker the impression is sometimes given that the only argument over Europe is whether Britain or any other country should ever have joined. In fact, although there always has been, and continues to be, a strong anti-European body of opinion in this and other countries of the Union, the real arguments that have influenced development over the years, and which continue to dominate discussions, are over different views as to the nature of EU membership:

- Should Europe be a federation or a confederation?
- Are politicians federalists or functionalists?
- Should the institutions of the EU be supranational or intergovernmental?

It must be stressed that the position on these matters adopted by individuals, parties, or even entire countries, does not follow a consistent pattern but tends to move according to the political climate or economic realities of the time. The labels given to these conflicting attitudes and institutions are terms that will be used throughout this book, so it may well be advisable to clarify their meaning at this point.

- **Federalists:** This is the name given to those who have, either explicitly or implicitly, the ultimate aim of creating a full political and economic union of Europe, with considerable powers in the hands of a federal government. On the whole federalists believe that the national interests of component states should be subordinated to the general good of the European Union as a whole. Used as a pejorative term by opponents, the 'f-word' is sometimes replaced by the term 'eurocentrism' to suggest the overthrow of national liberties by authoritarian centralisation in Brussels.
- **Functionalists** or **pragmatists:** These are those who, to put it crudely, are members of the Union for what they can get out of it. For them the institutions of the Union should be meetings of equals which negotiate the agreed outcomes that will best satisfy the individual needs of member states.

Functionalists are unwilling to surrender any aspect of national sovereignty but, for reasons of history, chauvinistic pride or for some other cause, believe in the supremacy of the centralised nation-state. Functionalists adhere to the Union for the pragmatic reason that it is more effective to co-operate than to face cut-throat competition in the modern industrial and commercial world, although it can also be seen as old-fashioned self-interested nationalism.

- **Supranational institutions:** These are the bodies favoured by federalists. Officials staffing the institutions are encouraged to think of themselves as loyal only to the Union, ignoring their former national loyalties: the policies they advocate are in the interests of all and take precedence over national positions. The Commission and Parliament of the EU are supranational institutions.
- **Intergovernmental institutions:** These are institutions where members discuss and negotiate as representatives of their national governments, retaining their national loyalties. These institutions are seen by functionalists as places where they can defend their national interests against the encroachment of federalism. The Council of Ministers and European Council are intergovernmental bodies.
- **Subsidiarity:** This is a concept that attempts to reconcile the federalist and functionalist positions and was enthusiastically embraced by John Major in the immediate aftermath of the Maastricht Agreement to show that functionalists can adhere to the European ideal without embracing federalist beliefs. Subsidiarity agrees that Community policy decisions should be made at the centre but that the way in which those policies are implemented should be decided as close to the people as possible. In other words the Union-wide policy is decided in Brussels but each individual national government can interpret that policy in the way which best suits the individual state's interests. Ironically, since subsidiarity was evoked to challenge federalism, that definition of subsidiarity is what many people understand is meant by a federal system. Since the spread of devolution in Britain after 1997 the meaning of subsidiarity has come to have new significance for the Scottish parliament and Welsh assembly.

It is important that these perspectives are borne in mind while reading this book because the behaviour of those involved, whether individuals, parties or governments, whether in the past or today, can only be properly understood in relation to their stance on the nature of Europe.

Finally, while considering terminology, it might be worth mentioning the use of the terms 'European Union' and 'European Community'. The European Community is the older term and is taken to refer to the three original communities established by the Treaty of Rome and merged in 1967. The Union, as established by the Maastricht Treaty with its defence and security 'pillars', is the wider of the two and all citizens of member states making up the European

Community are *de jure* citizens of the European Union. But all the institutions we think of as European, from the Commission and European Parliament to the Court of Justice, belong to the European Community rather than to the European Union. When the alternative terms 'Union' or 'Community' are used in this book there is a very subtle distinction of meaning between them but, as far as the reader is concerned, they both essentially refer to the same thing and should be regarded as interchangeable terms. The same apparently indiscriminate use of both labels is to be found used in literature produced by the EU institutions themselves.

Part I

History and structure
of the European Union

1

The origins and growth of the European Community, 1945–85, from the British perspective

The Briand Plan for a Federal Union of European States, named in honour of the then French foreign minister, was drawn up in 1929 by Jean Monnet, a young Frenchman working for the League of Nations. The plan was presented to European governments in 1930 but came to nothing when set against the rampant nationalism of the 1920s and 1930s. However, the idea sparked off something in the mind of that same Jean Monnet who, thirty years later, became known as one of the 'Fathers of Europe'.

Another key figure in the growth of a European identity was Winston Churchill, who, in a famous speech in Zurich on 19 September 1946, claimed that the best way to counter the threat of a third and atomic world war was through the unity of the 'European family'; pointing out that the key to that unity would be reconciliation between France and Germany. 'The fighting has stopped; but the dangers have not stopped. If we are to form the United States of Europe, or whatever name or form it may take, we must begin now.'[1]

The enthusiasm with which this speech was received by a growing European movement in 1946 is not really understood by the more sceptical politicians of the 1990s, who overlook the intense war-weariness which permeated a Europe which had suffered the destructive impact of two world wars since 1914. In 1946 there was a burning determination that Franco-German rivalry should never again force the countries of Europe into war. Churchill's Zurich speech was enthusiastically received because he articulated an as yet imperfectly constructed belief and understanding that the peace of the continent and of the world depended on a Franco-German reconciliation within some form of European union.

Those who welcomed Churchill's speech and believed that he meant Britain to lead the growing European Movement read far more into it than the former prime minister had ever intended. It is true that Churchill had a clear vision of what Europe might become, but that vision did not include Britain. What Churchill had said in the 1930s was a truer reflection of his views. 'We see nothing but good and hope in a richer, freer, more contented European commonalty,' he said. 'But we have our own dreams and our own task. We are with Europe but not of it.'[2]

In 1949 he repeated this sentiment in a speech about the newly-founded Council of Europe:

> The French Foreign Minister, M. Schuman, declared in the French Parliament this week that 'Without Britain there can be no Europe' ... But our friends on the Continent need have no misgivings. Britain is an integral part of Europe, and we mean to play our part.
>
> But Britain cannot be thought of as a single state in isolation. She is the centre of a world-wide Empire and Commonwealth. We shall never do anything to weaken the ties of blood, of sentiment and tradition and common interest which unite ... the British family of nations.[3]

Churchill was a federalist as far as Europe was concerned, as were many other leading political thinkers at a time when 'federalism' did not have a pejorative sense, but his view of federalism did not necessarily see Britain forming part of that federation. In Churchill's eyes, Britain had a unique role in the Cold War as the only nation to occupy the space where three important and interlocking political groupings in the non-Soviet world all overlapped:

- an Atlantic alliance linking North America to Europe
- Europe itself
- the British Commonwealth.

In his study of Britain's relationship with Europe, Hugo Young points out that Churchill was not only a 'father of Europe' but also the 'father of British misunderstandings about Europe'.[4] Churchill still believed completely in the greatness of Great Britain and shared with the British people a misguided complacency about the wealth and power of a Britain which had won the war, despite the terrible costs involved. The British people could see why devastated countries of continental Europe would need to band together for mutual support, but Britain was different, one of the 'Big Three', ranking alongside the United States and the Soviet Union as a world power. According to that perspective, Britain did not need Europe.

That attitude was shared by everyone with power and influence, not least the Attlee government's foreign secretary, Ernest Bevin. A man of instinctively Churchillian opinions, Bevin spoke in friendly tones about European unity and Britain's role in that Europe, but meant simply that Britain should act as a friend and supporter, rather than as a participant. A sentiment often expressed in the late 1940s was that Europe had been fatally damaged by the war and that Britain should avoid 'chaining itself to a corpse'.[5]

The Benelux Agreement

In March 1947, Belgium, the Netherlands and the Grand Duchy of Luxembourg agreed to form a common market. This was not new, as an informal agreement on economic co-operation had been in force before the war, but it was the first concrete move towards integration between European states. Economic union for the three countries came into force in October 1947, followed by a customs union, with a common external tariff, on 1 January 1948.

Alongside the Benelux Agreement came hints of a wider European customs union and negotiations began in 1947, at the suggestion of the Americans. Ultimately Britain squashed the plan and ensured that it was forgotten until the Treaty of Rome, ten years later. The sticking point for the UK was a suggestion that the customs union should have a supervisory council or supranational assembly whose remit might diminish the sovereignty of member states. And here we have the dilemma which has plagued Britain's attitude towards Europe since the 1940s and which continues to dominate any debate about Europe today. First seen in the attitude of Bevin towards customs union in 1947 it finds obvious parallels in the attitude of eurosceptics towards monetary union in 1999.

- On the one hand there is a recognisable *economic* argument for support, co-operation and integration between nations in the face of the global market.
- On the other hand there is the *political* argument of national sovereignty, pushing in the opposite direction. 'Any union, in Bevin's view, had to be between sovereign governments, with no power ceded to a supranational body'.[6]

After 1948, attitudes towards European union were affected by evidence of Soviet expansionism such as was seen in the Greek Civil War, the Berlin blockade and the *coup d'état* against Jan Masaryk in Czechoslovakia, and the integration of Western Europe came to be seen as a necessary safeguard against this expansion. Also, as the Cold War intensified, the need emerged for some kind of third world force, interposed between the super-states of the USA and USSR.

On 22 January 1948, Ernest Bevin made an important speech to the House of Commons calling for an alliance of the nations of Western Europe to resist the encroachment of the Soviet bloc. This speech led directly to the Treaty of Brussels, signed on 17 March 1948 by Britain, France and the Benelux countries. Basically it was a treaty of mutual assistance in the event of any one of the signatories being attacked, but the signatories went beyond this defence agreement and examined the idea of a unified defence policy and military alliance for the non-communist countries of Europe, to be known as the Western European Union. And, while creating this defence community, they also explored the possibility of economic and political co-operation, with an assembly or 'parliament' to provide some form of co-ordination and democratic control.

For a time Britain seemed to favour the idea, with even Attlee speaking of 'pooling some degree of authority' for the sake of the Western Union. The Foreign Office, however, at Bevin's behest, made it very clear that the community was for defensive purposes only and, while Britain was happy to see a political union in Europe, that union would stop short at the English Channel. The parliamentary idea was strangled at birth and the suggested assembly was replaced by a largely ornamental Permanent Consultative Council.

When, in October 1954, full sovereignty was restored to West Germany, permitting German re-armament, the UK with France and the Benelux countries resurrected the Treaty of Brussels, admitting Italy and West Germany to the treaty and restructuring the Western European Union by creating a common assembly with the Council of Europe. At the time it seemed a major step forward in the process of European integration but, on the whole, the WEU has had very little importance until recently, when the Maastricht Treaty on European Union (TEU) and subsequent European Councils created a growing defence and foreign affairs role for the EU. Within that role the WEU has come to be seen as the military arm of the European Union and has played a not insignificant role in the troubles of the former Yugoslavia.

The Truman Doctrine

In 1947 the post-war recovery of Europe faltered. Countries which had tried to rebuild their economies too rapidly failed to meet the cost of imports, resulting in massive balance of payments crises and deficits in European gold and dollar reserves. The UK was particularly affected because of Britain's insistence on her role as a world power – which a country impoverished by six years of war could not sustain in the face of so many threats to peace as then existed. The economic crisis began to affect the ability of European countries to defend themselves. As early as 1947, the British government, worried by the civil war in Greece, the continuing crisis in Trieste and subversive agitation by the French and Italian communist parties, appealed to the United States, saying that, unless America was ready to see Europe fall victim to Soviet communism, then economic and military aid was urgently required.

President Truman's reply, in March 1947, promised full support and assistance to 'those free peoples who are resisting attempted subjugation by armed minorities or by outside pressures'. On 5 June 1947, the secretary of state, George Marshall, proposed a programme of financial aid to Europe in what was to become known as the Marshall Plan, a plan which came with the proviso that countries accepting any aid must work together in planning its use and distribution. In July 1947, representatives of eighteen non-communist

European countries met in Paris to formulate the European Recovery Program (ERP) and devise the institutions to execute that programme. By April 1948, with the beginning of Marshall Aid, a body had been set up to administer the ERP known as the Organisation for European Economic Co-operation (OEEC). This was an intergovernmental organisation, guided by a council which had one representative from each member state. Beneath the council was a network of committees and agencies whose task was to prepare reports for council decisions.

The OEEC was very successful, achieving its main objectives in three years and then building on its success so that, by the mid-1950s, it had completely transformed the economic situation in Western Europe and Britain. The complex organisation involved in setting up and administering the OEEC was an inspiration to European federalists, showing just what could be achieved by co-operative effort. The French, with American backing, wanted to give the OEEC its own secretariat, with an executive and decision-making capability, thereby forming a putative European governing institution. The European enthusiasts even chose their own candidate to run the OEEC – a Belgian enthusiast for European unity, Paul-Henri Spaak, guaranteed to make the OEEC a major force for European integration. However, Bevin and the Foreign Office, finding federalist enthusiasms 'embarrassing', not only opposed any attempts to make the OEEC supranational, but also vetoed Spaak's nomination as OEEC chairman in favour of a safe, anti-federalist 'mandarin' from Whitehall, Oliver Franks.

Always intergovernmental in scope and organisation, and with strong links to the USA, the OEEC belonged more to the Atlantic Community than to Europe. In 1960 its international nature was recognised by the admission of the USA and Canada to membership and by a change of name to Organisation for Economic Co-operation and Development (OECD). In 1964 the membership extended beyond the Atlantic Community with the entry of Japan. Since then, other members such as Australia and New Zealand have joined, making the OECD into a fully international body, albeit one with a formative influence on European development.

The other organisation to emerge from the Truman Doctrine was fully international from the start, even though its headquarters and zone of operation were located in Europe. Hopes felt in 1945 that the Soviet Union would be a useful ally in the peaceful reconstruction of Europe had been dashed by Soviet expansionism. The onset of the Cold War made it clear that the Russians were never going to be true partners and it became a matter of some urgency to re-engage the United States in the concerns of Europe. The Marshall Plan provided one way in which this was done and the North Atlantic Treaty Organisation (NATO), formed for the purpose of collective defence and security in a treaty signed on 4 April 1949, was the other.

The membership of NATO was made up of the five signatories of the Treaty of Brussels together with Denmark, Iceland, Italy, Norway and Portugal in

Europe, and the United States and Canada in North America, with the purpose of defending Western Europe against any Soviet threat. However, although obviously part of a common European defence structure, NATO covered the Atlantic Community as a whole, rather than Western Europe alone.

The attitude taken by Britain towards Europe and European matters towards the end of 1948 can still be observed today. Britain may claim to want to be 'at the heart of Europe', but any hint of integration leads to rejection and active counter-measures. During 1948 three of the events mentioned above exemplified the typical British response to European unification:

- the suppression of moves towards a European Customs Union
- the refusal to accept a 'parliament' or assembly for the Western European Union
- the refusal to accept the OEEC as a supranational institution and the rejection of Paul-Henri Spaak in favour of Oliver Franks.

The Council of Europe

The International Committee of the Movements for European Unity, better known as the European Movement, was formed in December 1947. Based on an idea of Winston Churchill's, the Committee proposed that a forum should be formed within which European nations could discuss their problems and difficulties, beginning to break down centuries of distrust through the open exchange of views.

On 7 May 1948, 663 delegates from sixteen European states attended a Congress of Europe in The Hague; delegates including such luminaries of the European Movement as Monnet, De Gaspari and Spaak. A keynote speech by Winston Churchill was delivered to a gathering containing eight former prime ministers and twenty-eight former foreign ministers. Significantly, Churchill's speech to the Congress put the strongest arguments yet heard for a partial surrender of national sovereignty in order to create 'that larger sovereignty which can also protect their diverse and distinctive customs ... and national traditions'.[7] This concept of 'pooled sovereignty', much used by advocates of European unity in the 1950s and 1960s, might have soothed the doubts of future eurosceptics if it had been adopted as the British position from the first. But Churchill was again being ambivalent, advocating European unity for all European countries – except Britain.

It was this Hague Congress which first proposed an assembly to debate European issues, guided by a council of ministers. Within weeks the suggestion had been taken up by the French government, who also offered the new council a home in Strasbourg. Within a year the idea had progressed so far that, with the initial agreement of ten governments – Belgium, Denmark, France, Great

Britain, Ireland, Italy, Luxembourg, Netherlands, Norway and Sweden – the Statute of the Council of Europe was signed in London in May 1949.

> The aim of the Council of Europe is to achieve a greater unity between its Members for the purpose of safeguarding and realising the ideals and principles which are their common heritage and facilitating their economic and social progress.
>
> This aim shall be pursued through the organs of the Council by discussion of questions of common concern and by agreements and common action in economic, social, cultural, scientific, legal and administrative matters and in the maintenance and further realisation of human rights and fundamental freedoms.[8]

Convened in Strasbourg on 10 August 1949 under its first president, Paul-Henri Spaak, the Council consisted of an assembly of 150 members, together with a guiding Council of Ministers who met in closed session twice a year. In 1952 this body, largely made up of foreign ministers, appointed permanent deputies who would provide continuity between meetings of the ministers themselves.

The Council of Europe plays an important role in the development of European institutions but was never central to integration. Its structure and purpose was always intergovernmental and, although it remains useful for airing important European issues, its decisions are not binding and it remains very much a powerless talking-shop. As one British MP nominated to the Assembly said, 'The Council of Europe was a body with a high moral content, inclined towards the passing of resolutions in favour of good causes ... it carried little weight'.[9]

The Council of Europe does have one important success to its credit. In 1950, the European Convention of Human Rights was produced, modelled on the United Nations 'Declaration of Human Rights', defining those civil and natural freedoms which should belong by right to the citizens of Europe. The Convention was signed by all member states and enforced by the European Court of Human Rights in Strasbourg, to which citizens of all Council of Europe members have the right to appeal, as an independent legal forum superior to the national courts of the member states. However, the Convention of Human Rights can serve as something rather more than a superior court of appeal and, since the election of the Blair government in 1997, legislation has been passed which integrates the Convention into British law as the equivalent of a Bill of Rights.

Within the context of this book it is important that the Council of Europe should not be confused with the European Council, which is the major legislative institution of the European Union. Nor should the European Court of Human Rights in Strasbourg be confused with the European Court of Justice in Luxembourg: the latter being concerned with constitutional and institutional matters relating to the European Union.

From its institution in 1949 the position adopted by the British government towards the Council of Europe was as equivocal as ever. Ernest Bevin, always fiercely anti-federalist, favoured a series of bilateral agreements in which Britain formalised relations with Europe one country at a time. In answer to a suggestion for strengthening the Council of Europe, Bevin made a statement, splendidly mixing his mythologies, in which he said, 'If you open that Pandora's Box you never know what Trojan horses will jump out'. Government policy was to remain one of co-operation with Europe, but it was to be a very limited co-operation.

The Schuman Plan and Jean Monnet

In 1949 Jean Monnet, the Movement's most prominent supporter, summing up the position *vis-à-vis* European integration, said, 'A start would have to be made by doing something both more practical and more ambitious. National sovereignty would have to be tackled more boldly and on a narrower front'.[10] His plan of action involved a 'sectoral strategy', tackling one economic sector at a time, until the various sectors meshed together into an integrated whole.

According to Monnet the first sector to be tackled should be heavy industry, rationalising economic recovery in France and Germany by forming a common market in basic industrial materials: specifically in the creation of a European Coal and Steel Community (ECSC). Explicitly this was a pragmatic agreement in the economic interests of member countries, but Monnet made it clear that economic integration was merely the 'narrower front' of which he had spoken. The implicit, more visionary purpose was ultimately to be political integration. The choice of coal and steel was symbolic in that the principal product of heavy industry has always been armaments and, to place heavy industry under joint Franco-German control, had the implied effect of ruling out the future possibility of war between the two countries.

Monnet was a bureaucrat, never an elected politician, operating best on the periphery and influencing rather than initiating the action. However, Monnet's ideas were taken up and promoted by a practical politician, Robert Schuman, French foreign minister since 1948. At a press conference on 9 May 1950, Schuman made what is known as the Schuman Declaration, announcing the establishment of a Franco-German Coal and Steel Community: 'The pooling of coal and steel production will immediately provide ... common bases for economic development as a first step in the federation of Europe ... The solidarity thus achieved will make it plain that any war between France and Germany becomes not only unthinkable but naturally impossible.' Originally, the proposed community consisted only of France and West Germany but Schuman insisted that any other country was welcome, although France and Germany would go ahead even if no one else cared to join them. Both he and Monnet made it clear that, quite apart from any economic benefits, the main purpose of the agreement was to create the first stage of political union. It is because of this explicitly supranational objective that Britain so decisively rejected the offer when an invitation to join the negotiations was extended in 1950.

There were reasons peculiar to Britain, and a Labour government in particular, which constrained them to reject the proposal. In 1950 the long-awaited nationalisation of the British coal and steel industries, a fundamental plank of Labour Party policy since the party's foundation, had just been completed. The Labour government which had finally realised that policy was not going to hand over these two key industries to international regulation. And, although the Conservative government that took office in 1951 was elected in time to reverse its decision on ECSC membership, it failed to do so.

The Treaty of Paris, establishing the ECSC, was signed in April 1951 by representatives of six countries – France, West Germany, the Benelux countries and Italy – without the participation of the UK. The Community had its headquarters in Luxembourg and Jean Monnet was appointed its first president.

- The principal body of the ECSC was the High Authority – nine experts appointed by the member countries, with at least one representative from each country.
- Alongside the High Authority was a Council of Ministers, one minister representing each member country. The Council was intergovernmental, and over the years gained strength and influence at the expense of the supranational High Authority.
- The ECSC also had a Consultative Assembly with members nominated by national parliaments rather than elected. The Assembly had few powers and was largely advisory.
- A Court of Justice, made up of seven independent judges, dealt with any disputes between member states or community institutions.

In forming the ECSC, a constitutional pattern was established for all later communities. All of them, down to the post-Maastricht EU, have been characterised by the four basic institutions of High Authority (later the Commission), Council of Ministers, Assembly (later the Parliament) and Court of Justice.

The Treaty of Rome

According to the softly-softly strategy of Monnet and Schuman, a long process of step-by-step economic integration was the best way to achieve political union. In 1955, as part of just such a process, the Benelux countries suggested that the ECSC consider extending the customs union created by the Benelux Agreement of 1948. The idea was referred to the next meeting of the ECSC Council of Ministers, which opened in Messina, Sicily, in June 1955. And the

Messina Conference put into words the goals towards which Monnet, Schuman and the federalists had been working for so long. The Messina Resolution stated that:

> The governments of Belgium, France, the Federal Republic of Germany, Italy, Luxembourg and the Netherlands consider that the moment has arrived to initiate a new phase on the path of constructing Europe. They believe that this has to be done principally in the economic sphere and regard it as necessary to continue the creation of a united Europe through an expansion of joint institutions, the gradual fusion of national economies, the creation of a common market, and the gradual co-ordination of social policies. Such a policy seems to them indispensable if Europe is to maintain her position in the world, regain her influence, and achieve a steady increase in the living standards of her population.[11]

On the basis of this resolution, a working party was set up, chaired by the Belgian, Paul-Henri Spaak. It has to be said that the project conceived at Messina was always going to be more than a common market, though that was the label best understood by the public. As Spaak said to the Council of Europe in 1964, 'Those who drew up the Treaty of Rome ... thought of it as a stage on the way to political union'.

Negotiations were complicated by national interests such as the French need for an agricultural policy, but determination and compromise on the part of the negotiators achieved success within a year. Two treaties, approved in Paris by prime ministers of the six countries in February 1957, went on to be signed in Rome on 25 March 1957. The more important, the Treaty of Rome, established the European Economic Community (EEC) – popularly known as the Common Market – while a second treaty set up the European Atomic Energy Community (Euratom). Only in France and Italy did ratification of the treaties meet any parliamentary opposition – and that was largely from the communist parties of both countries. Once ratified by all six states, the treaties of Rome came into force on 1 January 1958.

The institutions of the EEC were essentially those created for the ECSC.

- In the case of the Assembly and Court of Justice the existing institutions of the ECSC became the Assembly and Court of the combined communities of the EEC, ECSC and Euratom.
- The executive of the EEC was the Commission, which had two commissioners each for France, Italy and West Germany, one commissioner each for the other three.
- The Council of Ministers formed the legislature of the EEC and was normally made up of the six foreign ministers, who could be replaced by the relevant ministers when any specific topic was discussed – agriculture, trade, etc.
- The Assembly was not elected, the members being nominated, usually being chosen from members of the national parliaments. However, the Assembly had very little power, bar a certain degree of budgetary control.

Britain had not attended the Messina Conference since it was a meeting of the ECSC, to which Britain did not belong, but the UK was pressed hard to appoint a representative to the Spaak Committee. Harold Macmillan, the foreign secretary, was enthusiastic and wanted the British representative to be an active participant rather than an observer. But Eden and Butler, as prime minister and chancellor, were less keen and appointed an official rather than a politician. An under-secretary at the Board of Trade, Russell Bretherton, was sent to Brussels without plenipotentiary powers, in the firm belief that the Spaak Committee would collapse with nothing achieved. The position adopted by the British government towards the Spaak Committee was similar to that taken towards monetary union forty years later: the British government did not rule out 'joining eventually' but meanwhile 'reserved their position' and would 'wait and see what happened' – fully expecting the venture to fail.

Bretherton soon realised that the working party had achieved far more positive results than the British government had expected, but his response was limited by his watching brief. On 7 November 1955 there was a confrontation in the Spaak Committee about which there are conflicting stories. One version says that Bretherton stormed out of the meeting, allowing others to claim that Britain walked out of the Common Market before it even existed. In another version, it was Spaak himself who threw Bretherton off the committee because of his negative attitude, ruling out any UK participation in the Treaty of Rome. Probably neither story is true. Yet neither Bretherton nor any other British representative took any further part in the deliberations of the Spaak Committee after the meeting of 7 November.[12]

Towards the end of 1956, the new prime minister, Harold Macmillan, made it clear that Britain's main concern was still with Commonwealth trade links. At a NATO Council meeting in December 1956 the foreign secretary, Selwyn Lloyd, made a sort of functionalist counter-proposal in 'the Grand Design'. Under this proposal the various European institutions that had emerged would be rationalised, two of the main proposals being:

- a single European assembly to oversee all institutions
- a Free Trade Area to cover the whole of Western Europe.

After the signing of the Treaty of Rome, Britain, together with Portugal, Norway, Sweden, Denmark, Austria and Switzerland, did build on Lloyd's suggestion by creating the European Free Trade Area (EFTA) in November 1959. This, however, was simply a low-tariff common market with no political or integrationist implications.

EEC – the first phase

The EEC set itself four main targets on the route to integration, agreeing that they would be achieved by 1970:

- removal of internal tariffs and trade restrictions, forming a common market
- creation of a Common External Tariff, so that imports from outside the Community pay duty according to the same tariff, regardless of the importing country
- legislation to outlaw practices preventing free competition between members
- free movement of goods, persons, capital and services.

All four targets were achieved by 1 July 1968 – nearly two years ahead of schedule. In April 1965 the three communities – the EEC, the ECSC and Euratom – were brought together when the members signed the Merger Treaty. This established a single Commission and a single Council for the three communities which already shared a common Assembly and Court of Justice. The Merger Treaty took effect in June 1967, the merged communities becoming known *de facto* as the European Community (EC).

In the early 1960s the French president, Charles de Gaulle, sought to establish a French hegemony over the institutions of the Communities by fully exploiting the intergovernmental nature of the Council of Ministers. In the Council a unanimous vote of all six members was required for new structural measures, meaning that a single adverse vote became a national veto. De Gaulle repeatedly used that veto to force through measures that were in the interests of France and to block any measure he believed was against French interests. Most notably that veto was used by de Gaulle to refuse Britain's entry into the EEC – twice!

Britain – the first application

Britain signed the agreement setting up the European Free Trade Area in Stockholm during November 1959, and it came into force in April 1960. Europe was thereby divided into two rival trading camps or, according to the press at the time, Europe was 'at sixes and sevens'. Britain claimed to admire the 'economic and commercial freedom' of EFTA as against the 'political straitjacket' of the EEC. And yet, within a year, Macmillan was to change his mind and apply for British membership of the EEC.

Many factors changed the attitude of the British government, the following being the most important.

- The Suez affair in 1956 led Britain to realise that her days as a world power were over. The press began to write about Britain having 'suffered a crisis of identity' and 'needing to find a new world role'. For many people that new role would seem to be in Europe.
- While the late 1950s and early 1960s were boom years in Britain, growth was even healthier elsewhere and economic commentators asked what was

wrong with Britain when, in comparison, EEC members had almost doubled their standard of living inside ten years.

- British politicians watched the EEC create a series of political and economic institutions while building a ring fence against outsiders. It was felt that, if one day it became necessary to join the European Communities, Britain would have to face a Europe formed without any British input. In 1959, Harold Macmillan stated, 'For the first time since the Napoleonic era the major continental powers are united in a positive economic grouping ... which, though not directed against the United Kingdom, may have the effect of excluding us both from European markets and from consultation on European policy'.[13]
- Britain assumed that the so-called 'special relationship' between the UK and USA would ensure that, in trading with Europe, the Americans would favour EFTA with its British connections. However, President Kennedy privately informed Macmillan that he was annoyed by Europe's divisions. If the US were forced to choose between EEC and EFTA, the USA would choose the more important EEC.

In July 1961 Prime Minister Macmillan announced Britain's application for EEC membership. Three other countries applied at the same time: the Republic of Ireland, whose currency (the punt) was pegged to sterling; and Norway and Denmark because they depended on British trade. In November 1961 Edward Heath was appointed to negotiate Britain's entry and talks began in earnest. Almost immediately they became bogged down over protectionism for British trade links with the Commonwealth. De Gaulle saw this as a British plot to destroy the Community's agricultural policy, claiming in his memoirs that the UK had only applied to join in order to wreck the Community, 'Having failed, from the outside, to prevent the birth of the Community, they [the British] now plan to paralyse it from within'.[14]

Ironically, if there were anyone intent on wrecking the Community, it was de Gaulle himself. Not only did the French president fear that Britain would be too powerful a partner, he also looked askance at the three smaller countries of Denmark, Ireland and Norway. While he could manipulate a Community of six nations, he was less sure of controlling ten. Above all else, however, the French president distrusted all things Anglo-Saxon: to him Britain was a Trojan Horse, part of the USA's plan to gain control of European affairs.

In December 1962 de Gaulle told Macmillan that he intended to veto Britain's application unless Britain broke with the American alliance. In response Macmillan took the opposite path, flying to a meeting with President Kennedy in the Bahamas. The resulting Nassau Agreement secured an increased stake for Britain in NATO's nuclear programme by America's offer of the Polaris missile. Macmillan returned from Nassau in triumph, having renewed the 'special relationship', able to dismiss as irrelevant the press conference of 14 January 1963 at which de Gaulle confirmed his veto.

Throughout these negotiations the UK's position was not helped by British attitudes towards Europe. Instead of adopting the position of humble suppliant in applying to join the Communities, Britain gave the impression of doing Europe a favour by the application. As one political commentator has recently said, 'It was in many respects as if Britain had decided that the EEC was worthy of British membership, and not the other way around.'[15] It is an attitude that has pervaded the UK's relationship with Europe ever since and which was certainly the position adopted by Margaret Thatcher in her relations with Europe.

The Common Agricultural Policy

It was a personal decision of the French president to reject Britain, made without the consent of his European partners, and naturally enough they were angered by his attitude. But it was typical of a period during which French policy virtually undid all the existing groundwork on EC integration, the problem being the Common Agricultural Policy (CAP).

The principles underlying the CAP were laid down in 1960:

- free trade within the Community in all agricultural products
- common guaranteed prices for most commodities
- protective heavy levies placed on all imported agricultural products
- purchase by the Community of all commodity surpluses.

For critics of the European Community, the second and fourth points together came to represent all that was wrong with the Community. The fact that the Community would not only pay guaranteed prices but would itself guarantee the purchase of any unsold surplus produce, would not have mattered if the Community had also laid down limits on production. But the French held out for there to be no such limits and it represented an open invitation for farmers to produce more than could be sold on the open market, in the certain knowledge that the Community would buy any surplus at the full market rate! It is this which produced things like the 'butter mountain' and the 'wine lake'. It also led to two-thirds of the EC budget being swallowed up by the CAP and, in the 1980s, almost led to bankruptcy.

Small countries within the Community tried to argue the case over the CAP but the policy was favourable to French farmers and had the support of de Gaulle. Whenever negotiations became bogged down he instructed French ministers to walk out of Council meetings until they got what they wanted. Since French withdrawal affected other policies as well as the CAP this was to be avoided and the CAP was finally agreed in January 1962.

This forcing through of the CAP, together with the veto on British membership, alienated other members of the EEC. They did not like the way de Gaulle did things without consultation and found it hypocritical that he should condemn Britain for 'not being truly European' while proving himself more chauvinistically nationalist than anyone. De Gaulle did all he could to reduce the influence of supranational institutions and stated forcefully that he did not want an integrated Europe but a loose association of nation states; a *'Europe des Patries'* – a position later adopted as her own by Mrs Thatcher.

In 1965, during a row with France over the sale of surplus wheat to Russia, it was proposed that the agricultural budget should be taken away from the Council of Ministers and placed under the joint control of the Commission and European Parliament. This proposed transfer of power from intergovernmental to supranational institutions inflamed de Gaulle. He announced his 'policy of the empty chair' by which France withdrew from the Council of Ministers. Since the constitution of the Community demanded the unanimous decision of all Council members, French withdrawal was immediately effective. As Aidan Crawley said, 'Europe had come to a full stop.'[16]

The deadlock lasted from July 1965 to January 1966. The Luxembourg Compromise which ended the dispute gave member states the right to exercise the veto if national interests were threatened. The de Gaulle years weakened the federalist position in Europe and encouraged a substantial transfer of power from supranational to intergovernmental institutions, setting a benchmark for the British position under Margaret Thatcher.

Britain – the second application

In Britain, the Labour Party narrowly won the election of 1964. Traditionally Labour was hostile towards Europe, or at best disinterested. Under Gaitskell's leadership the sentiment was expressed that, for a Labour government to join Europe would be like 'turning one's back on a thousand years of history'. However, while the party's grassroots remained hostile, over the three years between 1964 and 1967 the leadership and parliamentary party began to change their minds for a number of reasons:

- as more and more former colonies gained their independence, trade with the Commonwealth was rapidly declining
- the economies of Europe, especially West Germany, were booming, while Britain's growth was weak
- trade between Britain and EEC member countries was at a near standstill because of Britain's exclusion
- the special relationship with the United States was damaged by America's involvement in Vietnam
- Harold Wilson had won two elections on slogans involving the term, 'technological revolution', but research and development work in major technological industries such as aerospace was so expensive that it needed

international joint funding. Projects such as Concorde were done in association with the French and there were similar projects with other members of the Community such as Italy and West Germany.

In 1967 the Wilson government re-opened negotiations for Community membership. On this occasion de Gaulle acted after just five months. As before he neither consulted his fellow members nor did he go through the correct channels. He simply held a press conference at which he announced 'it would be impossible to bring the Great Britain of today into the Common Market as it stands'.

Unlike in 1963 the other five members of the Community let their displeasure at de Gaulle be known. It was made clear to Britain, Denmark, Ireland and Norway that their applications would be left in place, with the understanding that, while the application could not proceed while de Gaulle remained in power, the days of the general were numbered. In fact, shaken by the student protests of 1968, de Gaulle resigned in 1969. Within the year, the new French president, Georges Pompidou, had met the new British prime minister, Ted Heath, and a rather broad hint was dropped that France would no longer oppose British membership.

Edward Heath was probably the only prime minister Britain has had who truly believed one hundred per cent in the European ideal. Under his guidance and his negotiator, Geoffrey Rippon, negotiations went smoothly and remarkably quickly; Britain being able to sign the Treaty of Accession in Brussels on 1 January 1972. Britain's fellow applicants were also accepted but all three announced that they would consult the people by holding referendums on the subject. In Ireland, voting in May 1972, 82 per cent of those voting said 'yes'; in Denmark, voting in October 1972, those in favour were 63 per cent. In Norway, however, there was a bitter argument about membership terms. In the Norwegian referendum, in September 1972, only 46 per cent voted 'yes' as against 54 per cent voting 'no'. Norway withdrew from membership.

Accession and after

There could hardly have been a worse time for Britain to join the EC. The oil crisis of 1973 quadrupled the price of oil, producing a world recession and slowing down economic growth. Britain joined the EC in an attempt to share in the economic growth of the 1960s, only to find in the 1970s that there was no longer any growth to share. Without economic growth the less attractive aspects of EC membership, such as the CAP, became more evident and arguments in favour of British membership were much harder to sustain. During the recession there was a slowing down of Community development and the problems of the period came to bear the nickname 'eurosclerosis'.

In 1974 the Labour Party very narrowly defeated the Conservatives in both of the elections of that year. Since its rejection in 1967 the Labour Party had reverted to a policy of outright opposition to Europe and it fought the 1974 elections with a manifesto commitment to withdraw from the EC. However, faced once more with the 'realities of office' Wilson found that it would be very difficult to break with Europe. In order to save face and avoid too blatant a *volte face*, he announced that Labour was not opposed to Europe in principle but only to the unsatisfactory terms obtained by Ted Heath. Wilson proposed that the terms should be re-negotiated and that the government would then do what Heath should have done in 1972 by putting the revised terms to the people in a referendum, the result of which would be accepted by the government, whatever the verdict may be.

Negotiations were in the hands of James Callaghan who in due course came back from Brussels with what he claimed were improved terms, although to the observer the changes were merely cosmetic. The referendum was held in June 1975 and despite what were held to be dubious manoeuvres, produced a positive result for the government. In a low turnout of only 64 per cent, 66 per cent of those who voted said 'yes' as against 34 per cent who said 'no'.

Britain and Europe in 1979

Very little changed in the wake of the referendum. The remaining Labour years under Wilson and Callaghan were passed in the midst of a domestic economic crisis that had begun with the 1973 oil crisis and which occupied the government's thinking to the exclusion of such issues as Europe. Since the global economic crisis affected both Europe and the UK to an equal extent, the EC remained sunk in eurosclerosis and Britain seemed to suffer all the negative aspects of EC membership without reaping any of the positive benefits. But, at the end of the Labour years, three events made 1979 particularly significant:

- the European Monetary System (EMS) came into operation, representing the first step in a process intended to lead to economic and monetary union
- the first direct elections to the European Parliament took place; meaning more democracy
- the British general election produced a Conservative government that would have a major effect on relationships between Britain, the Conservative Party and Europe.

The European Community in 1979 was the antithesis of everything advocated by Margaret Thatcher. Ironically, Roy Jenkins, a former Labour minister and then president of the Commission, originally believed that Mrs Thatcher would be more amenable towards Europe than the previous prime minister, Jim Callaghan. Like many other politicians, Jenkins misread Mrs Thatcher. She had declared often enough that she was opposed to compromise and would remain committed to her chosen policies, but no one believed her, dismissing it as a political stance she would readily abandon when faced with the reality of office.

As it was, Mrs Thatcher had been in office for three years before realisation dawned that she meant exactly what she said:

- she despised committees
- she refused any compromise or consensus
- she would not do any deal which detracted from her demands
- her position in any argument was that she was right; everyone else was wrong.

This was so contrary to the way in which the Community operated that Britain's European partners were in turn shocked, repelled and alienated. Mrs Thatcher may have had right on her side but she also held to the view of Britain's superiority to Europe mentioned earlier. There is little doubt that her behaviour in successive European Council meetings throughout the 1980s led to a growing isolation of Britain in Europe. Mrs Thatcher's relationship with the European Community is clearly described by Roy Jenkins in his account of her first European Council meeting at Dublin in 1979, a meeting which defined the ways in which she would invariably deal with her fellow European leaders:

> Towards the end Mrs Thatcher got the discussions bogged down by being too demanding. Her mistake ... arose out of her having only one of the three qualities of a great advocate. She has the nerve and determination to win but she does not have a good understanding of the case against her ... her reiterated cry of 'It's my money. I want it back' strikes an insistently jarring note. She lacks also the third quality ... of not boring the judge and jury ... She only understood four out of the fourteen or so points on the British side and repeated each of them twenty-seven times during the evening.[17]

The British Budgetary Question

The question of Britain's contribution to the European budget arose at Mrs Thatcher's first European Council meeting and dominated discussions in the Council for five years, to the despair of Jenkins, the Commission and the rest of Europe. The issue was known in Brussels as 'the BBQ' which, according to Jenkins, meant 'the British Budgetary Question', but was more usually referred to as 'the Bloody British Question'.

The point was that, despite economic difficulties, Britain was making net contributions to Community funds quite as large as those being paid by Germany. This arose from the nature of Britain's agriculture, which is smaller and more efficient than that in most of Europe – and about twice as efficient than that of France. Payments to Britain out of CAP funds were comparatively so low that efficient farmers in Britain were heavily subsidising inefficient farmers in France. To make matters worse, EEC rules forced Britain, who imported more food from outside the Community than the others, to pay a much higher import levy than they did.

Soon after her election Mrs Thatcher instructed an under-secretary at the Treasury, Peter Middleton, to discover the exact size of Britain's contribution to the European budget, and to estimate just how much Britain ought to be paying. As a result of these investigations, Mrs Thatcher presented her first European Council in Dublin, November 1979, with the exact amount by which she wanted British contributions to be reduced – £1 billion. The Community offered a reduction of £350 million, which the prime minister rejected out of hand.

At this point Mrs Thatcher succeeded in shocking both her European colleagues and her own advisers. Repeated demands for what she called 'her money' made it clear that the sum she wanted was not negotiable and she would do no deals. As Christopher Tugendhat, the British commissioner, reported, she accused other European states of the outright theft of British money,[18] an accusation which horrified Foreign Office advisers who knew the rules of the European game. Under those 'rules' negotiations would improve on the £350 million offered by some deal on oil, or fishing rights, or the price of lamb.

However, there was to be no deal. Experienced negotiators were lost in what for them was an unprecedented situation. Among Britain's partners there were many who, while originally sympathetic, were subsequently alienated by such behaviour. As Jenkins said, 'on the merits Mrs Thatcher had right broadly on her side although she showed little sense of proportion, some of her favourite arguments were invalid and her tactical sense was as weak as her courage was strong'. Thatcher continued to demand her money throughout dinner and after. The Europeans retaliated – Giscard ignored her, Schmidt pretended that he was asleep and Jørgensen, the Danish prime minister, shouted insults. The complete breakdown of the Council was only prevented by postponing a decision on the BBQ until the next year.

That Dublin meeting set the tone for Britain's relationship with Europe throughout the Thatcher years. Her behaviour was deplored by the other Community members and indeed, at one point, would lead the French prime minister, Jacques Chirac, to call for Britain's expulsion from the Community. Attitudes towards Thatcher rubbed off onto Britons in general. Even the europhile Roy Jenkins found that his colleagues in the Commission were treating him and Christopher Tugendhat as potentially hostile.

Over the winter of 1979–80 the Commission worked for a resolution of the BBQ. The answer they came up with was that Britain should get a rebate on budgetary contributions to the value of one billion ecus (£700 million). Efforts were then made on the one hand to persuade other members to agree to this, and on the other to persuade Mrs Thatcher to accept what she insisted on regarding as only two-thirds of what was rightfully hers.

At Luxembourg, in April 1980, all seemed more promising. Mrs Thatcher was less strident, Schmidt duly made the agreed offer to Britain and Giscard added that they were willing to increase that rebate to 2,400 million ecus over two years. Everyone confidently expected that this would settle the matter but, at five in the afternoon, after a full day's discussion, she rejected the offer outright. She wanted a permanent agreement, not one for two years, and she wanted her demands paid in full. 'We must look after British interests', she said.[19]

Matters were then left in the hands of the Council of Ministers and the Foreign Office. Mrs Thatcher herself had nothing more to do with the negotiations, which were entrusted to Lord Carrington, supported by Sir Ian Gilmour. Negotiations in Brussels were long and hard, culminating in an eighteen-hour session that continued through the night of 29–30 May 1980. Ironically, the agreement, when it came, was almost identical to that rejected by Mrs Thatcher in Luxembourg. When Carrington and Gilmour took the news to the prime minister at Chequers they were shouted at for three-and-a-half hours. Gilmour describes her as 'incandescent' and believes she would have rejected the agreed terms had he not leaked the story to the press, so that she was faced with the *fait accompli* of tabloid headlines praising her 'success' in extracting such good terms from Europe.[20]

BBQ – the issue resolved

The immediate problem of Britain's over-payment was resolved by the agreement of May 1980, but the cause of the problem would not go away. Britain may have got a rebate, but that did not alter the fact that it was paying too much in the first place. As Mrs Thatcher said to a dinner given for MEPs in Strasbourg in 1984, 'I am tired of this being described as a British problem, the problems are Europe-wide. I want an agreement but I don't want to paper over the cracks. I want to get rid of the cracks. I want to rebuild the foundations.'[21]

When she reopened negotiations in 1983, Mrs Thatcher's two main opponents had changed. The new West German chancellor, Helmut Kohl, and the new French president, François Mitterand, did not as yet have the experience or sense of close partnership that typified the Schmidt-Giscard axis of 1979–81. Even so, the process dominated no fewer than four European Council meetings in a twelve-month period. A complication was that, following the example set by de Gaulle, Britain made it clear that no agreement on any other problem such as the CAP would be allowed until the BBQ had been settled to Britain's satisfaction.

At Stuttgart, in June 1983, the European Council passed a vague resolution on European Union but nothing else. At Athens in December there was not even a final communiqué; the first time that this had happened. In March 1984, at a European Council meeting held in Brussels, French and British officials working together had put together a practical formula. In the event, the Germans put forward an impossible alternative, the Irish walked out, Mrs Thatcher resumed her hectoring stance and the Council ended in mutual recriminations. Jacques Chirac, the French prime minister, wanted the EC to expel Britain and, although this was unlikely to happen people were beginning to talk about a 'two-speed' Europe in which those countries prepared to progress would go ahead without others.

The Fontainebleau Summit of June 1984 began as though it would also fail but, as is often the case in Council crises, there was an eleventh-hour agreement under which Britain would receive a permanent rebate worth 66 per cent of the difference between what Britain paid into the Community and the amount Britain got back from the Community. The same agreement increased Community resources by raising the levy on VAT from 1 per cent to 1.4 per cent. The matter was finally settled after five years and Britain could be said to have 'won' and indeed was said to have 'obtained much more than was reasonable'.[22] The agreement, however, was only achieved at considerable cost to future relations between Britain and Europe. The insistent demands made by Mrs Thatcher and her domineering and insulting treatment of her supposed partners had at times almost turned Britain into a pariah in European circles.

Summary – developments up to 1985

The late 1970s saw something approaching stagnation as far as moves towards European integration are concerned. It was a time when some EC mechanisms, particularly the Common Agricultural Policy, were questioned and there was a serious delay in creating a Common Fisheries Policy. Yet the twentieth anniversary of the Treaty of Rome was marked with a sense of solid achievement.

Out of the vague aspirations towards a new Europe that marked the immediate post-war period sufficient strands had emerged to show that European cooperation and integration had become a permanent feature of international relations. Such initiatives as NATO and the OEEC ensured that, at least in the fields of defence and the economy, some surrender of national sovereignty to ensure mutual benefits was seen as both necessary and possible. The Council of Europe, with its important European Convention on Human Rights, also required states to surrender some aspects of sovereignty for a greater good.

Thanks to the sectoral strategy developed by Monnet and Schuman the growth of the European Community had been an evolutionary rather than a revolutionary process. The softly-softly approach to integration and enlargement avoided the disruption of major change and created a Community strong enough to survive such strains as the position adopted by France under de

Gaulle. In the 1970s, the EC emerged as 'a geographically significant, econom-ically powerful and politically durable unit'.[23]

The nature of the Community was changing, as was inevitable with enlargement. In 1973 the six had become nine with the addition of the UK, Ireland and Denmark. With the late 1970s came the prospect of increasing to twelve with the applications of first Greece and then Spain and Portugal. Each enlargement altered the balance between federalists and functionalists with, generally speaking, the larger states – particularly France and Great Britain – in favour of intergovernmental perspectives, while the smaller states such as the Benelux countries tended to look more favourably on the supranational viewpoint.

The stance adopted by the United Kingdom in this developmental period was anomalous and often contradictory. Despite the original impetus given to European integration by Churchill's Zurich speech and the commitment of a few enthusiasts such as Edward Heath, the British proved to be very reluctant Europeans. The interesting lesson to be learned from the history of these early years is to discover just how long-standing is Britain's ambivalent attitude – wishing to seem to be a major part of Europe without wanting actually to take part. The trouble with the confrontational attitude adopted by Margaret Thatcher which so alienated her European colleagues was that it had proved so successful over the issue of the budget rebate. For some time after Fontainebleau she went on believing that her success on this one issue meant that she could control and guide her European colleagues along lines favourable to British interests on all matters. It was only later, in the rapid reso-lution of the Single European Act, that the facade began to crumble and, as Hugo Young says, 'there began to emerge the unsettling sense that she didn't know what she was doing'.[24]

Notes

1   Churchill's Zurich speech, quoted in M. Gilbert, *Never Despair – Winston S Churchill 1945–1965*, Heinemann, London, 1988, pp. 265–6.
2   Quoted in the *Saturday Evening Post*, February 1930.
3   Speech of 28 November 1949, quoted in Gilbert, *Never Despair*, p. 496.
4   Hugo Young, *This Blessed Plot*, Macmillan, London, 1998, p. 6.
5   Quoted by Young, *This Blessed Plot*, p. 32.
6   The episode of the customs union is described by Young, *This Blessed Plot*, pp. 36–7.
7   Much quoted by a wide range of sources, including Young, *This Blessed Plot*, p. 20.
8   Article 1 of the Statute of the Council of Europe, London, 1949.
9   Julian Critchley, *A Bag of Boiled Sweets*, Faber and Faber, London, 1994, pp. 124–5. As a Conservative MP Critchley served as a nominated member of the Assemblies of the Council of Europe and the Western European Union between 1972 and 1979.

10 Jean Monnet, *Memoirs*, Collins, London, 1978.
11 Text of the Messina Resolution, quoted in Neill Nugent, *The Government and Politics of the European Community*, Macmillan, London, 1991.
12 The full story of Russell Bretherton and the Spaak Committee can be found in Young, *This Blessed Plot*, p. 88–94.
13 A letter from Harold Macmillan to Selwyn Lloyd, December 1959, quoted by Young, *This Blessed Plot*, p. 118.
14 Charles de Gaulle, *Memoirs of Hope*, Weidenfeld and Nicolson, London, 1971.
15 Alistair Jones, 'UK relations with the EU, and did *you* notice the elections?', *Talking Politics*, Winter 2000, p. 312.
16 A. Crawley, *De Gaulle*, Collins, London, 1969, p. 443.
17 R. Jenkins (Lord Jenkins), *European Diary 1977–1981*, Collins, London, 1989.
18 C. Tugendhat, *Making Sense of Europe*, London, 1986.
19 Reported in Hugo Young, *One of Us*, Macmillan, London, 1989, p. 189.
20 Carrington and Gilmour related the story in a television programme, *Thatcher, the Downing Street Years* (part one), shown on BBC Television in the autumn of 1993.
21 A conversation of March 1984, quoted in Young, *One of Us*, pp. 383–4.
22 A view expressed by the Secretary-General of the European Commission, Emile Noel, during an interview with Hugo Young and quoted in *This Blessed Plot*, p. 325.
23 G.N. Minshull, *The New Europe – into the 1990s*, Hodder and Stoughton, London, 4th edn, 1990.
24 Hugo Young, *This Blessed Plot*, p. 326.

2

1985–99 – the single market, Maastricht, monetary union and Agenda 2000

Slow progress

It is sometimes said that the main problem created by the British budgetary issue was that the European Community failed to progress while the matter remained unresolved. This is not totally true, although progress during the first half of the 1980s was certainly tentative in nature. What progress as there was can be summarised as follows.

- Greece became the tenth member of the Community on 1 January 1981, while work continued on applications from Spain and Portugal.
- The EC signed the second Lomé Convention with fifty-eight ACP (Africa, Caribbean and Pacific) countries, mostly former British or French colonies.
- In 1983 a Common Fisheries Policy was agreed, establishing members' national areas within twelve miles of their own shores and acting in the interests of conservation by fixing allowable catches, divided into national quotas. The quotas would prove controversial.
- The Stuttgart Council in June 1983 issued a declaration on European Union and, in February 1984 the European Parliament (EP) approved a draft treaty for such a union.
- The EMS was working towards convergence between the economies of EC members with the ultimate goal of economic and monetary union. An important element of the EMS was the Exchange Rate Mechanism (ERM) by which EMS members undertook to keep their currencies pegged within fairly narrow bands, only a limited degree of divergence being allowed before intervention to maintain parities was invoked.

The Common Agricultural Policy

One area where progress was essential was the reform of the CAP, whose problems by the mid-1980s had reached crisis point. Any problems created by a combination of over-production and subsidies paid to small and inefficient peasant farmers were made worse by the imminent accession of Mediterranean countries. A new problem was that more efficient, scientific farming, especially in the use of chemical fertilisers, was creating environmental difficulties. When Spain and Portugal joined the Community in January 1986, the CAP was costing the EC more than 70 per cent of its total budget.

Reform was begun by Agriculture Commissioner Andriessen, who published a Commission Green Paper, *Perspectives for the Common Agricultural Policy*, in 1985. This recognised that limits would have to be placed on production, and made it clear that farmers had a part to play in conserving the environment and rural resources. In December 1986, during Britain's presidency of the Community, the Council of Agriculture Ministers produced a package of measures that included some production quota limits, amounting to something like a 6 per cent cut in milk production, and also some cuts in guaranteed prices, as with a 13 per cent cut in the guaranteed price of beef. Just over a year later, in March 1988, a special summit in Brussels approved a five-year reform package:

- farm expenditure limited to 74 per cent of the EC's growth in GDP
- production to be cut by as much as 15 per cent
- farmers compensated for 'set-aside' land.

By 1993 the reforms had been re-structured yet again by a new commissioner, Ray MacSharry of Ireland. The MacSharry proposals were based on compensation paid for land withdrawn from agricultural use: with extra payments for converting set-aside land to other uses such as leisure activities.

From the 66 per cent of Community expenditure being spent on the CAP in 1988, spending had been reduced to 55 per cent by 1992, while expenditure on the CAP in 1993 was reported to be down to 49.5 per cent.[1] Much remained to be done but a start had been made.

The Single European Act

As the 1980s progressed, 'the EC emerged from a period of stagnation into one of dynamism. This relaunching of Europe was largely based on the attempt to complete the Single Internal Market.'[2] Negotiations over the British budget and CAP had been the long overdue clearing away of dead wood and the Community was now ready to complete what had been its aim since the the Treaty of Rome – the creation of a single internal market within the Community. Statements favouring the idea had been issued by the Council, Commission or Parliament at regular intervals since 1970 but it was only after 1985, when Jacques Delors became president of the Commission, that progress towards the single market became rapid.

The Commission's White Paper on the Single European Market was presented to the Council of Ministers in June 1985 by the British Commissioner, Lord Cockfield, a former civil servant who had been chief executive of the Boots drug company before being appointed secretary of state for trade: a man much favoured by both Delors and Thatcher. He worked so quickly that a Single European Act, proposing the creation of a single market by the end of 1992, was drawn up in time for the December 1985 European Council in Luxembourg. During the following year the proposed act was ratified by the various national parliaments, the British act being steered through Westminster by Sir Geoffrey Howe. The Single European Act (SEA) became law in July 1987; the single market becoming operative on 1 January 1993.

In the light of its importance for the future development of an integrated European Community, it is worth noting the ease with which the SEA was accepted by Mrs Thatcher, the Conservative party and British parliament. The bill ratifying the act took a mere six days to pass through the Commons in April 1986 while, on the third reading, less than 200 MPs voted on the motion – 149 in favour, with 43 against.[3]

The market is essentially based on what are known as the 'four freedoms' – the freedom of movement for goods, people, capital and services without the restrictions of internal borders or customs regulations. The aspect which most obviously affected the general public was a relaxation on the amounts of tobacco and alcohol that could be purchased in other member states of the EC, a relaxation that led to a boom in cross-Channel shopping. But the SEA also affected the public through a reduction in administrative costs, both in the movement of goods and through minimal passport controls. However, details surrounding the SEA concerned more than just the single market. In what was essentially a tidying up operation, the act produced fundamental changes in the constitution and operation of the Community and represented the most far-reaching moves towards European integration that there had been since 1957. For example, the SEA:

- included many changes to the European Parliament, increasing its role in the legislative process and requiring EP assent for such things as enlargement of the Community
- increased the legislative and decision-making powers of the Council of Ministers
- extended the ability of the Council to make decisions by a qualified majority vote
- limited the power given to larger member states by the national veto
- gave legal recognition to the twice-yearly European Council summit meetings, for the first time since they began in 1975.

At that time, it has to be stressed, all these measures were purely bureaucratic in nature because they were not incorporated by Treaty and it was for that purpose that the Community moved on to consider a Treaty for European Union.

One can only assume that Mrs Thatcher accepted the Single European Act so readily because she was so pleased to be within reach of her two main aims in Europe – the reform of the CAP and the formation of a single internal market – that she ignored the supranational nature of that to which she was agreeing. Speaking some years later about Britain's acceptance of the SEA, Michael Heseltine was to say that Mrs Thatcher was responsible for 'the biggest transfer of sovereignty undertaken in any period of our history'.[4] In 1991 Lady Thatcher (as she had then become) was to claim that she had not understood the SEA when she signed it and, furthermore, that she would not have signed it if she had understood.

This attempt to plead ignorance, however, is rather questionable. Ten years later, Sir Michael Butler, for a long time Britain's permanent representative in Brussels, was to say on television, 'I never remember an occasion in the six years when I worked for her when she negotiated something without knowing exactly what it was she was talking about'.[5] Perhaps she was most guilty of misreading the character of Lord Cockfield. Originally a close confidant of Edward Heath he had proved an ardent convert to Thatcherism very shortly after she had taken over as party leader. Misled by his enthusiasm into thinking him a committed loyalist Margaret Thatcher did not see that his opinions could change again, every bit as quickly, 'effecting as swift a transfer from the Thatcher project to the Delors as he had from the Heath to the Thatcher'.[6]

The Delors presidency and the Bruges speech

In 1985, a French socialist and ardent European, Jacques Delors, became president of the Commission, a post he was to hold for a record ten years. It was an appointment that had a considerable effect, not only on the speed with which the EC began to move towards union, but on the relationship with Europe of both major political parties in Britain. From the start there were those who were highly critical of Delors because, as Nugent says:

> [Delors] has the requirement of a forceful personality, but he has also displayed traits and acted in ways which, many observers have suggested, have had the effect of undermining the team spirit of his Commission: he has indicated clear policy preferences and interests of his own; he has made important policy pronouncements before fully consulting with his colleagues in the Commission; and he has sometimes appeared to give more weight to personal advisers than to Commissioners.[7]

A committed social democrat, Delors was dedicated to the social and welfare dimension in the Community and was to produce the Community Charter of the Fundamental Social Rights of Workers (known more simply as the Social Chapter) in 1989. Early in his presidency Delors visited Britain as a guest of the TUC and made a speech to the Labour Party at a time when they, under Neil Kinnock, were moderating their policies. Thwarted as they were by the attitude of the Conservative government, both the Labour Party and the TUC found a meeting of minds with Delors, with a consequent euroenthusiast attitude adopted by Labour. On the other hand, given that Delors was a socialist, intellectual, French and a man, 'it is difficult to think of a collection of attributes less calculated to appeal to Mrs Thatcher'.[8] This conflict of attitudes led to a situation where Delors 'became, in the European context, the enemy Mrs Thatcher often seemed to need for the successful prosecution of the politics of battle'.[9] It is ironic to realise that Delors was only appointed because France's first choice as president of the Commission, Claude Cheysson, had been eliminated by Mrs Thatcher's use of the veto in the European Council. Delors, on the other hand, was initially very popular with the British government who believed that he 'began imposing our policies as a finance minister after our own hearts'.[10]

Jacques Delors soon proved that he was a euroenthusiast and a federalist. In particular, he made it abundantly clear that he favoured two specific measures that were alien to beliefs held by the Conservative government in Britain:

- European political and monetary union
- the social chapter in all EC policies and legislation.

Nothing could be more opposed to Mrs Thatcher's view of Europe, everything Delors said and did confirming her in the belief that the EC was imposing socialism onto Britain 'through the back door'. In June 1988 Jacques Delors was entrusted with studying how the Community could move towards Economic and Monetary Union (EMU). The move, which ignored all her own statements on the subject, infuriated Mrs Thatcher.

In September 1988, during a speech to the College of Europe in Bruges, the prime minister vented her anger on integrationist tendencies in Europe, saying that she had not spent nine years rolling back the frontiers of the state in Britain in order to allow that work to be overset by the manoeuvres of European bureaucrats. The Bruges speech marked a decisive turning point. Mrs Thatcher's attitude changed from a reluctant acceptance of Europe to one of outright hostility, opposed to anything that might place a restraint on the independence of the component nation-states. The greatest impact of the Bruges speech was, of course, on the Conservative party itself as it moved from a mild form of euroenthusiasm to one of euroscepticism: a sea-change of attitude that will be considered in more detail later.

The Delors Plan

Economic union for the EC was first proposed in 1969, but it was 1978 before anything concrete emerged in the form of the EMS, which was intended create monetary stability within the European Community. The EMS had three bases:

- the European Monetary Cooperation Fund (EMFC) which was intended to buy and sell EC currencies, minimising or eradicating major fluctuations in exchange rates
- the ECU or European Currency Unit, used for accountancy purposes only and based on a weighted basket of currency values
- the ERM as an agreed parity of exchange rates within which the rates of one member country would not diverge more than 2.25 per cent from those of any other member.

Britain did not join the EMS at first. Nor did Margaret Thatcher's new euroscepticism augur well for British acceptance of the proposed Economic and Monetary Union that was advocated by Jacques Delors in 1989. This proposal, arising from the negotiations which created the single market, was just part of a programme sometimes known as the Delors Plan, the mere mention of which could produce a mood of incandescent rage in Mrs Thatcher.

In April 1989 the committee chaired by Jacques Delors, which had been examining possible ways forward to achieve economic and monetary union, produced its report. This envisaged a three-stage progression towards EMU:

1 increasingly co-ordinated economic policies between EC members, within the ERM
2 foundation of an independent European Central Bank, using the US Federal Reserve Bank as a model
3 Introduction of a single European currency.

Mrs Thatcher went to the European Council meeting of June 1989 in Madrid determined not to accept the Delors proposals for monetary union. As she said in a newspaper interview, 'The Delors proposals would not command the support of the British Cabinet'.[11] On the other hand, she was accompanied to Madrid by two members of her cabinet who did wish to accept the Delors Plan – the foreign secretary, Geoffrey Howe, and the chancellor of the exchequer, Nigel Lawson. Lawson had been in favour of the ERM for some years and, although he was regularly and repeatedly denied permission to join, he had been attempting unofficially to shadow the German currency, maintaining the value of the pound at around three deutschmarks.

In Madrid both men combined against the prime minister and threatened to resign if she did not agree to the Delors Plan. Furious at what she regarded as betrayal, Mrs Thatcher was forced to sign the agreement; although she did manage to lay down four fairly stringent preconditions before Britain could join the exchange rate mechanism:

1 internal market arrangements must be completed
2 all exchange controls should be abolished
3 there should be a free and open market in financial services
4 there must be a strengthening of competition policy.

After returning from Madrid Mrs Thatcher had her revenge for what she saw as her humiliation. The following month Geoffrey Howe was demoted from foreign secretary and replaced by Mrs Thatcher's protegé, John Major. In October Nigel Lawson also felt that he too was being undermined and he resigned, to be replaced in his turn by John Major. And it was John Major, on 5 October 1990, who finally took Britain into the ERM, albeit at what many people felt at the time was a dangerously high rate of DM2.95 to the pound.

From the fall of Mrs Thatcher to Maastricht

At Strasbourg, in December 1989, the European Council accepted Delors' social chapter and agreed to set up an intergovernmental conference (IGC) on economic and monetary union, decisions that were confirmed at the Dublin Councils in April and June 1990. On all three occasions Britain was the only country opposed to the Delors proposals and an isolated Mrs Thatcher was again voted down by eleven votes to one.

In October 1990, the Italians, who held the presidency, called a special European Council in Rome to prepare for the official Council meeting which would set up the all-important IGC in December. Mrs Thatcher had been highly critical of the way in which Italy was conducting the presidency and now the Italian prime minister, Bettino Craxi, had his revenge by calling a simple majority vote on stage two of the Delors Plan, despite warnings from both Delors and Kohl not to isolate the British. Irritated by Margaret Thatcher's confrontational style, the other European leaders lined up behind Craxi to vote against her and, inevitably, Britain found herself alone against the other eleven. Mrs Thatcher was furious at the turn of events and particularly over the decision that the Community would aim to have a single currency in place before the end of the century.

In her statement to the House of Commons about the Rome Council of 15 December 1990 (at which two IGCs had been convened, one on economic union and the other on political union) Mrs Thatcher adopted a reasonable attitude at first. She was still opposed to a single currency but she was quite prepared to consider a common currency of account. The breaking point came when Neil Kinnock, as leader of the Opposition, described a different view of the Delors proposals put forward by Sir Leon Brittan, once a close political ally of Mrs Thatcher but now one of Britain's European commissioners. At this point the prime minister failed to stay calm and almost exploded with the pressure of her own frustrated anger:

> Yes, the Commission wants to increase its powers. Yes, it is a non-elected body and I do not want the Commission to increase its powers at the expense of the House, so of course we differ. The President of the Commission, Mr Delors, said at a press conference the other day that he wanted the European Parliament to be the democratic body of the Community. He wanted the Commission to be the Executive and the Council of Ministers to be the Senate. No. No. No.[12]

It was his repudiation of this speech which led to the resignation of Sir Geoffrey Howe and his own resignation speech, which played such an important part in the downfall of Margaret Thatcher.

The IGCs convened in Rome which had so upset Mrs Thatcher formulated amendments that needed to be made to the treaties establishing the European Communities, if economic and political union were to be achieved. Measures proposed by the IGC, as amended by Britain and others, were agreed by the European Council which met at Maastricht in the Netherlands on 11 December 1991. The IGCs re-convened in February 1992 to draw up an actual treaty embodying what had been agreed. It is this treaty, known as the Treaty on European Union, that was presented in its final form on 7 February 1992, creating a major landmark on the long road of European unification. The Treaty would come into force on 1 January 1994, at which point the Communities covered by the treaty would become known as the European Union. The principal aim of the Treaty, as set out in Article A, is that, 'this Treaty marks a new stage in the process of creating an ever closer union among the peoples of Europe'.[13]

There are three 'pillars' forming the European Union, defence and security one and policing and immigration policy another; neither area being dealt with by any of the original treaties. The main pillar finally established the European Community in law by incorporating the provisions of the Single European Act into the Treaty of Rome. There were also attempts to reduce the so-called 'democratic deficit' in the Community, modifying some of the more stultifyingly bureaucratic aspects of the SEA:

- the Council of Ministers acquired a greater freedom to act by the use of qualified majority voting
- increased powers were given to the European Parliament
- enhanced powers were given to the European Court of Auditors.

In the year which followed Mrs Thatcher's departure, the new prime minister, John Major, managed to stifle debate on Europe, concentrating his efforts on achieving an outcome in the IGC that would more or less satisfy all the varying

British attitudes. In particular there were two proposals in the Treaty to which Britain could not agree and John Major negotiated at length for the Treaty to be amended by the addition of two protocols. One of these removed the need for Britain to move towards economic and monetary union, while the other dealt with those social policies which require members to work towards improvements in the proper use and development of human resources, including employment and working conditions. This second protocol was binding upon eleven members of the Community, but the United Kingdom was specifically excluded for as long as the Conservatives remained in power and indeed remained until the policy was reversed in the Amsterdam Treaty of 1997.

The forward momentum of first the Single European Act and then the Treaty for European Union had been so swift and relatively trouble-free, transforming the entire European venture from head to toe in little more than seven years, that there were those who labelled the mood of the time as 'europhoric'. Yet, as soon as agreement was reached at Maastricht things began to go wrong. Lady Thatcher and right-wing Conservatives, now totally opposed to the Delors proposals, campaigned vigorously for the British people to be allowed to vote on Maastricht in a referendum along the lines of the two member countries – Denmark and Ireland – who were constitutionally required to hold referendums prior to ratification.

John Major ruled out the idea of such a thing for the UK but elsewhere the referendum issue began to cause problems. In the referendum of 2 June 1992, Denmark rejected the Maastricht proposals by a margin of 40,000 votes. Two weeks later the pendulum may have swung the other way when Ireland voted very positively, with 68 per cent of those voting saying yes, but the damage had been done. The Community was faced with the need to re-negotiate Danish terms for the Treaty and these in turn had be submitted to another referendum. Further political problems arose when France also decided to hold a referendum and a French rejection began to seem quite possible. In fact, when the referendum was held on 20 September, the vote was for acceptance, but only by the very small majority of 51 per cent to 49. One commentator could write, 'Public disquiet about the Treaty, expressed in the EC's "Eurobarometer" opinion polls, and in the Danish and French referendums, lends support to the claim that European integration is an élite-led process, viewed with indifference or hostility by the peoples of Europe'.[14]

German re-unification and a British exit from the ERM

In mid-September 1992 serious flaws within the ERM began to show themselves. Since 1979 the ERM had largely maintained parity between currencies, mostly because of a strong deutschmark and the controlling hand of the Bundesbank. When economic union was first mooted a necessary precondition of membership was satisfying 'convergence criteria', by which the economies of at least seven members had to sustain a stable parity of currencies over a period. Until then interim members only allowed exchange rates and levels of inflation and growth to diverge within very narrow limits, correcting any drift by fiscal measures such as interest rates. The strength of the German economy meant that the deutschmark and Bundesbank formed the main reference points for regulating the European economy.

Between 1989 and 1990 the Soviet bloc collapsed, the Berlin Wall came down, the communist government of East Germany (DDR) fell and Germany was reunited by redesignating the DDR provinces as *länder* of the Federal Republic. Economic problems associated with the DDR were made worse by Chancellor Kohl's insistence that the exchange rate between east and west versions of the deutschmark should be on a one-for-one basis. The vast sums of money expended in this currency exchange combined with other factors to throw the German economy into crisis.

Many countries in the EC slumped into recession and, during the summer of 1992, the weaker currencies within the ERM – the pound sterling, the Italian lira and the Spanish peseta – proved to be overvalued in comparison with the deutschmark and came under heavy pressure from currency speculators. The mechanisms of the ERM demanded that the EC central banks should intervene and buy those currencies under threat. But rigid anti-inflationary measures introduced by Germany to ease re-unification meant that the Bundesbank could not provide the necessary support.

- In September 1992, the adverse Danish and French referendums created uncertainty in the money markets and there was a massive movement out of weaker currencies into the deutschmark.
- Over the weekend of 13–14 September Italy devalued the lira by 6 per cent and pressure increased on the pound and French franc.
- On 16 September (Black Wednesday) desperate measures raised the British interest rate twice in the same morning, taking it to an astonishing 15 per cent. At the same time the Bank of England intervened on the money markets and spent millions of pounds in an attempt to prop up its value. In the afternoon the British government bowed to the inevitable, cut interest rates to where they had started and withdrew from the ERM. The same day Italy also 'temporarily suspended' its ERM membership.

For Britain the value of the pound fell rapidly to find its true level and the crisis was over. There was talk of returning to the ERM when conditions were better but, unofficially, most people said that they could not envisage conditions becoming right in the foreseeable future. On 1 August 1993 an emergency meeting of EC finance ministers agreed that ERM constraints should be relaxed and fluctuation of 15 per cent allowed.

Debating Maastricht

The currency crisis was inextricably entwined with negotiations over Maastricht, as witness two European Council meetings during the British presidency in the second half of 1992. In Birmingham on 16 October, an emergency meeting was called to resolve the Danish crisis. In the event, the ERM dominated the Birmingham Council and the Maastricht Treaty was carried forward to Edinburgh on 11–12 December. At that meeting Major got most of what he wanted: Denmark gained an opt-out on EMU like that obtained by Britain, concessions were made on the defence and security pillar and other adjustments were made in advance of the second Danish referendum of May 1993, adjustments which ensured that the Danes accepted Maastricht by 56.8 per cent to 43.2.

As a counter-weight to any suggestions of federalism or centralism embodied in the Maastricht Treaty Major promoted subsidiarity at Edinburgh; subsidiarity meaning:

- proposals by the centre in Brussels should be implemented according to the decisions of national or regional government
- no major policy decision should be made in Brussels if it is more properly the concern of national or regional government.

Article A of the Treaty now reads, 'creating an ever-closer union among the peoples of Europe, *in which decisions are taken as closely as possible to the citizen*'.

The debate on Maastricht which now resumed in the British parliament was not strictly necessary for ratification and was much more about internal Conservative policies than about Europe and will be discussed more closely in the chapter on party attitudes. The process took up 204 hours of debate, 163 of these in one twenty-three-day Committee of the Whole House. It also involved seventy divisions, one of which was lost by the government, and another of which became a vote of confidence in the government. It was 2 August 1993 before the UK could ratify the Treaty but Germany was actually the last to ratify on 12 October 1993. Despite the problems, the Treaty became operational as planned on 1 January 1994, the European Community thereby becoming absorbed within the European Union.

Enlargement

A major factor affecting Europe in the 1990s was that the process of enlargement seemed to be accelerating, with an increasing number of countries applying to join, carrying the potential membership to between twenty-five and thirty; a different situation from the first thirty years, which is how long it took for membership to increase from six to twelve.

The first enlargement of the EC by Britain, Ireland and Denmark was delayed by de Gaulle. It has been claimed that the second and third enlargements of the 1980s, by Greece, Spain and Portugal, were delayed by the fact that all three countries were somewhat less than democratic when they first became eligible for membership; Greece being ruled by a military junta and the other two having fascist dictators. In fact, the real cause of delay in processing the Greek, Spanish and Portuguese applications was probably less to do with democracy than because all three countries had weaker economies than the existing members. In particular, a lot of complex negotiations proved necessary in order to extend the CAP to countries with a Mediterranean agriculture.

After the accession of Spain and Portugal in 1986 the movement toward enlargement gathered additional momentum, until there were three groups of would-be members.

- The first group consisted of Turkey, who applied in 1987, and the islands of Malta and Cyprus, who applied in 1990. In December 1989 the Commission advised the Council of Ministers to reject the Turkish application, partly out of doubts over human rights violations. The applications of Cyprus and Malta remained on the table but were elbowed to one side by other developments.
- The second group of aspirants to membership were former members of the Soviet bloc, most of whom negotiated 'Europe Agreements' with the EU giving them favourable trade terms. The countries most enthusiastic for membership were the Czech Republic, Hungary and Poland. After the accessions of 1995 these three countries together with Slovakia, Bulgaria, Romania and Slovenia, became the focus of attention.
- The third group of applicants consisted of former EFTA countries who, concerned at the implications of the single market, and freed from fears for their neutrality by the end of the Cold War, applied first for associate status and then for full membership. The applicants were Austria, Finland, Norway, Sweden and Switzerland, who would initially join the single market to form a European Economic Area (EEA). Britain was very keen on these five applicants because:
  - enlargement would dilute the federalist tendencies of the Union
  - all five countries are wealthy and potential net contributors to the Community budget, easing the strain for existing net contributors.

As a result of a referendum in December 1992 Switzerland withdrew their application to both the EEA and EU. However, Austria, Sweden and Finland pressed ahead and opened negotiations on 1 February 1993, with Norway following on 5 April. Negotiations were rapid, agreement on Finnish and Swedish entry being reached by 28 February 1994 and the Austrian application following the next day, while negotiations with Norway extended for a further week. All was settled by early March 1994 and accession for all four countries was fixed for 1 January 1995, at which point Britain, with some backing by Spain, demanded that there be no change to majority voting procedures in the Council of Ministers.

The dispute threatened a serious delay because, unless the position could be resolved quickly, the accession treaties could not come before the EP before it was dissolved for the June 1994 elections. This was another round in the Conservative Party's internal argument over Europe and was less about European voting rights than about keeping face in the eyes of party critics at home. The British position, however, was non-sustainable – concessions were made at the eleventh hour and a compromise agreed.

Once the dispute over voting rights had been settled, the accession of the four applicants could proceed, although the applicant countries still had to seek the approval of their own citizens. Referendums in Austria, Finland and Sweden approved the accession agreements, although by very small majorities in the latter two cases. Then, on 28 November, the people of Norway voted against membership, as they had done in 1972. Norway joined Switzerland, Leichtenstein and Iceland in being the only Western European countries not belonging to the EU, retaining the trading benefits of EEA membership, but without any power to influence decisions of that body.

Norway is often cited by eurosceptics as an example of a country which manages to reap the trading benefits of EEA membership, without the adverse factors of EU membership; suggesting that such an arrangement would make an ideal solution for the UK. However, as Hugo Young has pointed out, the idea that Norway has all the advantages of membership without any of the disadvantages is the reverse of the truth. 'The entire apparatus of EU rules on immigration, transport, manufacture and trade in goods and services applies in Norway. Norway's courts and companies live under law as interpreted by the European Court in Luxembourg. This is the precondition for Norway's trade with the EU, unmediated, however, by the presence of any Norwegian ministers at the political table.'[15]

Appointment of the Santer Commission

The main business of the European Council held on the island of Corfu in June 1994 was the election of a new president of the Commission to succeed Jacques Delors. According to tradition the presidency of the Commission is held alternately by someone coming from a large member country and someone from a small country; by someone on the left and someone on the right. Since 1984 the Commission had been headed by a French socialist and it therefore followed that the new president should be a centre-right politician from one of the Benelux countries.

The most obvious candidates were Ruud Lubbers, the Dutch prime minister, and Jean-Luc Dehaene, prime minister of Belgium. Unfortunately, Mr Lubbers had upset Chancellor Kohl in a dispute between Germany and the Netherlands and, at a meeting in early June Chancellor Kohl and President Mitterand of France had decided that the post should be given to Mr Dehaene. Several EC members, particularly the Dutch, Italians and Spanish, were unhappy at this Franco-German manipulation and were prepared to vote against Dehaene on the first ballot, although knowing they would ultimately have to accept the majority choice.

Not so Mr Major. Supported by Douglas Hurd, he stated bluntly that, if he could not have the British commissioner, Leon Brittan, he might settle for Ruud Lubbers, but he would never accept Jean-Luc Dehaene and he would be prepared to use the British veto to prevent the Belgian from becoming president. The British stressed that there was nothing personal in their rejection of Mr Dehaene: the objection, said Douglas Hurd, was the way in which Kohl and Mitterand had done a secret deal that the rest were supposed to accept without question.

The other members interpreted Britain's stance as due to Major's need to look tough and resolute in the eyes of the eurosceptics in his own party at home. However, they assumed that, having proved his virility by waving the big stick, Major would back down and accept Dehaene. Instead, the British prime minister stuck to his threat and duly employed the veto. It was a significant moment in Britain's relations with the Community because, by using the ultimate weapon of the veto for party political purposes, John Major had just broken the unwritten rules of the EC club.

Once the Germans had taken over the presidency from the Greeks in July intensive discussions ensured that, by the time the ministers met in Brussels, it was to rubber-stamp a previously determined choice in Jacques Santer, prime minister of Luxembourg.

On 20 July the EP, newly elected in June, chose to exercise the right granted to the Parliament by the Maastricht Treaty, and voted on whether to accept the nominee for Commission president. The British Labour Group of MEPs voted to reject Mr Santer on the grounds that he had been appointed by the Council of Ministers without the consultation procedures written into the TEU. The Labour Group's lead was followed by the Socialist Group as a whole and, since the Socialist Group formed the largest party grouping in the EP, there looked to be a real danger that Mr Santer might be rejected. The Parliament's rejection would not be binding but it was hard to see how Mr Santer could carry on with any credibility once he had been rejected. As it was, Santer was accepted by a mere twenty-two votes and the crisis was over. But the chain of events that began in Corfu made three important points:

- John Major's use of the veto may have restored his personal standing with the Conservative Party but it weakened Britain's standing in Europe
- in the aftermath of the Delors era the Council of Ministers was perfectly willing to see the Commission weakened and marginalised

- the EP now had real powers for the first time, and intended to use them.

Another legacy of Corfu was that, for the two-and-a-half dying years of the Major government eurosceptics in the Conservative ranks seized on the national veto as the last bastion of sovereignty, while majority voting was something to be resisted. Tory ministers represented the right of a British minister to block the wishes of other member countries the last ditch defence of British sovereign rights. As part of its strategy to force Europe to abandon the ban on British beef in 1996, the British government made great use of its veto to block any decision making by the Council of Ministers. This conduct merely ensured that the BSE crisis continued to the year 2000 and beyond.

New Labour and the people's Europe

Maastricht had laid down a timetable for monetary union, with the first wave of members joining in 1998, as well as establishing those convergence criteria which member countries would have to satisfy before being allowed to join. At the time of Maastricht the UK won an opt-out clause in the Treaty which meant that Britain did not have to join if it did not wish to do so. At that time of economic recession in Britain it seemed that the UK could never satisfy the convergence criteria so no one worried overmuch about an issue which might never happen. As the UK economy improved, however, the possibility of the UK joining EMU in the first wave became ever more real, making eurosceptics demand even more stridently that membership of EMU should be ruled out, at any time and under any conditions.

Europe therefore became a major issue in the 1997 general election but not in the way that anyone might have expected.

- The debate on Europe was initiated by eurosceptics in the Conservative party, encouraged by the tabloid press but later Labour introduced the topic, knowing that a mere mention of Europe provoked a Tory response that was both self-destructive and self-defeating.
- Discussions concerning Europe were almost exclusively about the single currency, about which the general public had no firm opinion. Other European issues like fish quotas and beef bans, which really were of some concern to the electorate, were largely ignored.
- There is no evidence that the British people are as europhobic as the right wing of the Conservative Party think they are. The British people dislike foreigners, particularly the Germans and French; they do not like the idea of 'losing the pound' and they can get very annoyed with the 'nit-picking' bureaucracy of Brussels. However, abstract arguments over concepts such as national sovereignty come a very poor second to bread-and-butter election issues like taxation or education.

In contrast to the increasingly europhobic position adopted by the Conservative Party in opposition, the re-establishment of Britain's position in Europe was one of the first priorities of the Blair government after the 1997 victory.

- Within days of becoming foreign secretary Robin Cook had committed the British government to signing the Social Chapter and agreed to extensions of majority voting. Doug Henderson was appointed as the first specifically European minister at the Foreign Office and it was made clear that in future intergovernmental talks Britain would be represented by Henderson as a minister, rather than by a civil servant as had been the case under the Conservatives, thus bringing UK procedures into line with other member states.
- Within a month Robin Cook had gone further than any British minister had gone before by appointing an MEP as his European parliamentary private secretary to handle liaison with the EP.
- These concessions, together with a willingness to negotiate and accept compromises rather than seek confrontation, sent out hints to Europe that Britain would henceforth be far less obstructionist than had been the case in recent years. This change in relations between Britain and the EU was more a change of style and attitude rather than one of substance but it proved acceptable to the other member states and Tony Blair's first European Council meeting in Noordwijk seemed bathed in goodwill. The prime minister was still basking in the glow of European approval when he faced his first summit meeting at Amsterdam in July when the IGC set up to succeed Maastricht was to be resolved.

In negotiations to draw up the Amsterdam Treaty this new mood of give and take meant that other member states were more ready to accommodate British positions on contentious issues. The Amsterdam Council was hailed as a triumph for Tony Blair and his government in that, without surrendering a tough negotiating stance, the Blair team showed a willingness to listen to the arguments, an ability to compromise when required and a reluctance to employ the British veto. It was obvious that this honeymoon effect would wear off and Europe would become more critical of Blair and his government, but such criticism as there has been has fallen far short of the outright hostility engendered by the Thatcherite tactics typical of the later Conservative years.

At the heart of New Labour's approach to the problems facing the European Union is the need to reform EU institutions and procedures in order to meet the issues created by a wider union. Very shortly after his election victory, Tony Blair announced that, just as he had modernised his party and created New Labour, he now wanted to create a new kind of Europe: a People's Europe that would empower its own citizens. And Blair stressed the central role he wanted Britain to take in the creation of this new Europe.[16]

In the first half of 1998 the UK assumed the presidency of the European Union, taking office at a critical time for the Union since, within the six month period of the presidency:

- the outcome of the Amsterdam IGC had to be finalised and assessed, completing work begun at Maastricht
- the go ahead for monetary union (EMU) had to be given
- the Central European Bank had to be established
- the nature and number of member states willing and qualified to become members of EMU had to be determined
- moves had to be made with regard to the enlargement of the Union, with eleven states competing for accession, many of them with serious problems over meeting the conditions for entry.

With all that to do, the British government was aware that it had been in power for little more than seven months when it took over the presidency and could therefore be considered as totally inexperienced. The Blair government had not only to lead the EU through a series of vitally important community decisions but had to do so while simultaneously proving its own European credentials in the wake of an outgoing government that was ambivalent about Europe to say the least. Most interestingly and paradoxically, the UK had to negotiate and administer the start of monetary union while retaining the UK's opted-out determination not to join in the first wave of participants.[17]

The Amsterdam Treaty

At the intergovernmental conference in Amsterdam:

- agreement was reached on a range of internal security measures, including freedom of movement, immigration, political asylum and harmonisation of civil laws such as divorce
- '*The IGC has incorporated into the Treaty the Agreement on Social Policy which previously only applied to fourteen Member States*' – in other words, Britain gave up its solitary opt-out on the Social Chapter
- strong measures were introduced against discrimination on the grounds of gender, race, religion, sexual orientation or age
- policing remained with national governments but a supranational Europol was inaugurated
- Britain and Ireland, as island members with a terrorist problem, were allowed to retain their external border control
- plans by France and Germany to make the Western European Union into the defence arm of the European Union were blocked by Britain, Finland, Sweden and Ireland, leaving NATO as the safeguard of European defence

• new anti-unemployment measures were introduced across Europe. The European Investment Bank will make £700 million available to underwrite pan-European job creation schemes and an employment chapter written into the revised Treaty for European Union.[18]

The Amsterdam Council failed to agree on new constitutional structures for the EU prior to current applicants for membership being accepted into the Union. There was a feeling that a general willingness to allow for Blair's inexperience led the other leaders to give the prime minister an easy ride, giving ground in a number of controversial areas, such as the constitutional matters mentioned above, as well as defence and security, and leading to a bland treaty that left unresolved quite a few of the issues carried forward from Maastricht.

It was to continue the examination of these issues that Jacques Santer went before the EP on 16 July 1997 to outline the Commission's strategy for strengthening and widening the Union in the early years of the 21st century. This strategy is known as 'Agenda 2000'.

Agenda 2000

The document submitted by the Commission is 1,300 pages long and makes a detailed assessment of what needs to be done in the wake of the Maastricht and Amsterdam treaties.

1 The enlargement of the union through the accession of new member states. Five countries were judged to be ready for serious negotiations to begin in 1998: Hungary, Poland, the Czech Republic, Slovenia and Estonia. Also included in this first phase of negotiations was Cyprus, which had had the implicit approval of the Commission for some time. Forming a second phase of applicants were five more countries from eastern or central Europe: Bulgaria, Romania, Latvia, Lithuania and Slovakia. When negotiations for this second phase of applicants were completed at Helsinki in December 1999, Malta had also been reinstated as applicant after a change of government and, in a surprise move, thirty-six years after the country's first application, Turkey was also given the go-ahead for membership negotiations to begin. The first accessions envisaged by Agenda 2000 are unlikely to take place before the years 2002 or 2003.

2 A greater pro-active role in foreign affairs. The international community has expressed disappointment with the part played by the EU in a wide range of international crises such as:

• wars in Bosnia, Kosovo and elsewhere in the former Yugoslavia
• the Palestinian peace process

- the financial and economic crisis in the Far East
- a code of conduct for arms sales and so on.

All too often the member countries have failed to develop a united policy and the United States has been permitted to impose its own views and policy on the rest of the world, rather than developing a clear, alternative European strategy. At the Helsinki summit in December 1999 a decision was made to set up the EU's own rapid-reaction force, which could take action if NATO and the USA were unwilling to be involved.

3 Further institutional and constitutional reform. Certain reforms or changes need to be made in order to streamline the EU prior to enlargement. There also needs to be some form of community accountability to remove a long-standing democratic deficit. Two reforms in particular need to be:

- Reducing the number of Commissioners.
- A more general use of qualified majority voting in the Council of Ministers.

4 Effective action is needed to create employment and reduce unemployment. A new deal would include increased:

- education and training
- flexibility of working conditions and hours
- mobility, recognising that EU citizens have the right to work in any member country.

5 Further reform of the Common Agricultural Policy. This is vital if the European Union is not to be bankrupted by enlargement. Even after widespread reforms of the early 1990s had transferred aid for rural communities from the CAP to regional funds, the CAP still accounted for more than 50 per cent of the EU budget, while agriculture itself represented a mere two per cent of the EU's gross domestic product. In addition, even more alarming possibilities loomed through enlargement: the accession of Poland alone could, in itself, almost double the amount of subsidy paid out to peasant farmers.

Negotiations which began under the German presidency in early 1999 were extremely bitter, largely because Germany was no longer willing or able to act as the EU's major net contributor and, along with Britain, wanted a system of co-financing introduced whereby national governments would have to make up for any EU reductions. Those proposed reductions in subsidies were hard-fought, however, and by the time of the Berlin summit in March had been severely trimmed back. For example, beef subsidies were reduced by just 20 per cent rather than the 30 per cent proposed. In addition, the reforms were to be phased in over seven years and would not be in place until 2006.

Monetary union

With the Treaty of Maastricht, progress towards EMU moved into phase two of the Delors Plan. Under the guidance of the Economic and Finance Council (Ecofin) of the EU, EMU would create three institutions:

- the European Central Bank (ECB) to operate monetary policies such as the setting of interest rates for the EMU as a whole
- the European System of Central Banks (ESCB), made up of the fifteen central banks of EU member states, in conjunction with the ECB, and is intended to be the overall coordinating body determining monetary policy for EMU
- a common currency, the euro, its value initially based on the ECU basket of currencies.

Of all the integrationist measures proposed for Europe, this is the one most distrusted by the eurosceptics. Emotionally, the sceptics use patriotism to argue against monetary union, refusing to 'give up the pound' in favour of some alien imposition. However, the retention of the pound is largely irrelevant. The valid political argument of those opposed to EMU is that the existence of a European central bank would mean that the British government would lose control of the British economy, forfeiting the right to set budgetary measures such as tax and interest rates.

At Maastricht John Major won an opt-out for Britain by which this country could choose whether or not to join monetary union, if and when it ever happened. A similar opt-out was also obtained by Denmark, joined by Sweden after their accession. From 1995 onwards, government policy was that Britain was lucky enough as to be able to wait and see what was on offer before deciding on whether to join or not.

After Labour's 1997 victory government policy officially remained the same, because Tony Blair accepted Major's wait-and-see approach and made it his own (see Appendix 6). According to the Labour government Britain would not join EMU with the first wave of countries in 1999 but would make a decision regarding entry at a later date 'when the time was right'. The Labour government also undertook to put the issue to the country in a referendum before joining.

It has long been accepted that Tony Blair was more in favour of EMU than against it, while Gordon Brown, the chancellor, was enthusiastically and increasingly in favour, alongside the Treasury team and the entire business and political community. Yet the government remained strangely reticent, possibly for fear of sceptics in the tabloid press such as the *Sun*, and a suspicion that to advocate European unity is to court electoral rejection. 'Now, by sidelining EMU from immediate decisions, he [Blair] was pre-empting a Murdoch onslaught which, he feared, might undercut his prospects of a second term'.[19] To political commentators it seemed as though Tony Blair was in essence buying time since the success or failure of the single currency would be so manifest by the year 2002 that Britain's course of action would be blindingly clear.

As far back as the 1950s when the Treaty of Rome was proposed, eurosceptics have comforted themselves with the thought that any movement towards unity could never happen. Now the same sceptics confidently predicted that not more than one or two countries would be able to meet EMU convergence criteria. As recently as May 1997, even a europhile like Kenneth Clarke was saying that EU members were in such economic difficulty that the single currency would probably never happen. It was, however, whistling in the wind.

On 1 May 1998 the European Monetary Union was created at an Ecofin meeting in Brussels. Only one country – Greece – had failed to meet the convergence criteria. Despite being qualified to join, Denmark and Sweden decided to side with Britain and opted out of EMU for the moment, and so eleven countries actually signed the agreement on 1 May. One irony of the situation was that, with Britain holding the EU presidency at the time, Gordon Brown had to take the chair for the actual ceremony creating monetary union but then had to withdraw from the room while the ESCB members of Ecofin discussed matters related to the euro which the UK is barred from discussing.

Just one day later, on 2 May 1998, EMU plunged into its first crisis. It had been agreed that the first president of the European Central Bank should be a respected Dutch candidate, Wim Duisenberg, the preferred choice of the Germans. At the last minute the French claimed the position for their own nominee, Jean-Claude Trichet, and a bitter argument broke out between the French and Germans. There was awkward confrontation for a time and the British presidency was much criticised for a dispute in which the views of smaller member countries were sidelined. Finally, however, the contenders reached a classic EU compromise with the two men agreeing to split the eight-year term as first president between them. As if to show that such disagreements do not count for anything in the financial world, the euro soared in value on the money markets.

Once EMU had been agreed and the euro became a reality on 1 January 1999, there was a sense in which British involvement became inevitable. Europhobes may demand that Britain preserves its own currency and has nothing to do with the euro, but the fact remains that it will inevitably use and trade in the common currency if only because the eleven EU members who have agreed to the common currency represent a trading bloc with which Britain conducts 60 per cent of its trade. British citizens are at liberty to open euro bank accounts, to pay their bills in euros and if, like a good half of the country, they holiday in France, Italy or Spain, not to mention the Republic of Ireland, they will become accustomed to dealing in euros. It was always possible that Britain will drift into acceptance and usage of the single currency – almost by default.

On the other hand, the new currency did not achieve success at first. From the start it was weak on the world markets and began to lose value against the dollar. By January 2000, the euro had slid below parity with the dollar to be worth little more than 98 cents. Several economies, and particularly that of Germany, had performed so badly that lines of convergence which had worked so well before 1998 began to diverge again. To the phobes and sceptics the moral was clear and no doubt the case for British membership was weakened. The question of monetary union nevertheless remains as one of the two major features of the EU's future.

Reform of the Commission

Typical of what has been called a 'democratic deficit at the heart of European institutions' has been the European Parliament, a body without power or accountability, easily dismissed as 'just a talking-shop'. Until 1979 and the first direct elections of MEPs, delegates to the EP were nominated by national governments, with no democratic mandate at all. Since then, despite agreements like the Maastricht Treaty, the EP is still very limited in what it can do since its powers have always been restricted by the member states for fear that a strong Parliament would weaken national parliaments. The EP is supposed to scrutinise legislation proposed by the Commission and Council of Ministers but, although about 75 per cent of EP amendments are accepted by the Commission, less than 20 per cent get past the Council into final legislation.

However, at the end of 1998 and early in 1999 a series of events culminated in a dispute between European Parliament and Commission that lent such serious democratic credibility to the Parliament, at the expense of the Commission, that Martin Walker of the *Guardian* felt able to say, 'The commission's 40 year reign ended this week'. In mid-December 1998 the Parliament chose to block the Community budget by refusing to approve the Commission's handling of the 1996 budget by 270 votes to 225. There are two important points to be made about this protest.

- Initially a French commissioner, the former prime minister, Edith Cresson, was accused of fraud associated with the *Leonardo* education scheme, a Spanish commissioner, Manuel Marin, was accused of misusing Mediterranean funds and the Swedish and Finnish commissioners, Erkki Liikanen and Anita Gradin, were judged negligent by the auditors. Even the name of the president of the Commission, Jacques Santer, cropped up in the course of an enquiry by the Luxembourg police.
- Strictly speaking individual members of the Commission cannot be dismissed; the only sanction available to the EP being to dismiss the Commission in its entirety. However, such a measure seemed to be a little over-severe when the Commission was due to retire in June 1999. Most national governments did not wish to see the Commission embarrassed and

a significant number of European Socialists, led by the UK's Pauline Green, announced that they would not vote for any motion of censure against the Commission.

That should have ended the matter, since the EP would obviously not get the two-thirds majority needed to dismiss the Commission, but the Irish MEP Pat Cox, leader of the European Liberals, discovered a way to censure individual selected commissioners. An alliance of Greens, Liberals, German Social Democrats and about half the parties of the right introduced a motion on 14 January 1999 condemning Cresson and Marin for their individual faults and censuring the Commission in general and Jacques Santer in particular. Cresson and Marin survived the individual votes, but the overall vote of censure, while defeated by 293 votes to 232, nevertheless forced the Commission to make significant concessions:

- commissioners must now publish a register of interests and end patronage for family and friends
- the Commission must accept inspection teams of MEPs with the right to demand the sight of all documents and dossiers
- any commissioner found guilty of fraud or malpractice will be instantly dismissed
- a committee will be appointed by the EP to oversee all Commission financial arrangements.

For the moment Santer and his Commissioners survived. But in early March an independent review and audit of the incidence of fraud in the Community, by the so-called Committee of the Wise, came up with a report which 'found the Commission guilty of lax management at the highest level'.[20] By using the phrase 'highest level' it was saying that Jacques Santer himself was deeply implicated in the mess of corruption and mismanagement revealed by the report. In fact, of the twenty commissioners, less than half survived with a completely clean record. An outraged European Parliament demanded and obtained the resignation of the entire Commission.

To everyone's astonishment, Jacques Santer stated that the report described him as 'whiter than white' and declared that he had every intention of staying on as a 'caretaker' until the end of the year. The most clearly guilty commissioner, Edith Cresson, dismissed her own guilt by saying 'Maybe I was a little careless'. Infuriated at this attitude the president of the European Parliament, Jose-Maria Gil-Robles, announced the unanimous decision of all political groups that the Santer Commission should go and be replaced by a new Commission within the month.

In the choice of a new president there were early indications of horse-trading, with Germany and Britain favouring a candidate from the Netherlands whereas the majority favoured the idea of a president from a southern

European country. But Tony Blair made it clear that he did not want the sort of haggling that had characterised Corfu and resulted in the appointment of Jacques Santer. On the opening day of the Berlin summit, 24 March, there was a rapid and unanimous decision to appoint a former Italian prime minister, Romano Prodi.

Prodi and the caretaker team he appointed had to face intensive questioning from the EP and, what is more, the new Commission he appointed after the June elections faced an even more intense scrutiny under the new procedures (see Appendix 4). Prodi was given a hard time but there were several factors operating in his favour, suggesting he is likely to be a suitable president to lead the EU into the twenty-first century:

- Prodi is a centrist and the centre-right EP elected in 1999 is likely to favour him more than the outgoing socialist-dominated parliament
- Prodi is dedicated to reforming the institutions of the Community and has appointed Neil Kinnock as his deputy-president with the special responsibility of administrative reform
- Prodi has strong federalist principles and favours a European army, co-ordinated tax systems and a genuine single market.

Notes

1 Figures based on those given in Victor Keegan and Martin Kettle, *The New Europe*, Fourth Estate, London, 1993.
2 Daniel Wincott, 'The Conservative Party and Europe', *Politics Review*, April 1992, p. 12.
3 Hugo Young, *This Blessed Plot*, Macmillan, London 1998, p. 334.
4 Michael Heseltine in an interview with the *Independent*, 10 October 1989.
5 Sir Michael Butler, speaking on *The Last Europeans*, Channel 4 Television, July 1995.
6 Young, *This Blessed Plot*, as above, p. 328.
7 Neill Nugent, *The Government and Politics of the European Community*, Macmillan, London, 1991, pp. 70–1.
8 Alan Watkins, *A Conservative Coup*, Duckworth, London, 1992.
9 Hugo Young, *This Blessed Plot*, p. 327.
10 Lord (Geoffrey) Howe, speaking on *The Last Europeans*.
11 *The Times*, 27 June 1989.
12 Mrs Thatcher to the House of Commons, *Hansard*, 30 October 1990.
13 The full text of the Treaty is published in English by the Office for Official Publications of the European Communities, Luxembourg, 1992.
14 P. Lynch, 'Europe's post-Maastricht muddle', *Politics Review*, November 1993, p. 2.
15 Hugo Young, *This Blessed Plot*, p. 504.
16 Colin Pilkington, 'Europe', in Steve Lancaster (ed.) *Developments in Politics, Vol. 10*, Causeway Press, Ormskirk, 1999.

17 Material presented to those attending People's Europe 98, a conference of non-governmental organisations held at the London School of Economics, 5–7 June 1998.

18 Taken from the communiqué detailing agreements reached at Amsterdam, published by the Council of Ministers and to be found on the EU website: http://europa.eu.int

19 Hugo Young, *This Blessed Plot*, p. 494.

20 Martin Walker and Michael White, 'Chaos, fraud, failure but the man at the top says: I'll stay', *Guardian*, 17 March 1999.

3

The institutions of the European Union at the turn of the century

The organisational structure of the European Community[1] as it was made up of Assembly, Council, Commission and Court of Justice, together with the advisory Economic and Social Committee (ESC), was formally established by the Treaty of Rome in 1957, although the basic structure was already in existence, being that devised for the ECSC in 1951. Outwardly, these institutions have changed very little over nearly forty years of existence, despite the mutation of the Assembly into the European Parliament, but, behind their apparently unchanging facade, their underlying nature and functions has been subject to a fundamental process of change which continues still – as was the case in 1979 when the Parliament became directly elected for the first time. In addition, new institutions have emerged over the last twenty years, such as the European Court of Auditors, the European Investment Bank, the European Ombudsman, the Committee of the Regions and the European Central Bank.

One aim of Maastricht was supposed to be the re-definition of the institutions of the EU in the light of these organisational changes, formalising the resulting amendments by incorporation in the Treaty. Even so, it was not possible to complete a full review of the institutions at Maastricht and, like other aspects of the Treaty, this was one of the tasks passed to the IGC which reported at Amsterdam in 1997. And even that was not completed.

Two constitutional problems influence the re-structuring of the EU's institutions:

1 the so-called 'democratic deficit' of those institutions
2 the vexed question of the rights belonging to individual member nation-states.

Most of the bodies involved in the policy and decision-making processes of the EU are not directly accountable to the peoples of the Union. Until 1979 the Assembly was appointed rather than elected and, even after the introduction of direct elections, the European Parliament was left with very few powers to control the Commission, and even less to control the Council of Ministers. As Nugent says 'It is the case that Community decision-makers are less directly accountable than are national decision-makers'.[2] Constitutionalists would argue that the Council of Ministers, composed of elected ministers of the member countries, can be considered accountable in that those ministers are answerable to the electorate of their own countries. The subtext, however, is that countries such as Britain argue against giving too much power to the European Parliament because by doing so the sovereignty of national parliaments is undermined.

Another issue generating supranational versus intergovernmental arguments concerns the comparative powers of member states that are of disparate sizes and populations. Germany has a population of 80 million, while Luxembourg has 400,000. If each state were to have equal voting rights then Luxembourg would have an influence equal to that of a country 200 times greater. On the other hand, to giving member countries an influence weighted for comparative size would mean that larger states could trample at will over the wishes of smaller countries.

The eighteenth-century solution arrived at by the Federalists drawing up the United States constitution was to create two houses of Congress in which one, the House of Representatives, represents the population through constituencies of roughly equal size; while the second, the Senate, represents states' rights by having equal representation (two senators) for each state of the union. There are those in Europe who would like to replicate this system by granting full legislative powers to the European Parliament and Council of Ministers, the EP taking the role of the House of Representatives and the Council acting as Senate. This, however, met with opposition from anti-federal national governments and, although the EP has gained a considerable number of additional powers and legitimacy since Maastricht it has not been sufficient to remove the democratic deficit, let alone make the Parliament a true legislative body.

The Commission

The College of Commissioners

The Commission is the executive arm of the European Union and is sometimes perceived as the 'government' of the Community, while others see it as the 'civil service'. In fact it is neither. In policy-making decisions the Commission differs from a civil service in that it formulates statements of policy but, unlike a government, it is powerless to control the vote on acceptance or rejection of that policy.

There are twenty members of the College of Commissioners, forming the political arm of the Commission and representing all fifteen member countries.

The five largest member states – France, Germany, Italy, Spain and the UK – have two commissioners each and all the rest have just one. Those people nominated to be commissioners are experienced politicians, often having held ministerial office in their home countries before going to Brussels.

The number of commissioners, having started as nine in 1957, is growing all the time and this remains a major problem in view of the possible enlargement of EU membership to as many as twenty-six within the next decade. As long ago as 1977 Roy Jenkins was complaining that there were more commissioners than there were suitable portfolios for them, and that was when there were only thirteen commissioners in all.[3] At Helsinki in 1999 it was agreed that the present Commission would be the last in which any country would have more than two commissioners and the question was passed to the IGC as to whether the smaller states might not have to share commissioners between themselves.

Since January 1995 commissioners have been appointed to serve for five years: prior to that the period was four years. This five-year term now coincides with the life of the European Parliament, although the commissioners take office in January; six months after the June parliamentary elections. This delay is so that the commissioners-designate can be vetted by the new Parliament before they take office.

In theory, according to the Treaty of Rome, appointment to the Commission is a collective decision of all member governments. In fact, the appointments are usually the result of nominations by individual countries. Those member states which have one commissioner normally appoint a member or supporter of the government or majority party. Those states which have two commissioners have their individual arrangements: the practice for Britain having been to nominate one commissioner each from the Conservative and Labour parties.

The Commission is a supranational body and anyone appointed to the Commission must forget their national origins and serve only the Community: newly appointed commissioners swearing an oath of independence, undertaking that they shall 'neither seek nor take instructions from any government or from any other body'. Furthermore, 'Each Member State undertakes to respect this principle and not to seek to influence the members of the Commission.'[4] While it is only natural that commissioners maintain links with former colleagues at home and remain sympathetic to their own national interests, the Commission cannot function if its members are too nationalistically inclined. On the whole, commissioners are community-minded, often to the despair of the governments that appointed them. As a former British commissioner, Sir Leon Brittan, said, 'I may be a British Conservative but I do not agree with the Conservative government on many European questions'.[5]

Each commissioner is given a portfolio, which is to say that they are placed in charge of some function of the Commission's work (see Appendix 4). In that respect they are rather like government ministers, although with greater freedom. As Brittan said in the same article quoted above, 'Commissioners do have somewhat greater personal political autonomy than a cabinet minister – you do not have to clear things with the top'.[6]

To assist them, commissioners have a small group of aides or advisers known as a *cabinet*. The word here is used in its French sense and would be better translated into English as 'private office'. The members of a commissioner's *cabinet* are mostly civil servants who have been seconded, either from the commissioner's own national civil service or from another part of the Community's bureaucracy. Members of the *cabinet* are often fellow-nationals of the commissioner, although convention expects at least one to be from another member state. One of the first moves made by Romano Prodi on taking office in 1999 was to state that he wanted his commissioners' *cabinets* to be truly international and not packed with officials and cronies from the commissioners' own countries. As an example to his team Prodi appointed an Irishman, David O'Sullivan, as his own *chef de cabinet*.[7]

The president of the Commission

> The governments of the Member States shall nominate by common accord, after consulting the European Parliament, the person they intend to appoint as President of the Commission.[8]

Before Maastricht the original rules stated that a new president should be chosen from the ranks of the existing commissioners. This was never a practical possibility since the office of president is so important that member governments need to spend a long time over their choice: it would be impossible to wait until an entirely new Commission was in place before beginning that selection process. As it is, the process of lobbying and negotiation begins well over a year in advance of appointment, the nominee traditionally being announced at the European Council held in the June prior to the January appointment. A convention has grown up over the years under which the office of president alternates between citizens of large and small countries, and between representatives of the right and left. Normally the appointment of a new president is tacitly agreed between the member states before the European Council meets to announce the appointment but there have been two occasions when this preliminary agreement has not been reached; the chosen candidate being vetoed by one country – Britain on both occasions. In 1984 the French candidate, Claude Cheysson, was vetoed by Mrs Thatcher (ironically enough to be replaced by Jacques Delors), and in 1994 the Belgian Jean-Luc Dehaene was vetoed by John Major.

Although with limited powers, the president of the Commission is the nearest thing the EU has to a head of government. Probably the true head is the president of the European Council but, since that post circulates on a six-monthly rota, the president of the Commission is a more clearly identifiable figurehead for the Community as a whole. And it has to be said that the definition of the president's role is sufficiently vague as to allow a strong personality to dictate his own agenda. Delors was strong, while Prodi also came into office aiming to create a quasi-prime ministerial role for himself, heading a cabinet-style administration in which he had the powers to fire or re-shuffle individual members of the College of Commissioners.[9]

The more easily identified duties of the president of the Commission are:

- to chair weekly meetings of the College of Commissioners at which proposals are adopted, policies finalised and decisions taken
- to co-ordinate the work of the various commissioners; an even more arduous task than it might appear since the commissioners often have partisan interests and ideological positions at variance with those of the president
- to allocate portfolios at the start of a new Commission, a process that requires all the president's skills of negotiation and political judgment since there is always a shortage of portfolios, or at least a shortage of important portfolios, compared with the number of commissioners available. One of the fascinations of the Jenkins diary[10] is the picture he paints of the months of negotiation involved in fixing jobs for the commissioners
- to represent the Commission with other institutions of the EU, including an annual State of the Union address to the European Parliament, and by attendance and participation in meetings of the European Council. At these meetings the president has the same status as other heads of government
- to represent the European Union at international gatherings such as the G7 or G8 economic summits
- to give a sense of direction to the supranational development of the EU. Strong presidents can give a real lead to policy initiatives, in the way that the Delors Plan would lead to the single market, Monetary Union and the Maastricht Treaty.

The bureaucracy

About half the staff employed by the EU serve with the Commission. Despite the public perception of a massive bureaucracy, the actual size of the Commission's staff (about 15,000 people)[11] is remarkably small, being no larger than the average government ministry in one of the member states or the administrative staff of a medium-sized city.[12] One factor that swells the numbers required is the question of translation and interpretation. Although the Commission's working languages are French and English, there are larger meetings where interpreters are required and, of course, all documents of record must be issued in all the eleven official languages of the Union; all citizens having the right to know of, and have access to, the workings of the EU.

As a result almost 3,000 staff are involved in the translation and interpreting services. A survey in 1994, by the pressure group promoting Esperanto as a universal language for the Community, found that the EU generates more than three million words a day at a cost in translation and interpretation of £1.2 billion a year.

Staff of the Commission are permanently employed and are mostly appointed on merit. In the case of senior or specialised staff, that merit is judged by means of a highly competitive open examination. There is a career structure and most promotions are internal but the ever-present question of national jealousies prevents the organisation being truly meritocratic. Something in the nature of a national quota system does exist, at least for those senior administrators who can initiate legislation and it is still not unknown for outsiders to be seconded from their national civil services into the service of the Commission in order to preserve the balance of nationalities.

The Commission administration is divided into twenty-three policy responsibilities, similar to government ministries, each headed by a director-general. These directorates-general are not known by their area of responsibility but by a Roman numeral preceded by DG for Directorate-General: hence DGVI for agriculture, DGXVI for regional policy, and so on. The normal hierarchical structure divides the directorates-general into directorates and the directorates into divisions. The pattern is not uniform, however, because the size of the directorates-general varies so much: DGIX for example, which deals with budgetary matters, has a staff of more than 2,500 while DGXXII, dealing with structural policy, has a staff of less than 60. Some of the smaller directorates-general have directorates but no divisions, while others have divisions but no directorate. Each director-general is answerable to a commissioner but there is no precise match between the areas of responsibility given to the directorates-general and the portfolios given to commissioners. Liaison between the College of Commissioners and the directorates-general is through the six officials forming each individual commissioner's private office or cabinet.

> The Commission is the archetypal multi-organisation, with each directorate-general anxious to preserve its own territory. This produces a chronic lack of co-ordination, and plenty of jurisdictional fights. The style and attitude of directorates can vary enormously and can change over time according to the nationality and personality of the director-general.[13]

Apart from the directorates-general there is quite a sizeable section of Commission staff which is organised into twelve or more specialised service units such as the translation and interpreting services mentioned above.

The internal career structure of the Commission's secretariat is similar to that of the British Civil Service. Members of staff are divided into four categories:

- **Category A** represents the senior administrative staff and is the nearest equivalent to a senior civil servant in the UK Home Civil Service. There is also a parallel **Category LA** for administrative grade officials working as translators or interpreters in the Joint Interpretation and Conference Service.
- **Category B:** executive grades.
- **Category C:** secretarial and clerical officers.
- **Category D:** manual and support service staff.

The tasks and duties of the Commission

- The most important duty carried out by the Commission is the drafting of policy documents for discussion and decision by the Council of Ministers, its remit being to initiate and formulate those policies that will promote the aims for which the European Communities were founded. The Commission is not the only source of policy to be presented to the Council, but the majority of issues discussed by the Council can only be accepted if they have been framed by the Commission.
- The Commission has an executive role after policy decisions have been made and will issue the regulations, directives and instructions by which Community decisions are executed in the member states. The Commission issues something like 5,000 of these legislative instruments each year, although most of them deal with very minor matters such as price levels for a single commodity in the CAP.
- The Commission is responsible for preparing the Union's annual budget and for the management of Community finances, including the various Structural Funds.
- The Commission must monitor the actions of member states in obeying and carrying out Community law. In the event of non-compliance or deliberate law-breaking it is up to the Commission to demand obedience or, if the offence continues, to prosecute the country or organisation through the European Court of Justice.
- Thanks to certain clauses in the Maastricht Treaty there are some areas of responsibility such as competition, agriculture and trade policy over which the Commission is autonomous and able to take decisions without consulting the Council of Ministers.
- Commissioners and senior Commission staff must attend meetings of the European Parliament and its committees. Commissioners must answer questions from MEPs as well as attending, and even participating in, debates which deal with the subject of the commissioner's portfolio.
- The Commission is represented and participates in the work of various international bodies such as the United Nations, the General Agreement on Tariffs and Trade, the Council of Europe and the OECD.

- The Commission deals on behalf of the EU with diplomatic relations with non-member countries. Just as a country would receive ambassadors from foreign countries, the Commission deals with diplomatic missions from over 125 foreign countries accredited to the EU. On the other side of the same coin the Commission itself maintains diplomatic relations with nearly a hundred non-member states. Through the Lomé Convention the Commission regulates relations between the EU and the developing countries of Africa, the Caribbean and Pacific (ACP).
- The Commission acts as the first check on new applications for membership of the EU. On receipt of such an application the Commission is asked to conduct an enquiry into all the implications of that application. Negotiations can only begin with the Commission's approval.

The Council of Ministers

The Council shall consist of a representative of each Member State at ministerial level, authorised to commit the government of that Member State.[14]

The Council of Ministers is the decision-making body of the European Community with a crucial role in the legislative process, although the Maastricht Treaty increased the role of the European Parliament through the co-decision procedure. However, to use the term 'Council of Ministers' as though there were only one institution of that name would be misleading. There are, in fact, as many as twenty-five different Councils, because the type of minister present varies according to the subject-matter of the meeting – transport ministers will meet to discuss transport policy, energy ministers to discuss energy, and so on. If there is such a thing as *the* definitive Council of Ministers it is the General Affairs Council, which is made up of foreign ministers from the member countries, although it deals with general policy issues rather than foreign affairs. Another important council is the Ecofin Council, made up of the economic and finance ministers and obviously dealing with matters such as EMU. The other councils – transport, energy, etc. – are known generically as technical councils.

There are Council meetings throughout the year, normally convening in Brussels, although meetings are held in Luxembourg during April, June and October. As an example of how busy the programme can be, there were about 100 formal ministerial meetings in 1994, during which 300 regulations, 50 directives and 160 decisions were adopted. The General Affairs Council, the Ecofin Council and the Agricultural Ministers' Council meet at least monthly, but some of the minor technical councils may not meet more than once or twice a year. Meetings seldom last more than one day and, even if the meeting extends over two days, it is usually from lunchtime to lunchtime. Advisory groups and working parties continue to operate between meetings and some groups, especially the foreign and finance ministers, will meet informally outside Brussels, perhaps within the context of a social weekend.

Leadership of the Council is vested in the presidency of the European Union, a position which rotates among member states, each holding the responsibility for a period of six months (for details of this rota see Appendix 5). During their tenure ministers of the country holding the presidency will call Council meetings, decide the agenda, introduce initiatives and take the chair for all Council meetings.

The Secretariat and COREPER

There is a vast bureaucratic input into Council meetings from a number of sources, including the 2,000 members of the General Secretariat, whose duties in servicing the Council consist of:

- preparing for meetings
- keeping records and giving advice
- providing all the services that might be looked for in civil servants
- providing some services peculiar to the European situation, such as the need to translate working documents into all eleven official languages.

Since the responsibility for arranging meetings and agendas lies with the presidency, the Secretariat works closely with the national officials of the state holding the presidency, the numbers of such national officials seconded to Brussels always increasing substantially during the relevant six months. The size of the supporting Secretariat turns Council meetings into very large affairs. Roy Jenkins wrote of the room in which the Council of Ministers met as reminding him of a crowded aircraft hangar.

Of considerable importance in the policy and decision-making processes of the Community is the body known as COREPER (Committee of Permanent Representatives). These are the diplomatic missions sent by member states to the Community. While civil servants seconded to the Commission must forget their national loyalties, and civil servants accompanying ministers to Council meetings are transient, the senior British diplomat sent to Brussels as permanent representative (UKREP) ensures the continuous representation of British national interests at all times. The permanent representative has a large staff including a delegation of up to forty officials, most drawn from Foreign and Commonwealth Office staff but with other policy areas also represented.

COREPER was originally set up to hammer out the details written into the 1957 Treaty of Rome, meeting informally, but was recognised as an official organ of the Community by the Merger Treaty of 1965 when a definition of COREPER's duties was written into the the Treaty and all its subsequent amendments: 'A committee consisting of the Permanent Representatives of the

Member States shall be responsible for preparing the work of the Council and for carrying out the tasks assigned to it by the Council.'[15] The committee is not only a vital part of the legislative process but is the principal channel of communication between the institutions of the Community and national governments.

COREPER has developed into one of the most powerful groups of officials in the world. Over the years the committee has begun to devolve some of its duties to specialists and, as a result, now comprises literally hundreds of officials, splitting for convenience in 1962 into two bodies, COREPER I and II. COREPER II was designated the senior, its core membership comprising the fifteen permanent representatives, while COREPER I became a forum for their deputies.

The two committees into which COREPER is divided are responsible for:

- keeping the EU's institutions and the governments and bureaucracies of the member states informed of each others' work
- ensuring that national and European policy are not at loggerheads
- finding compromises so as not to undermine core national positions.

In practice these different functions are difficult to separate and merge into a more general aim of keeping the Union working smoothly.[16]

The Council of Agricultural Ministers incidentally does not use COREPER but has its own Special Committee on Agriculture (SCA) made up of Brussels-based representatives of the member states who meet at least weekly.

Voting in the Council

There are three ways in which the Council of Ministers can vote to take a decision: by unanimous vote, by simple majority or by qualified majority. Originally, decisions of the Council needed to be unanimous, in effect giving a dissenting state the veto, a fact exploited by de Gaulle in the 1960s. The Luxembourg Compromise of 1966 reduced the need for unanimity, extending the number of issues that could be settled by qualified majority. Since then there has been a steady extension of qualified majority voting (QMV), most significantly in the Single European Act.

In pillar one of the TEU, unanimity is still required for:

- all new policies
- amendments to the policy issues of taxation and industry
- matters relating to regional and social funds
- where the Council wishes to agree or amend a policy against the wishes of the Commission.

Since Luxembourg in 1966 the member states have additionally insisted on retaining the right to veto any decision they can claim was against their national interests. However, for all but exceptions like John Major as British prime minister, the veto is regarded as being like a nuclear deterrent: held in reserve but never used.

For the other two pillars created by the Maastricht Treaty – Foreign and Security Policy (pillar two) and Justice and Home Affairs (pillar three) – the Council has the sole right to act as decision maker and unanimity is the rule.

Simple majority voting is not allowed on policy or legislative proposals; its use is mainly for procedural reasons.

It is QMV that is the most contentious of the voting methods, since it is directly related to the question of states' rights and the comparative strengths of small and large states within the Community. Under QMV the member states are given so many votes each, with a token acknowledgment of the comparative size of the member states. From the start it was agreed that for a decision to be passed it would require in the region of 70 per cent of the votes, representing something like 60 per cent of the population of the Community. The votes are distributed in such a way that the large countries acting together cannot out-vote the smaller, needing the combination of two major countries and at least one more to block the decision-making process.

The votes given to the member states increased with each enlargement of the Community and the required majority was adjusted to the 70 per cent mark each time. After the enlargement of 1995 the weightings given to the member states' votes were:

10 votes each	France, Germany, Italy, United Kingdom
8 votes	Spain
5 votes each	Belgium, Netherlands, Greece, Portugal
4 votes each	Austria and Sweden
3 votes each	Denmark, Finland and Ireland
2 votes	Luxembourg

87 votes

When a proposal from the Commission is involved, at least sixty-two votes must be cast in favour, creating a blocking minority of twenty-six. In other cases, the qualified majority is also sixty-two votes, but these must be cast by at least ten member states. The whole issue of qualified majority voting has proved a vexed topic in a series of IGCs and it remains one of the major issues to be resolved before the next enlargement of the Union.

Ironically, in the light of the controversy surrounding it, majority voting is very seldom used by the Council of Ministers, even in areas where QMV is expected. The Council prefers to give the appearance of unanimity by continuing discussion overnight or over successive meetings until a compromise on a consensus decision is reached. In 1994, for example, only about 14 per cent of legislation adopted by the Council was subjected to contested voting.[17]

The European Council

> The European Council shall provide the Union with the necessary impetus for its development and shall define the general political guidelines thereof.[18]

With all the media attention that surrounds its biennial summit meetings, the public could be forgiven if they believed the European Council to be the most important institution of the Community. It is therefore ironic to realise that the European Council only received official recognition in the Single European Act of 1987 and still does not form part of the legal framework of the EU. The European Council cannot legislate unless it transforms itself for the purpose into an extraordinary meeting of the Council of Ministers, and decisions of the European Council are not subject to the jurisdiction of the Court of Justice.

Throughout the 1960s the heads of government of the member states of the Common Market met from time to time in what were largely unofficial and informal summits. In the early 1970s, however, after the first enlargement, a feeling grew that there was a lack of leadership. The institutions of the Community coped well enough with detailed policy but there was no focus of authority to give direction and purpose to future developments. It was a new generation of heads of state or government, most notably the Franco-German partnership of Giscard d'Estaing and Schmidt, who proposed at the Paris Summit in 1974 that the occasional summit meetings should be formally institutionalised.

The term 'European Council' did not appear until the Single European Act of 1986, which had just one article defining the composition of the European Council and the frequency of its meetings. At that time there was no definition of the body's functions, clarification only coming with the treaties of Maastricht in 1993 and Amsterdam in 1999. However, since the European Union became established through these treaties the European Council gained a particular importance as the sole body which links, co-ordinates and integrates the three separate pillars of the EU. It was also Maastricht which clarified the difference between the European Council itself and a Council of Ministers made up of heads of government: 'The Council, meeting in the composition of the Heads of State or Government' does not mean '"The European Council'. It must be stressed, however, that the European Council is not part of the EU's organisational structure but simply a political body, albeit an important one.

It was established as early as 1986 that the European Council meets at least twice a year, the meeting usually being held in the final month of each six-month presidency and hosted by the country holding the presidency at that time. The meetings of the European Council have therefore come to represent a public statement on the performance of the presiding country during its half-year tenure. Since most member states now aim to satisfy some objective during their presidency, European Council meetings can be seen as passing judgment on the achievement of those objectives. During the UK's presidency in the second half of 1992 it was Britain's stated aim to amend the TEU to satisfy the doubts of countries such as the United Kingdom and Denmark; this being accomplished at Edinburgh with the strengthening of opt-out clauses and the doctrine of subsidiarity.

If an additional problem arises during a presidency an extraordinary European Council meeting may be called – this increasingly became the case during the 1990s. In March 1999, for example, an extraordinary special Council was called in Berlin to choose a new Commission president after the forced resignation of the Santer commission. At first the actual meetings were always held in the capital of the country holding the presidency and, if any special meeting were called, that was held in Brussels. Increasingly the host country tends to place the summit meeting in some other city, as has been the case with Edinburgh, Cardiff, Maastricht or Amsterdam. And, increasingly, special meetings are held in the presiding country rather than Brussels; as with Birmingham in 1992 or Noordwijk in 1997.

These meetings have become something of a public relations exercise; a successful European summit being seen to confer prestige on the host country. As a result, considerable amounts of time and money can be spent on the two days of the Council. The Edinburgh Summit in 1992, for example, cost the British government £9 million.[19]

Meetings of the European Council are much smaller than those of the Council of Ministers. Those attending are the heads of government for all member states (head of state for France where the president rather than the prime minister leads the delegation) together with the foreign minister of each country: although the foreign ministers can be replaced by finance ministers if EMU is to be discussed. The president and vice-presidents of the Commission also attend, along with the secretaries-general of the Council and Commission. Apart from these the national delegations can bring their own officials and advisers with them but only one at a time can attend the meetings. Records are kept by members of the Council and Commission secretariats, together with officials of the presiding country. This secretariat is, however, restricted to a total of six. Other than interpreters these are the only persons permitted to attend the negotiating sessions, so there are therefore not more than forty people in the main meeting room.

Attendance at Council sessions is restricted but the two-day meeting as a whole caters for a very large number of people being in proximity to the meeting's location. Each national delegation will consist of about fifty members, not to mention the 2000 or so journalists, television crews and photographers who wish to be on the premises. Nor should we forget the three interpreters needed for each of the eleven official languages of the Union. Accommodation is always a problem: translation booths were stacked in tiers to fit them into Edinburgh Castle in 1992, while at Fontainebleau in 1984 the typing pool was located in Marie Antoinette's bedroom.

Much of the work of the European Council takes place outside the meeting room. Some of the most important contacts take the form of informal head-to-head meetings between individual leaders, popularly known as 'fireside chats'. Most of the work, however, is accomplished by the officials of the presiding country working alongside officials from the various national delegations. There is always far too much on the agenda for the participants to debate at length. In the months preceding the Council teams of officials will have drawn up papers which they feel will be agreed by the members of the Council. If they are successful it is only the finer points of detail that need to be discussed in the meeting.

Since 1987 the proceedings of the European Council have always opened with an address by the president of the European Parliament who briefs the Council on how the Parliament feels about current issues. Having spoken, he withdraws to leave the European Council members isolated with a small number of officials. That first day's work is a 'plenary session' and involves a free exchange of views. There is no formal agenda, the only guidance being a letter from the presidency containing a list of possible topics for discussion. Close at hand throughout the session is a group of diplomats and COREPER assistants known as the Antici Group who liaise between the meeting and the national delegations.

At the close of the working day the heads of state or government dine together and discuss the issues of the day rather less formally. The foreign ministers dine in a separate room and begin to discuss and draw up the line to be taken by the official communiqués. After dinner come the 'fireside chats' that are the least formal aspect of the meeting, while the presidency and Council secretariats tidy up the official conclusions to be made public the next day.

The second and final day begins with a working breakfast for each delegation, followed by the traditional group photograph. A final plenary session attempts to finalise the text of the official communiqué and this can be prolonged beyond lunch in the need to reach agreement. The day finishes with a series of press conferences given by the presidency of the Council, the president of the Commission and by the national delegations.

The European Council does not take a vote nor apply the rule of unanimity, since they are essentially making political rather than legislative decisions. The members of the European Council reach agreement by consensus and this agreement is then passed on to the institutions of the EU in the form of guidelines. The documents produced by meetings of the European Council are usually phrased diplomatically, avoiding orders and using words such as 'invites', 'undertakes', 'encourages' or 'recommends'.

The Troika

This is a function of the European Council that has been in existence for some time but which is comparatively little used. In order to provide continuity when a six-month presidency proved to be too short for initiatives to be carried to a conclusion within, co-operation grew between the current presidency and those immediately preceding and following it. In origin an administrative device this trio was later employed as a sort of trouble-shooting team if there were deadlock in a dispute between member states. Later still, a potentially interesting use of the Troika was as an international mediation team during troubles in the former Yugoslavia. The first example of this came in 1991 when the foreign ministers of Holland, Luxembourg and Portugal jointly led missions to Zagreb and Belgrade in order to mediate between Serbia and Croatia.

The European Parliament

Until 1979 the EP was composed of delegates nominated by their national governments in the same proportions as the various parties were represented in their national parliaments; many members having 'dual mandate' member-ship of both European and national parliaments. It was the European Council of 1974 in Paris which decided to bring into force, as from 1979, the provision for direct elections that had been written into the Treaty of Rome. This may well have led to a greater legitimacy for the EP but what it did not produce was any strengthening of its powers. Throughout its life, the member states have always sought to hold back the powers of the Parliament through the Council of Ministers and European Council, for fear that a strengthening of the EP would mean weakening the sovereignty of national parliaments.

The EP has had three locations:

- the Assembly Chamber for plenary sessions in Strasbourg
- the committees structure in Brussels
- the General Secretariat in Luxembourg.

There used to be an Assembly Chamber in Luxembourg (it was the Assembly of the ECSC), abandoned when the size of the EP doubled on the introduction of direct elections. The Strasbourg Chamber in turn became too small in 1994, not only through the addition of forty-nine MEPs to allow for German re-unifi-cation but also because a further increase was pending due to the accessions of 1995. Many MEPs wanted to end their nomadic existence by transferring the plenary sessions to Brussels where there are ample facilities in the new parlia-ment buildings. However, as was said at the time, 'this possibility is being blocked by the French government which intends to force through the construction of a new parliament building in Strasbourg for the benefit of *la Gloire*'.[20] Although almost all MEPs wanted to centre their activities in Brussels, the new parliament building in Strasbourg had the support of the French government, which refused to ratify procedural matters relating to German re-unification unless the EP agreed to continue meeting in the new Strasbourg buildings. The French had their way and the new, prestigiously modern parliament building was completed and opened in time to welcome the intake from the 1999 elections.

An MEP spends one week of every month in plenary session and between one and two weeks in every month on committee work. The rest of the time is spent working with the political group they belong to, travelling with an EP delegation on a fact-finding mission, or consulting with EP officials in Luxembourg. Some MEPs, like the British, also do a certain amount of constituency work. In the Assembly Chamber there are debates, commissioners deliver reports, there is a question time and the plenary session votes quite often, using electronic means to do so. Yet there seems to be little interest in the debates: the perpetual language problem means that speeches are deprived of oratory or humour, the debates becoming uniformly dull and boring as a result. Any important work is done in committee, each MEP being assigned either to one of the twenty or so standing committees or to an *ad hoc* specialised committee. These have an important input into the legislative process since committee members draft reports on proposed legislation and put forward amendments, about a third of which, it is estimated, find their way into Community law.

The EP works closely with the Commission on proposed legislation but finds the Council less sympathetic. About 75 per cent of EP amendments are accepted by the Commission, whereas less than 20 per cent get past the Council into final legislation. This is part of the EP's 'democratic deficit' in that up until now no one has been legally obliged to listen to what the EP has to say and decisions have often been simply ignored by the Council of Ministers. A fuller account of the European Parliament's role in the legislative process can be found in Chapter 5.

Powers possessed by the EP include:

- the right to vote on the accession of new member states
- the right to be consulted by the Council of Ministers on the granting of associate status to other countries
- the EP can reject or amend Council decisions on matters relating to the single market, a move that can only be reversed by a unanimous vote of the Council if a proposal is rejected, or by qualified majority if it is an amendment
- most importantly, the ability to reject the Union's budget in its entirety or to amend any part of the budget that does not relate to a provision required by treaty.

The Commission must report to the EP every month and the EP has the ultimate weapon of being able to dismiss the entire Commission (although it cannot dismiss individual commissioners) on a two-thirds majority. The TEU also gave the EP the right to pass a vote of confidence or non-confidence in an incoming commission. These rights were exercised to the full during the controversy surrounding the Santer commission in 1999.

The democratic deficit of the European Parliament is being reduced but the largest contributor to the democratic deficit is the apathy of the public. The people not only do not seem interested in the workings of the EP but they are universally ignorant as to the function and identity of MEPs and, with the exception of those countries such as Belgium where voting is compulsory, their turn-out in European elections is pitifully small, while the issues on which people vote have more to do with national rather than with European factors (for turn out figures for the 1999 elections see Appendix 2). We shall return to the subject of European elections, parties and voting behaviour in Chapter 7.

The European Court of Justice

This court, based in Luxembourg, is not to be confused with the European Court of Human Rights, meeting in Strasbourg and an institution of the Council of Europe. The latter has nothing to do with the EU, even though all member states of the EU have signed the European Convention of Human Rights. The Court of Justice is exclusively concerned with the administration of Community Law.

The Court is made up of fifteen judges appointed by common agreement of the member states for a renewable term of six years: continuity over those six years is assured by a staggered replacement over a three-year cycle. Judges are nominated for appointment by the member states, those nominated being individuals whose independence is beyond doubt and who have usually either held high judicial office in their own countries or who are international jurists of a known competence. The judges choose one of their members to act as president of the Court, with a three year term of office. The presiding judge administers the work of the Court, in particular assigning cases to specific panels of judges and appointing the individual judge-rapporteurs who will be in charge of those panels. In charge of collecting documentary and other evidence for presentation to the judges, together with their own conclusions and legal judgments, are nine advocates general, also appointed by mutual agreement of member states.

Because of the pressure of business as the Community grew, a second court, the Court of First Instance, was introduced on 1 September 1989 in order to deal with the consequences of the Single European Act and specifically in order to protect individual interests, permitting the Court of Justice to concentrate on the interpretation of Community Law. The Court of First Instance also has fifteen judges as members but does not have advocates general, one of the judges acting in the capacity of advocate if required.

Cases can be brought before the Court by the institutions of the Community or by member states. Possibly the most frequent are cases brought by the Commission against member states for non-compliance with Community directives or regulations. Cases can, however, be brought by individuals or organisations who feel that their national governments are penalising them in breach of Community Law although these cases are usually held before the Court of First Instance. Many cases are referred to the European Court after they have failed on appeal in the national courts but the European Court emphasises that it is not a court of appeal and the only grounds for appeal against a member state's national courts is if there has been a misinterpretation of Community Law by those courts. Actual court actions, however, only form part of the Court's duties. More than half the work done by the Court arises from requests by member states for clarification or interpretation of some aspect of Community Law.

Only the most important cases, involving the Community institutions or member states, are heard before a full plenary Court, for which the quorum is seven judges. Most cases are heard in chambers before a panel of three judges in most cases; or five judges for more complex matters. Cases in the Court of First Instance are heard before any one of five chambers, each of which has a panel of three or five judges, although plenary sessions can be held for certain important cases.

The Court of Justice has five areas of competence:

1 rulings on the treaties which form the basis of the Community – Treaty of Paris, the two Treaties of Rome, the SEA, the Maastricht Treaty and the Amsterdam Treaty
2 regulation of any international agreements made by the EC as a Community
3 any problems arising from EC regulations
4 any problems arising from EC directives
5 rulings on decisions made by the Commission.

The Court of First Instance deals with more routine matters, including breaches of competition rules and disputes between the Community and its staff.

In a direct action the language in which the case is heard is chosen by the applicant while cases referred by a national court use the language of that national court. For clarity and to avoid errors with a possible eleven languages in use, most pleadings and submissions are initially made in writing. It is only at the end of a long written phase that cases are argued orally in open court. At the end of the hearing it is the advocate general assigned to the case who sums up the arguments submitted, interprets the relevant law and recommends a decision. The opinion of the advocate general is not binding on the court but it is very influential. The panel of judges consider the matter in closed session and then deliver judgment in open court. The text of the judgment includes the reasoning behind the decision and is then published in full, in all eleven languages of the Union.

Since the Court began as an institution of the ECSC in 1954, it has heard over 9,000 cases and delivered around 4,000 judgments. However, for the average individual or small business the Court of Justice is far too expensive (legal aid is not available) and the process is far too slow, even urgent cases taking two years to reach judgment.

The Court of Auditors

The European Court of Auditors is an important institution set up to scrutinise the conduct of Community institutions as the taxpayers' representative. As a single body it has only existed since 1977 and was less than powerful in its early years. Its powers, however, were strengthened by Maastricht in answer to calls for greater 'transparency' in the EU.

The Court has fifteen members – one for each member state – all of them suitably qualified and often being members of an official audit body in their own country. Nominees have to be approved by the Council of Ministers and the European Parliament. Appointment is initially for six years, after which time the appointment can be renewed. From among their number the Court elects one member to serve as president for three years.

The duties of the Court of Auditors are quite obviously related to auditing the Community's annual budget and validating the Commission's efficiency in administering that budget. There are groups within the Court of Auditors which deal with specific budgetary questions such as the CAP or the Regional Fund. Since being revised by Maastricht the Court has extended its activities away from mere concern over financial rectitude and is more involved in questions of policy effectiveness. To that extent the Court:

• checks that both revenue and expenditure observe the legal regulations laid down by the Community
• ensures that the Community is getting value for money by checking as to how far financial objectives have been met.

Every institution and body that has access to Union funds – now amounting to more than 100 billion euros each year – is subject to scrutiny. The Court is not restricted to Community institutions but must examine all administrations, national, regional or local, which manage Community funds, whether or not those administrations are member states of the Union. The Court carries out on-the-spot audits in Community institutions, the member states or even in those countries outside the Union receiving Community funds. The Court of

Auditors also produces an Annual Report each November which is the most important factor considered by the European Parliament in its annual review of the Commission.

The European Investment Bank

The European Investment Bank (EIB) provides long-term loans for capital investment and is controlled by a board representing all fifteen member states. Administering loan funds in the region of 33 billion euros the EIB is devoted to strengthening the economies of EU member states. To this end it has two principal areas of operation:

- underpinning regional development in the Union, over half of total lending going towards investment in the less favoured regions of the EU. These loans are done in co-operation with the Commission through the EU's Structural Funds and Cohesion Fund
- financing trans-European networks (TENs), large-scale and long-term projects in the fields of transport, telecommunications and energy. This investment is as a result of repeated requests from European Council meetings since that held at Essen in 1994 and is designed to help member states strengthen their economies and competitiveness and their capacity to create new jobs to combat unemployment. To assist in the work the EIB, in association with the Commission and the Community's banking sector, has set up the European Investment Fund (EIF).

Although the EIB is principally concerned with lending within the Union it also assists with the EU's financial involvement with non-member states. The Bank operates in more than a hundred countries, supporting development projects in four main areas:

- those countries in Central and Eastern Europe preparing for EU membership
- in Lebanon, Gaza and West Bank, in support of the Middle East peace process
- in the 70 APC signatories of the Lomé Convention, together with South Africa
- in Asian and Latin American countries which have signed EU co-operation agreements

The Economic and Social Committee

The Economic and Social Committee (ESC) was written into the Treaty of Rome because it was felt that the then Assembly would not represent fairly the various sectional interests of the Community. The resulting committee has two main functions within the EC:

- as a forum for special interest groups in the exchange of views and ideas
- as a body that has a minor but integral place in the policy and decision-making process.

Originally the ESC was regarded purely as a consultative body for the Council and Commission but successively the treaties of 1986 (SEA), 1992 (Maastricht) and 1999 (Amsterdam) have extended the range of mandatory issues that must be referred to the ESC. In addition, the Amsterdam Treaty allows for the ESC to be consulted by the European Parliament as part of the decision-making process.

The 222 members of the ESC are appointed by their national governments for a renewable four-year term of office, membership being roughly proportional to the size of the member state:

Germany, France, Italy, UK	24 members
Spain	21
Belgium, Greece, Netherlands, Portugal, Austria and Sweden	12
Denmark, Ireland, Finland	9
Luxembourg	6

It should be noted that all the numbers included in the national delegations can be divided by three because the membership is divided into three socio-economic groups:

- Employers (Group I) – of which about half represent industry, the other half being from commercial bodies or services in the public sector
- Workers (Group II) – which basically means representatives of trade unions
- Other interests (Group III) – of which about half represent protectionist groups in areas of importance to the Community such as agriculture and transport, the other half representing special interest groups such as the environment or consumer affairs.

Members of the ESC elect a president and two vice-presidents, chosen from the three groups in rotation, as well as an executive committee of thirty-six members (twelve from each group) known as the Bureau. The ESC meets in plenary session about ten times each year but most of its work is in sub-committee, drawing up opinions for the Council and Commission; something like 170 advisory documents and opinions being delivered each year. For operational purposes, the ESC is split into six sections:

1 Agriculture, Rural Development and Environment

2 Economic and Monetary Union
3 Employment, Social Affairs and Citizenship
4 External Relations
5 Single Market, Production and Consumption
6 Transport, Energy, Infrastructure and the Information Society.

There is a secretariat-general, headed by a secretary-general. which provides bureaucratic services to the committee. Although there are 135 staff working exclusively for the ESC, the committee does share a common staff of around 500 with the Committee of the Regions.

The Committee of the Regions

The Committee of the Regions (COR) is one of the newer Community institutions, set up in the aftermath of Maastricht in order to facilitate the doctrine of subsidiarity, and meeting for the first time in March 1994. It is an attempt to bridge the gap between Brussels and citizens of the Union, although anti-federalists argued against its institution, claiming that it was all part of a Brussels plan to undermine the nation-state.[21] It does, however, reflect the growing importance of the regions in many member countries and, indeed, for the new relationships encouraged by cross-border regions such as the Rhine-Meuse, created from parts of Belgium, Germany and the Netherlands; or the Atlantic Islands Council, created by the UK, Republic of Ireland, Scottish Parliament, Welsh Assembly and the Isle of Man.

The COR provides a body that must be consulted during the legislative process on any matter which it is felt has regional implications, the key issues being identified as trans-European networks, health, education, culture and economic and social cohesion. There are those who feel that in future the COR may become a directly elected body and form a second chamber in an enlarged and strengthened European Parliament.

Like the ESC the COR also has 222 members, provided by member states in exactly the same proportions and appointed for a four-year term. The criterion for appointment to the COR differs between member states, dependent on the degree of devolution already existing in those states. Germany already is a federal state and COR membership is represented by members of the *länder* governments. Belgium is also virtually a federation of the Flemish and Walloon communities. Other countries such as Italy and Spain are highly regionalised with semi-autonomous regional administrations and these countries will draw most of their COR members from regional governments. More centralised states such as Britain have appointed COR members from mayors of cities or chairmen of county councils. This issue was the cause of a defeat for John Major in the Maastricht debate because he had wished to send unelected quango representatives to COR; opposition parties demanding, however, that these representatives should obey EU guidelines and all be elected councillors.

The COR meets in Brussels for five plenary sessions a year, the work of the committee being organised by a Bureau that is elected for two years at a time. Much of that work is done through a structure of seven standing committees:

- Regional policy, structural funds, cross-border and inter-regional co-operation
- Agriculture, rural development, fisheries
- Trans-European networks, transport, information society
- Urban issues, energy, environment
- Social policy, public health, consumer protection, tourism
- Employment, single market, industry
- Education and training, culture, youth, sport, citizens' rights.

There is also a Special Commission on Institutional Affairs which has the duty of looking after regional interests in the current programme reforming the Community's institutions.

The COR is still a fairly new institution but it has already made an effective contribution to the democratisation of the EU. For Britain the major significance of the COR has lain in its work for those regions such as Scotland or Wales which have since gained their own devolved assemblies and governments. The COR is useful in gaining EU structural funds for the regions and can also work to exempt the regions from blanket measures aimed at national governments: for example, both Wales and Scotland wished to be treated differently from the UK over beef production during the BSE crisis. 'The widening wealth gap among regions is feeding demands for more radical action to redistribute wealth and refocus EU economic priorities. The poorer regions see greater decision-making power in Brussels not as an obstacle but as a pre-condition for greater autonomy'.[22]

The Ombudsman

The idea of appointing an Ombudsman for the EU was first mooted at Maastricht but, because of 'procedural delays', no appointment was made until 1995, when Jacob Söderman, a Finn, was appointed.

The Ombudsman's purpose is to reconcile the interests of EU citizens and EU institutions by investigating thoroughly any accusation of maladministration on the part of any EU institution other than the Court of Justice. He has wide-ranging powers of inquiry: the Community institutions being required to provide all the documents and other evidence that he might demand of them. If maladministration is discovered the Ombudsman will report in full to the institution concerned, together with any recommendations for correcting the fault. He can also refer the case to the European Parliament for further action.

In the first year of operation the Ombudsman and his staff dealt with nearly 700 complaints, the largest number of which came from Britain. Most, however, were ruled to be inadmissable.[23]

The European Central Bank

The European Central Bank (ECB) was instituted as of 1 July 1998, at a meeting of the Ecofin council in Brussels. Prior to that date work on monetary union had been carried out by the European Monetary Institute (EMI) supported by the combined forces of the central banks of all fifteen Community members, the European System of Central Banks (ESCB).

Based in Frankfurt the ECB is intended to serve as a normal central bank for those countries able and willing to participate in monetary union. As such the bank has three main areas of responsibility:

* the printing, minting, issue and administration of the new euro notes and coins, together with the ultimate withdrawal of the old currencies after the transition to a single currency, which is now scheduled for 1 July 2002
* the determination of fiscal policy, including the setting of interest rates, for all eleven countries initially making up the 'eurozone'
* maintaining a watching brief on the suitability for entry of countries currently outside EMU. Dependent on their own wishes, it is believed that Britain, Denmark and Sweden would be eligible to join in 2001 but that Greece and some of the other applicant states might not qualify for another ten years yet.

The ECB has an executive board and governing council which should be composed solely of representatives from those member states participating in stage three of EMU, but the European Council can give special associate membership to non-participating states, the UK for one being keen to have at least observer status.

At the head of the ECB is a president who is appointed for eight years. In May 1998 the European Council was ready to choose the Dutch candidate president of the European Monetary Institute, Wim Duisenberg, but the French submitted a last minute claim for their favoured candidate, Jean-Claude Trichet. For a while there was stalemate but it led to the usual compromise. The appointment went to Duisenberg but he issued a statement to say that, in view of his age, he did not wish to serve his full term and would step down after four years, having seen through the introduction of the single currency. It was also announced that, when Duisenberg stepped down he would be succeeded by Trichet, for the full eight-year term.

Foreign affairs, defence and internal security

The institutions described so far have all been first and foremost institutions of the European Community which is only one of the three pillars of the European Union; the other two pillars being a common foreign and security policy and a common policy relating to justice, home affairs and internal security. The only institution common to all pillars of the EU is the European Council and therefore, for the two sectors other than the EC, the TEU had to create new institutions, or rather to rationalise existing *ad hoc* institutions within a framework of intergovernmental co-operation. The task of co-ordinating policy under the leadership of the country holding the presidency was given to the European Council while a new foreign affairs political committee was set up to oversee the international situation and deliver opinions to the Council.

Common Foreign and Security Policy (CFSP)

This was established under Title V of the TEU to encourage co-operation between member states in the formulation of a common foreign policy, with the ultimate aim of implementing joint action by all member states where a common interest is recognised. Assumed in this process of increased co-operation is the need to safeguard the external interests of the Union through a common defence policy.

There are obviously problems concerning a common defence policy as far as the neutral status of countries such as Sweden is concerned, and naturally there are problems over applications for membership from former Soviet bloc countries, given the suspicions felt by Russia towards the EU and NATO.

In Amsterdam attempts were made to strengthen and improve the CFSP:

- the European Council became the main source of strategies to define the EU's common foreign policy
- the EU acquired the ability to negotiate and conclude international agreements in its own right
- work began on integrating the Western European Union with the EU in a common defence programme. At Helsinki in 1999 the suggestion was made that the EU might develop its own 60,000-strong reaction force to act in humanitarian crises and peacekeeping operations when the United States is unwilling to become involved through NATO.

Trevi, the Schengen Group and Europol

There is no suggestion that the EU is to set up its own police force, nor institute a common judicial and legal system. What the TEU did do under Title VI was to set up or formalise certain institutions for co-operation on matters of law and order. Since the main objective of the TEU is the right to free movement of citizens within the EU the areas of policy covered by co-operation procedures deal with terrorism, immigration, drug traffic, political asylum and border controls.

The TREVI group has been in existence since 1975 when it was set up to exchange information on international terrorism and violence. The name is supposed to stand for Terrorism-Radicalism-Extremism-Violence-International but is really a joke on the name of the French justice minister, Fontaine, who helped set up the group at a meeting in Rome close to the Fountain of Trevi. The group functions as part of the Council of Ministers, although more in the exchange of information between officials than in meetings between ministers.

The Schengen Group was formed in 1985 in the town of Schengen on the Luxembourg–German border. It was a reaction to the reluctance of some EC members to see the removal of internal border controls. At Schengen, France, Germany and the Benelux countries agreed to abolish border controls between their countries. In 1990 they were joined by Italy and, in 1991, by Spain and Portugal. The TEU accepted the Schengen principle as part of its home affairs policy, with the intention of extending its provisions to the whole of the EU. But some countries were reluctant to join for fear of giving assistance to the free movement of terrorists, drug traffickers and illegal immigrants. Under the treaty signed at Amsterdam, Schengen established freedom of movement for twelve member states: the UK, Ireland and Denmark reserving the right to exercise border controls on the movement of people. In late 1999 Belgium temporarily suspended the Schengen Agreement because of trouble with immigrants.

Maastricht also instituted the European Police Office (Europol), initially with the prime object of exchanging information and ideas to control drug traffic. Since it began operation in 1992 its remit has been widened to include the exchange of criminal intelligence of all kinds. Europol has a Co-ordinating Committee of senior officials, reporting to the Council of Ministers. There are many problems concerning the development of Europol as a union-wide police body since there are not only questions of language and incompatible computer systems, but the basic difference in legal systems between member states.

Notes

1 Detailed information on the institutions and organisation of the European Union can be found on the Internet from links listed on the home page of the Europa website: http://europa.eu.int
2 Neill Nugent, *The Government and Politics of the European Community*, Macmillan, London, 1991, p. 309.
3 R. Jenkins (Lord Jenkins), *European Diary 1977–1981*, Collins, London 1989.
4 TEU, Title II (amendments to the Treaty of Rome), article 157, clause 2.

5   Quoted by John Palmer, *Guardian*, 23 March 1994.
6   Ibid.
7   Quoted in the *Observer*, 11 July 1999
8   TEU, Title II, article 158, clause 2.
9   Julian Coman, 'Prodi lays foundations for "United States of Europe"', *Observer*, 11 July 1999.
10 Jenkins, *European Diary 1977–1981*.
11 No one source seems able to agree on the exact size of the Commission staff – figures quoted range from 13,000 to 16,000, the figure chosen depending on variable factors. The figure I give is that officially used in literature produced by the Commission itself. This vagueness, however, does not invalidate the point that, for a busy bureaucracy with wide-ranging responsibilities, the Brussels establishment is in fact very small.
12 According to figures released in April 1998 the number of civil servants employed by the Department of the Environment, Transport and the Regions totalled 15,215, almost exactly the same as the numbers employed by the Commission. Even the annual budget of 97 billion euros administered by the Commission is only half the budget spent by the British Department of Social Security. Figures given in Colin Pilkington, *The Civil Service in Britain Today*, Manchester University Press, Manchester, 1999.
13 Sonia Mazey and Jeremy Richardson, 'Pressure groups and the EC', *Politics Review*, September 1993.
14 TEU, Title II, Article 146.
15 TEU, Title II, Article 151, clause 1.
16 Details of Coreper are taken from an article by Alistair Keene in Europa, a discussion journal published by the European Commission, 1997.
17 Details of voting in the Council of Ministers is taken from the web pages of the Council, to be found within the general Europa website: http://europa.eu.int
18 Article 4 of the common provisions of the TEU.
19 A useful insight into the organisation of European Council meetings was provided by a BBC Television documentary showing the workings of the Foreign Office. This programme, *The Minister*, shown on BBC2, 28 April 1994, followed the then Minister of European Affairs, Tristan Garel-Jones, during Britain's tenure of the presidency in 1992.
20 Matthew Engel, 'Parliament of snoozers', *Guardian G2*, 25 January 1994.
21 John Carvel, report on the first meeting of the COR, *Guardian*, 7 March 1994.
22 John Palmer, 'Devolved power redraws map', *Guardian*, 7 March 1994.
23 Duncan Watts, *Introducing the European Union*, Sheffield Hallam University Press, Sheffield, 1996, p. 173.

Part II

The impact of Europe on the British political system

4

Sovereignty and constitutional change

In 1972, by signing the Treaty of Accession, the British government tacitly accepted as part of British law some forty-three volumes of European legislation, made up of more than 2,900 regulations and 410 directives; the sum total of legislation agreed by the Community over the twenty years since its formation. Admittedly, much of this legislation was trivial: most regulations or directives from Brussels deal with points of detail such as intervention prices for commodities within the Common Agricultural Policy. Nevertheless, there were some major issues involved and, in any case, the triviality of certain details is unimportant compared to the basic principle that here was a solid *corpus* of law that became binding upon the peoples of the United Kingdom, despite that law never having been scrutinised or debated by the British parliament. It was a massive breach of the constitutional convention which holds that parliament is the supreme, and indeed only, law-making body in the UK.

Ironically enough, this major shift in the constitutional position was hardly noticed at the time. In the early years of British membership, most complaints about Europe concerned the operational faults and absurdities of the Community. People complained that Europe was too bureaucratic, too time-wasting, too remote from the people, too undemocratic, far too expensive. That which most alienated public opinion was the cost and irrationalities of the CAP. The CAP was seen as criminally wasteful, with three major drawbacks:

- it penalised the British taxpayer to the benefit of profligate foreigners
- it gave over-generous aid to French and other inefficient peasant farmers
- it produced the so-called 'mountains' and 'lakes' of food surpluses.

This perception of cost and waste became fixed in peoples' minds and many of the criticisms levelled at the Community in the early years were value judgments, based on preconceived ideas that often did not stand up to serious scrutiny. Such fears and criticisms were almost exclusively practical matters relating to the working of the Community. Very few people understood or concerned themselves with constitutional theory and it was only old-fashioned parliamentarians such as Enoch Powell who concerned themselves with the issue of sovereignty and the constitution at that time. It is only in recent years that concern has been expressed as to the extent to which membership of the EU has led to a transfer of sovereignty from Westminster to Brussels.

Sovereignty

'A dictionary definition of the word sovereignty is "supreme and unrestricted power residing in an individual or group of people or body".'[1] To be precise it is the legislative or judicial body that has no superior body able to over-ride legislative or judicial decisions made for the territory over which it is sovereign. In Britain, parliament is held to be sovereign because no other body has the right to pass and implement laws. So jealously does parliament guard the right to be the only legislative body that other governmental or quasi-governmental bodies which need to pass laws, rules and regulations, such as local government or transport undertakings, can only do so through the device known as delegated legislation. Through delegated legislation, parliament grants to other bodies the facility to pass laws, but only laws specifically related to the jurisdiction of the authority concerned. In strict legal parlance they are not laws, but by-laws. As the nineteenth-century constitutional writer, A.V. Dicey, put it:

> The sovereignty of Parliament is the dominant characteristic of our political institutions ... [Parliament] has, under the English constitution, the right to make or unmake any law whatever, and, further, that no person or body is recognised by the law of England as having a right to override or set aside the legislation of Parliament.[2]

Sovereignty is difficult to define precisely. In Classical Greece Aristotle distinguished between two kinds of sovereignty; one based on personal rule and the other on impersonal institutions. 'Rightly constituted laws should be the final sovereign.'[3] In more modern political theory these two types of sovereignty are distinguished as:

- legal sovereignty – which, in unitary states, is usually vested in the legislature. The source of legal sovereignty in federal or supranational states is harder to define, although the general belief in the United States is that the Constitution is sovereign
- political sovereignty – which is vested in a person or persons. At one time the monarch was sovereign but with democracy has come the belief that sovereignty is vested in the people. Implied in this concept of the constitution is a belief that no change can be made in the nature of the state without consulting the people through a referendum or plebiscite.

In Britain sovereignty is said to be vested in 'The Crown in Parliament', conjuring up visions of the State Opening of Parliament, with the Queen enthroned in the House of Lords, surrounded by both her Houses of Parliament. In practice, the term 'Crown' no longer refers to the monarch but to the body which now exercises the royal prerogative on behalf of the monarch: in other words, the crown equals the government. This highlights an anomaly in any dispute over the surrender of sovereignty. In the face of 'the ability of the Government to whip its own backbenchers through the voting lobbies to support its policies',[4] it is only fair to say that what is called by ministers 'parliamentary sovereignty' is rather more accurately 'executive' or 'governmental' sovereignty. David Judge has claimed that this is the 'contradiction at the heart of the British Constitution: of the principle of parliamentary sovereignty being used by executives to minimise their accountability.'[5]

This ambivalence over the definition of sovereignty can lead to problems in that those who believe they are arguing about sovereignty from a common basis can in fact be arguing about two quite different things:

> Sovereignty has two meanings in UK politics, whereas it has only one in other European countries ... (therefore) ... debating sovereignty is more difficult in the UK than elsewhere in Europe because of its other reference to parliamentary sovereignty.[6]

Any government which speaks about the need to preserve sovereignty is almost certainly talking about parliamentary sovereignty, and therefore about the government's fears of a curtailment of its own powers. Those opposed to Europe, however, tend to speak in terms of national sovereignty, playing upon the chauvinism inherent in the British people.

Lady Thatcher, for example, tended to wrap herself in the Union flag when speaking of Europe, hinting that the freedom of Britain was at stake. 'Willing and active co-operation between independent sovereign states,' she said in her Bruges speech, 'is the best way to build a successful European Community.' Some of Lady Thatcher's supporters were even more willing to play the xenophobic card to maintain national independence, often by playing on anti-German prejudices that have lingered since the last war. In July 1990 there was a furore over an interview given to Dominic Lawson, of the *Spectator* magazine, by the late Nicholas Ridley, then a government minister. In the midst of other anti-European remarks Ridley went so far as to say, 'I'm not against giving up sovereignty in principle, but not to this lot. You might just as well give it to Adolf Hitler.' The implied suggestion was that the surrender of British sovereignty to the Community was akin to the Germans using the EC to fulfil the dream of world domination pursued by Hitler in the Second World War. The sense of outrage which greeted Ridley's comments, particularly in Germany, led to his resignation but his words re-awakened the natural distrust of foreigners on the part of the British, leading in turn to thinking of Europe as representing foreign, particularly German, domination.[7]

What the europhobes tend to obscure in this debate is the position that any surrender of sovereignty that has taken place so far is only partial and that, quite irrespective of the European Community, all nations in the modern world are inevitably having to surrender some aspects of their sovereignty. The multi-national nature of life in the late twentieth century, particularly in the fields of defence, trade and the economy, has forced most countries into a series of compromises between independence and dependency. One result is a marked decline in the nature and status of the nation-state. And, as the nation-state has declined, so too have the more chauvinistic aspects of nationalism.

The nation-state

In medieval Europe the concept of a politico-geographical entity composed of people with a common ethnicity, religion, language and culture was unknown. Everyone paid lip service to a vague concept known as Christendom, within which the Emperor represented secular power and the Pope spiritual dominion. Within that dual hegemony, loyalties and allegiances were personal, made up of the reciprocal oaths, duties and obligations of the feudal system. When the nation-state began to emerge, as early as the fourteenth century, it was largely due to a breakdown in feudal relationships through disputed allegiances.

The dispute between France and England over the overlordship of Aquitaine known as the Hundred Years War transformed a feudal quarrel between two kings into a bitter war between two countries each of which developed a strong sense of national identity as a result. Early examples of nation-states came about through war, revolution, or the expulsion of an alien power – England, Scotland and France discovered their national identities in fighting one another while Spain and Portugal emerged through expulsion of the Moors from Iberia.

Yet, although a handful of nation-states existed as early as the fifteenth century, the development of the nation-state to the point at which it was perceived to be a part of the natural order of things, is a fairly recent development. In Europe the oppressive Austro-Hungarian Empire or the crumbling Ottoman Empire led to the rise of liberal nationalism in the nineteenth century, leading to successes such as the independence of Greece and the unification of Italy, in the creation of what Mazzini called 'a sovereign nation of free and equal beings'.

The heyday of the nation-state, however, undoubtedly came after 1918 when the collapse of the Austro-Hungarian, Russian and Ottoman Empires created a wealth of new nations. Even more productive was the period of de-colonisation which followed the Second World War, with even more to come with the collapse of the Soviet bloc in 1989.

Between 1870 and 1914 there were only about 50 sovereign states in the world,
16 of them in Europe. The figure barely fluctuated over the period. By the end of
the first world war the community of nations had grown by 10 as new states
emerged in Europe. When it was founded in 1920 the League of Nations had 42
members: its successor the United Nations, was established in 1945 with a
membership of 51. By 1960 this figure had grown to 82; by 1973 it was 135 and
in 1992 it stood at 183.[8]

The supranational institution of the European Union has therefore to be placed
in the context of a period when the nation-state internationally was seen as the
normal political unit. As John Major said in 1994, 'Europe's peoples in general
retain their favour and confidence in the nation state ... I believe the nation
state will remain the basic political unit for Europe. The European Union is an
association of states, deriving its basic democratic legitimacy through national
parliaments.'[9] Yet, by the start of the twenty-first century, the nation-state
has come under threat from two separate directions: on the one hand over-
shadowed by supranational and multi-national organisations, and on the other
undermined by the minor nationalisms of regions, religious groups or ethnic
minorities.

> The state survives, but it is no longer the supreme authority within a defined
> territory. Increasingly, it finds itself bargaining with multi-national companies
> strong enough to play one state off against another, and sharing power with sub-
> national provincial or regional authorities on the one hand and with the proto-
> federal institutions of the EC on the other. It has ceased to be the sole, or even the
> chief, custodian of the interests of its citizens.[10]

Therefore, it has to be said that the use of euroscepticism to defend national
sovereignty against the encroachment of an alien Europe is flawed because the
nation-state, instead of reaching its apotheosis in the modern world, is in
decline in the face of international reality.

The decline of the nation-state

The impression given by the opponents of European Union is that Europe is the
only threat posed to national sovereignty and that withdrawal from the EU
would leave the country once more independent of foreign influences. This is
to ignore the realities of the modern world and the extent to which Britain, in
common with most other countries, has surrendered vital aspects of its sovereignty quite independently of EC membership. In the latter part of the twentieth century it is no longer possible for a country to exist in glorious isolation: in
defence, economics and the development of trade the countries of the world
are inter-dependent.

- After 1945 Britain, France and other European countries were dwarfed militarily by the superpowers of the USA and USSR. Defence in the post-war world was only possible through the collective security of international alliances such as NATO. Elements of national sovereignty were sacrificed, part of the nation's armed forces was put under international control and national defence policy was subordinated to strategic decisions made by a supranational body – in this case the North Atlantic Council for NATO.
- As far as international trade and commerce is concerned, few national economies are strong enough to survive in a world of unrestricted market forces and, indeed, all nations have found that it was in their interests to subordinate themselves to GATT (the General Agreement on Tariffs and Trade) and its successor the World Trade Organisation (WTO).
- In any country a hallmark of sovereignty is the ability of the country's government, banks and financial institutions to dictate the nature of economic and fiscal policy within that government's jurisdiction. In 1976 the economic situation facing the Labour government became so grave that Britain was on the verge of what, in an individual, would have been called bankruptcy. In order to escape from its difficulties the government, in the person of the chancellor, Denis Healey, appealed to the United Nations agency, the IMF (International Monetary Fund) for help and Britain was granted a loan to extricate the country from the situation in which it found itself. But the loan came with conditions attached, one of these being that the Treasury would receive a team of advisers from the IMF who would have the power to dictate certain aspects of British economic policy. A programme of cuts in both services and public expenditure followed which represented economic policy and legislation that was not originated by the government and which was not subject to amendment by parliament.
- In signing the European Convention for the Protection of Human Rights and Fundamental Freedoms in 1950, and in accepting the subsequent establishment of the European Court and Commission of Human Rights, the British government acknowledged a source of law other than parliament and a final court of appeal other than the House of Lords. Since 1997 the Convention has been absorbed into British law but, in accepting and implementing the decisions and judgments of a supranational Court and Commission for so many years, the British government voluntarily surrendered the main theoretical plank defining parliamentary sovereignty.

Bearing these factors in mind it can be said that any surrender of sovereignty resulting from accession to the European Community was merely part of a more general recognition that a modern state cannot be nationally self-sufficient but that states are now essentially interdependent. In that light the more enthusiastic Europeans tend not to talk of surrendering sovereignty but of pooling sovereignty. In other words, the nation-state retains its separate identity in the more general sense, while sharing sovereignty with other states in certain agreed areas.

At the same time as the nation-state is diminished by the pooling of sovereignty over major policy matters there is also a sense whereby the nation-state is undermined by the growth of regional autonomy, or separatist movements on ethnic, linguistic or religious grounds. Most European countries have powerful regions or separatist movements:

- within Britain there are Scottish and Welsh Nationalist parties, as well as the problems of Northern Ireland
- France has language-based separatist movements in Brittany and Languedoc
- Belgium's division between Dutch and French speakers has turned the country into a *de facto* federal state, with separate assemblies for Flanders and Wallonia
- in Italy the Lega Nord was popular for a time with a programme of federalisation through a division of Italy into North, South and Central
- in Spain, regions such as Catalonia have become semi-autonomous, while the Basques continue to fight for independence.

There is therefore a sense that the monolithic power of the nation state, while being vigorously defended against the external threat of a federal Europe, is crumbling and fragmenting under internal pressures. This dual attack on the nature of the nation-state leads to many anomalies. National governments, in defending themselves against the centralising powers of Brussels, claim rights for themselves which they deny to those of their own regions that are seeking autonomy. Thus Conservative Party policy protested at regulation from a distant and remote Brussels but still insisted on Westminster's domination of Scotland's affairs, even though London is as remote to the Scots as Brussels is to the English. It has to be said, however, that these difficulties arise from different interpretations of the term 'federal'. For ardent adherents of the nation-state such as the British Conservative Party, federalism is equated with a centralised super-state in Brussels, eating away at the independence of member nations. The view of federalists on the other hand is that the federal state is a necessary prerequisite for decentralisation. In their view a federal structure provides the means by which the power to take decisions may be devolved, to national governments if need be, but equally to regional or local administrations, where that is more appropriate. As Lord Thomas said at the time:

> it seems that when John Major talks of disliking a centralised federal Europe, he must actually be saying nothing, since the essence of the word 'federal' is that it is not centralised. If a group of states wish to act in common in some ways and, at the same time, want to preserve national identity, how can you avoid having a

[federal] polity ... There is thus a paradox if those who say they want to preserve national identity insist, at the same time, that they are against a federal solution in Europe. Surely only a federal structure can preserve the identity of peoples.[11]

The loss of sovereignty

By signing the Treaty of Accession in 1972, Britain accepted the treaties of Rome and the other foundations of European Community Law. Since then the UK government has signed for itself the Single European Act and the treaties of Maastricht and Amsterdam. In so doing Britain has accepted a diminution of sovereignty in that:

- laws enacted by the Communities are directly applicable in Britain
- the UK parliament is barred from passing laws in areas where Community law already exists or where national law would be inconsistent with Community law
- British courts must accept and enforce decisions of the European Court of Justice.

As Community law states:

> On the basis of the powers thus conferred on them, the Community institutions can enact legal instruments as a Community legislature legally independent of the Member States. Some of these instruments take effect directly as Community law in the Member States, and thus do not require any transformation into national law in order to be binding, not only on the Member States and their organs, but also on the citizen.[12]

This surrender of sovereignty is not, however, all-embracing. The Community works according to the principle of the *specific attribution of powers*. This means that the scope and parameters of Community competence are limited and vary according to different tasks.

- some areas are not defined in the founding treaties where Community law has no relevance
- in other areas Community law is directly applicable and has clear primacy over national law
- in between are areas where Community decisions lay down the general aims of the law but where national governments are permitted considerable latitude as to how those decisions are applied.

Regardless of this, however, the argument can legitimately be advanced that sovereignty is not abandoned when Community law is made by the Council of Ministers on which all member states are strongly represented.

> The Member States have pooled certain parts of their own legislative powers in favour of these Communities and have placed them in the hands of Community institutions in which, however, they are given in return substantial rights of participation.[12]

It must be said, however, that those eurosceptics who comfort themselves with the thought that the transfer of sovereignty to Europe is limited and of no great importance are embracing false comfort. It has long been established that, if there were a conflict between Community law and national law then, constitutionally, Community law has primacy. In one important test case in 1991 the judgment clearly stated that 'Under the terms of the 1972 Act, it has always been clear that it was the duty of a United Kingdom Court to override any rule of national law found to be in conflict with any directly enforceable rule of European law'.[13]

Over the forty years or so that the European Communities have been in existence there has been a succession of judgments, by both the European Court of Justice and the various national courts, that have helped to build up a formidable *corpus* of case law concerning the relationship between Community and national law.

- Member states have transferred sovereign rights to a Community created by themselves. They cannot reverse this process by means of unilateral measures inconsistent with the general interests of the Community.
- No member state may call into question the status of Community law as being a system uniformly and generally applicable throughout the Community.
- Community law, enacted in accordance with the treaties, has priority over any conflicting law of the member states.
- Community law is not only stronger than earlier national law but has a limiting effect on laws adopted subsequently.[14]

The most obvious constitutional change brought about by membership of the European Union is therefore a surrender of the UK's parliamentary sovereignty to the primacy of Community law. One interesting argument put forward prior to 1972 was that advanced by Harold Wilson. In reply to the accusation that membership of the EEC would diminish British sovereignty, particularly parliamentary sovereignty, he said:

> Accession to the Treaties would involve the passing of United Kingdom legislation. This would be an exercise, of course, of Parliamentary sovereignty ... Community law, past and future, would derive its force as law in this country from that legislation passed by Parliament.[15]

The suggestion would seem to be that the Act of Accession which gave entry into the British legal system for all past, present and future Community law, was little more than an advanced form of delegated legislation. In other words, Community law can be applied in Britain without detracting from British parliamentary sovereignty because the right to apply that law was originally granted by a law passed by the British parliament. Harold Wilson was an astute politician and a past master of sophistry but it has to be said that to see Community law as yet more delegated legislation is a delusion. The fact is that the British parliament cannot refuse to accept Community law, nor debate it, nor repeal it, unless Britain were to cancel the Treaty of Accession and withdraw altogether from the European Union.

So it must be accepted that the UK has surrendered both parliamentary and national sovereignty through the act of joining the European Union. That loss of sovereignty and thereby the loss of national identity is the main complaint about membership now brought by those hostile to the European ideal whether they are known as eurosceptics or as europhobes. However, to speak of sovereignty in such simplistic terms is to ignore a more recent perspective which would first ask whether it is real or theoretical sovereignty that is being talked about, given the extent of current globalisation.

Real and theoretical sovereignty

The difference between the two has been described as follows: 'real sovereignty is the degree of control which a nation can exercise over its own destiny, while theoretical sovereignty can be best described as symbolic control, signifying little if any substance.'[16] Very often the loss of sovereignty which seems to cause the most concern is theoretical by nature. In their book on British attitudes towards Europe, Anderson and Weymouth cite two important instances where symbols of British sovereignty can be said to be theoretical rather than real.

The first of these is the so-called 'independent' nuclear deterrent, which was said to guarantee Britain's independent defence and security strategy in the post-war world. Yet, from the 1950s onward, control of Britain's nuclear arsenal was shared with the United States and it is unthinkable that nuclear weapons could ever have been used without American permission. Indeed it is far more likely that they would have been used as a result of orders emanating from Washington. So much for Britain's independence of action: the image of Britain as a major world power with sovereign control over its own defence capabilities was in fact a fairly transparent fiction maintained simply in order to bolster British self-esteem.

The other area where sovereignty is illusory concerns the maintenance of the strength and importance of the pound sterling. The eurosceptic argument against British membership of EMU is based on the undesirability of the British government and Bank of England surrendering control of British taxation or interest rates. And it is true that a Britain within the EMU would lose the ability to deal with short-term economic issues through fiscal measures such as the exchange rate. But the fact is that the British economy lost the ability to deal alone with medium to long-term issues many years ago. The sterling crises of 1967, 1986 and 1992 had comparatively little to do with decisions made within the British economy and much more to do with global problems associated with the German, Japanese and US economies.

The sovereignty which has quite clearly been lost or surrendered to the European Union is almost entirely of a theoretical nature. Anderson and Weymouth suggest that the European concept of pooled sovereignty might well mean the definite loss of theoretical sovereignty but in reality could actually mean an increase of real sovereignty. According to this viewpoint, real sovereignty in a collective organisation like the EU is something that is open to negotiation and 'real sovereignty in some areas of governance should be *traded* in order to secure a greater overall level of real sovereignty'.[17] Ironically enough, Margaret Thatcher recognised the tactics of negotiation when she signed the Single European Act and gave ground on the controversial issue of qualified majority voting in return for an application of market forces that was suited to the British view of the single market.

Critics of the European Union seem to concentrate on the loss of British sovereignty as though no other member state of the EU had sovereignty to lose. Yet every country has its own particular interests which are often in conflict with the interests of other countries. The countries which have been most successful in the growth of the European Union are those which have realised from the start that some aspects of real sovereignty must be surrendered at the negotiating table in return for gains in other aspects within the Union's pooled sovereignty. The history of Britain's relationship with Europe has been all too often one of delaying membership until after all the negotiations are over. Perhaps the feeling in Britain that there is a constant drain on British sovereignty through EU membership is due to the fact that Britain was never there in the early stages of forming the union, when participating members were trading-off some aspects of sovereignty in return for others.

There are elements of paranoia and pessimism in the eurosceptic view of things. In arguing against British participation in EMU and the common currency the sceptics say that it is undesirable in that it would give a measure of control of the British economy to other countries – and Germany is usually meant. They do not consider the reverse of that position and the possibility that, if Britain had been involved from the start at the negotiating table, then rather than simply seeing it as Germany controlling the British economy it could be represented as equally true that Britain might have a certain measure of control over the German economy.

That view, however, has not gained much ground and much of the development of Britain's place in Europe over the past decade has been coloured by the

Major government's determined efforts to counter or ameliorate the degree to which the Community could impinge upon the country's independence of action.

Defending the national identity

It was Lady Thatcher when she was still prime minister who first expressed the government's determination to defend British national independence and oppose federalism, which she stigmatised as 'centralisation'. Yet the irony is that, as is stated above, it was Margaret Thatcher who signed the Single European Act which, more than any other agreement on Europe, made a loss of sovereignty inevitable. As a prominent student of the EU stated: 'If you remove internal barriers you let illegal as well as legal substances cross Europe. If you want to police that, you have to have co-operation and this will affect the law-making authority of individual countries.'[18]

When John Major succeeded Lady Thatcher as prime minister he made much of his commitment to Europe by maintaining Britain's place 'at the heart of Europe'. Nevertheless, it was not long before the Major government, faced with the opposition of eurosceptics on the Tory bankbenches, became just as opposed to European integration as the Thatcher administration had been. From being mildly euroenthusiast in his views, John Major became what Hugo Young called 'a pragmatic eurosceptic'. In November 1992 the Foreign and Commonwealth Office (FCO) published a pamphlet to mark Britain's presidency of the EC. Called *Britain in Europe*, it purported to explain the European Community and the Maastricht Treaty to the general public. In fact it represented a statement of government policy.[19]

> The original Community treaties aimed at an 'ever-closer union among the peoples of Europe'. The Government are committed to closer co-operation with our Community partners. This has brought political and economic benefits. But the Government don't want, and won't have, a United States of Europe.

In negotiating the Maastricht agreements and in subsequent relations with Europe the Major government moved steadily away from federalism towards a militant defence of national identities against encroachment from Brussels, a move that was driven by the disproportionately influential band of thirty or so eurosceptics led by Bill Cash. The Major administration proceeded to defend national interests through a variety of devices such as:

- agreeing opt-outs from the Maastricht agreement
- promoting the concept of subsidiarity
- a stalwart defence of the national veto in the Council of Ministers
- and the possibility of multi-speed European development.

Opt-outs and variable geometry

Having agreed the terms of the Maastricht Treaty, a number of member states negotiated protocols giving them exemptions from certain clauses in the Treaty. Some of these were quite minor, as with France, Spain and Portugal who all negotiated exemptions for those overseas territories such as the Canary Islands or the Azores who are themselves unable to meet the Community's economic objectives.

A much more serious exemption, however, was granted to the UK over monetary union. Protocol 11 of the TEU states, 'The United Kingdom shall not be obliged or committed to move to the third stage of economic and monetary union without a separate decision to do so by its government and Parliament'. The most important effect of this opt-out is to preserve the independence of the Bank of England from moves to establish a European Central Bank. On the other hand, as was outlined earlier in this chapter, there is a contrary argument which says that the opt-out prevents the UK from having any say in the development and nature of the European Central Bank or on the form taken by an economic union that Britain may well have to join in the future.

The constitutional issue involved in economic and monetary union is that of economic sovereignty – meaning that the government, governor of the Bank of England and Chancellor of the Exchequer surrender control of the British economy to central European institutions. The relevant issue as far as the public is concerned, however, is the far more emotional matter concerning whether a common currency would mean having to give up the pound and penny. In their pamphlet the government were re-assuring in this, 'Britain is not committed to joining a move to a single currency. If we choose we can stay out indefinitely'.

The same exemption from the need to follow the other member states into economic union was granted to Denmark, on the grounds that Denmark could only enter into negotiations over economic union if required to do so by a referendum of the Danish people. It is to be noted that neither the UK nor Denmark see these opt-outs over economic union and the common currency as necessarily permanent: both countries retain the right to rejoin the process at a time which suits them best. The two countries are exercising their sovereignty to the extent of ensuring that any future pooling of that sovereignty will be done at the wish of the member country and at a speed set by the member country.

A more significant opt-out at the time was over the so-called Social Chapter, the programme for social protection in the workplace and elsewhere, which was accepted by all the other member countries. The UK government claimed that the Social Chapter, particularly in its provisions for a minimum wage and legislation on maximum working hours, was potentially harmful to the competitiveness of British industry. As such, the British negotiators at Maastricht did not so much opt-out of the agreement on social policy, as never opt-in in the first place. In the final Treaty, the Agreement on Social Policy is described as 'Concluded between the Member States of the European Community with the exception of the United Kingdom of Great Britain and Northern Ireland'. As it happens, this was the very first Conservative amendment of the Treaty to be swept aside by the Blair government after the 1997 election. Very little fuss was made about the reversal of policy: the press release issued by the IGC which reported to the European Council and formed the basis for the Amsterdam Treaty, states quite simply, 'The IGC has incorporated into the Treaty the Agreement on Social Policy *which previously only applied to fourteen Member States*' (my italics).

This approach – of only signing the parts of a treaty with which you agree – opened up the possibility known in Community jargon as *variable geometry*. This was an option originally devised for applicant members in Eastern Europe, who might never become members if they had to wait until they had parity of economic strength and stability with the countries of Western Europe. Under variable geometry member states would progress towards integration at a speed suitable for each individual state. According to Philip Lynch:

> The 'variable geometry' approach envisages European integration as a Chinese meal at which some diners take large portions of each dish but are left still wanting more, while the more sceptical steer clear of those bits they cannot stomach. This option may prove an attractive proposition for a British government eager to claim economic benefits without paying for them through further losses of national autonomy. But inherent in this is the danger of being relegated to Europe's 'second division'.[20]

This was the pattern John Major appeared to advocate during the 1994 European elections campaign when he claimed that the best way forward for Britain might lie in a multi-track, multi-speed Europe. Those members who wanted it could proceed towards integration without involving those members who are less sympathetic to a federalist approach. In 1994 the French prime minister put forward just such a three-tier plan for a centre-core, fast-track integrated Europe consisting basically of France, Germany and the Benelux countries, a peripheral, slow-lane second-tier for the more reluctant members like Britain and a third tier made up of other European countries that are not yet members. From what he had been saying it might have been expected that John Major would welcome the plan. Instead of which he was the first to condemn it and made a major speech in the Netherlands in which he denounced any suggestion that Britain should not be 'at the heart of Europe'.[21]

Subsidiarity

The concept of subsidiarity was principally developed to counter British fears of what was seen as the committed pro-federalism of Maastricht. In Britain federalism was actually equated with centralism, giving rise to fears of a powerful federal administration in Brussels imposing its will on the member states, without regard to the wishes of national parliaments. What developed at Maastricht was the doctrine of subsidiarity, defined in the Treaty itself as:

> In areas which do not fall within its exclusive competence, the Community should take action, in accordance with the principle of subsidiarity, only in so far as the proposed action cannot sufficiently be achieved by the Member States and can therefore, by reason of the scale or effects of the proposed action, be better achieved by the Community. Any action of the Community shall not go beyond what is necessary to achieve the objectives of this Treaty.[22]

At the time the Treaty was signed in February 1992, the British government felt that this definition of subsidiarity was inadequately expressed. The British presidency in the second half of 1992 was used to strengthen and refine the principle, much of the Birmingham and Edinburgh European Councils being given over to the matter. The communiqué issued at the conclusion of the Edinburgh meeting stated in clarification that, 'the Community [is] to act only when member states cannot achieve the desired goal themselves'.

The intention has been to ensure that an important role remains for national governments in the legislative process. Any proposed legislation in Brussels must now be first scrutinised for its subsidiarity and, if action would be best dealt with by national governments then the proposal must be passed down to the most appropriate authority.

It is here that the proponents of subsidiarity have made a rod for their own backs. Simply because a proposal is thought to be inappropriate for Community action does not necessarily mean that action by national governments is any more appropriate. It could well be the case that regional or local action might be even more suitable and the Committee of the Regions was established in 1994 to assert the rights of regions and districts within the member states. Certainly, the Scottish parliament and Welsh assembly have both adopted the concept of subsidiarity with enthusiasm, insisting on direct negotiations with Brussels without an intervening English body over such matters as the beef crisis or regional funds. And the anomaly in the situation was that, although the Major government advocated subsidiarity to prevent centralisation in Brussels, that same government was very ardently centralist in their management of the affairs of the United Kingdom.

The veto

The use of opt-outs and the doctrine of subsidiarity are useful weapons for national governments in their fight to retain sovereignty, but their ultimate weapon, as proved by de Gaulle in the 1960s or John Major at the Corfu

Summit in 1994, is in the use of the national veto in the Council of Ministers. The original plan for decision-making in the Council of Ministers was that there should be unanimity or the proposal would fail, thus effectively giving each member state a veto and the ability to block decisions even when they are approved by all other members. In the 1960s the use of the veto by Charles de Gaulle not only blocked British accession on two occasions but effectively stymied progress by the Community in any direction that did not suit French interests.

The reaction to de Gaulle's use of the veto was to move towards extending the number of areas that could be decided by majority voting instead of by unanimous decision. Because the smaller member countries were concerned that a simple majority voting system would disadvantage them in any confrontation with the larger countries, a qualified majority voting system was introduced. This gave differential numbers of votes to the countries, roughly dependent on size, and required a coalition of around 30 per cent of the total number of votes in order to block a proposal. The figures were so arranged that it would take a coalition of at least three member states to prevent a decision from going through. It was on this basis that the use of QMV was steadily extended, particularly in the SEA, to the extent that decisions requiring unanimity, and therefore subject to veto, were increasingly confined to major constitutional matters involving changes to the original treaties. QMV was becoming accepted as the norm until the mid-1990s, when the issue of voting and the veto became the sticking-point for a Conservative government attempting to appear firm so as to allay the fears of eurosceptics on its own backbenches.

In 1994 the crisis over voting rights erupted because it was proposed to enlarge the Community by admitting four more countries to membership, these four countries being given weighted votes in the Council of Ministers in accordance with the rule of thumb previously applying: Austria and Sweden getting four votes each, and Finland and Norway three each. At the same time it was proposed that the blocking majority should be raised to twenty-seven, so as to remain at 30 per cent of the new total of ninety.

Britain at once objected, claiming that the change would weaken the position of the large countries within the Community. The argument which followed threatened to overthrow the timetable for entry of the new applicants since the position of the British Conservative Party seemed to be that the veto in the Council of Ministers was the last remaining safeguard of national sovereignty. Ultimately, Britain had to agree to a compromise in which the blocking minority rose to twenty-seven (which became twenty-six when Norway withdrew) but member countries retained a strengthened right to apply the veto if they could show that their national interests were threatened.

Only a short period later, Britain emphasised the importance of the veto by being the one country at the Corfu European Council to block the appointment of Jean-Luc Dehaene, prime minister of Belgium, as president of the

Commission. As has been said in a previous chapter, it was a significant moment in Britain's relations with the Community because, by using the ultimate weapon of the veto for party political purposes, John Major had broken the unwritten rules of the EC. It was a crisis that was quickly resolved at the time but its effects lingered on. It was originally intended that the issue of the veto would be settled by the IGC due to report at Amsterdam in 1997, but the crisis inspired by Major's actions delayed things considerably and the issue was included in Agenda 2000 for resolution in the year 2000.

Accountability

Eurosceptics, in their criticism of Europe, often use the terms 'unelected' and 'undemocratic' in talking about the institutions of the Community and the need for Britain to defend its parliamentary sovereignty. At least the British parliament can claim to speak for the British people, they say, since it was the British electorate which elected that parliament. But for whom can the European Commission claim to speak when its members are appointed rather than elected, and to whom is the Commission accountable?

There is, however, an anomaly in the situation when national parliamentarians criticise the Community for its lack of democratic institutions; the so-called 'democratic deficit'. There are three simple solutions to accusations of non-accountability and they are:

1 strengthen the powers of the European Parliament
2 make more European institutions answerable to the European Parliament
3 open up even more European legislation to scrutiny by MEPs.

Yet, despite the simplicity of the solution, proposals to strengthen the European Parliament are bitterly opposed by national parliaments:

• to increase the democratic nature of the European Parliament would be to legitimise its activities, so that it could no longer be dismissed as 'unrepresentative'
• to legitimise the EP is to strengthen it in relation to national parliaments to the extent that national parliaments could easily become irrelevant in time.

So we end with the ironic situation that the very ministers who can criticise the Community for being 'undemocratic' are the same people who, as members of the Council of Ministers, refuse to legislate for democracy within the Community.

The ultimate in accountability, however, is the referendum: much used in parts of the Community where it is, indeed, required by constitutional law. The referendum is primarily used in those states where sovereignty is said to be vested in the people and where the constitution will often state that, if major constitutional changes are to be made then it can only be done with the approval of the people as shown in a referendum. There are those in Britain, the Liberal Democrats among others, who believe that changes in the British constitution, including those brought about by EU membership, should similarly be subject to referendum. Most of those who advocate referendums are, however, those who hold very strong opinions which the government will not accept but which their advocates believe have the support of the public. Referendums, therefore, are a way to appeal to public support over the heads of government in order to get a desired result.[23]

British parliamentarians have always been opposed to referendums, which are seen as something alien, antipathetic to representative democracy and liable to undermine the British Constitution. When opposing calls for a referendum, the principle of parliamentary sovereignty is evoked, as it was in reply to calls for a referendum on Maastricht such as the Irish, Danish and French had had, and which appeared in the government pamphlet *Britain in Europe*, already mentioned.

> The British system is a parliamentary democracy: the Government are accountable to Parliament and Parliament is accountable to the electorate. The House of Commons approved the British negotiating stance before Maastricht and the results afterwards. Parliament will have a thorough and detailed discussion of the Bill ... The Government believe that this is the right way to proceed in a parliamentary democracy.[24]

The reasons advanced for this position were expressed by the foreign secretary in the Commons debate as to whether to hold a referendum on Maastricht:

> As Parliament is sovereign it is clear that it could decide to hold a referendum, which it could either accept or reject. It could certainly choose, as it has before, to ask for advice from those who sent us here. But I return to the fact that we owe our constituents our judgment, and if we decline to exercise that judgment we are to some extent damaging the authority of Parliament.[25]

The expression 'as it has before' referred to the previous occasion on which the government had resorted to a referendum: indeed, the one and only instance of a national referendum for the whole of the UK. This was the referendum of June 1975, in which Harold Wilson's Labour government asked the British people to endorse the 're-negotiated' terms for continuation of British membership of the EC. On that occasion the British people had voted for membership two-to-one although, on a turnout of 64 per cent, that meant that only 43 per cent of the electorate had voted in favour, as against 22 per cent of the electorate opposed to membership.

There were special circumstances associated with the 1975 referendum. It only took place because Harold Wilson was determined to keep Britain in Europe despite having fought the two elections of 1974 with Labour committed to British withdrawal. Wilson only kept his party with him by promising to consult the people of Britain before reversing party policy. There is also the point that it is a psychological quirk of referendums that people are more likely to vote for the status quo than for change and prefer to vote 'yes' rather than 'no'. At the time of the 1975 referendum Britain was already a member of the EC, and the question posed to the electorate was so phrased that continuation of membership received the 'yes' while withdrawal demanded the 'no'.

In 1993, at the height of the Maastricht debate, the issue of a referendum was brought up again by rebel eurosceptics in the Conservative Party. Led by Lady Thatcher, once the most scathing critic of referendums, the eurosceptics said that they would withdraw their opposition to the ratification of Maastricht if the government laid the issue before the electorate in a referendum. Naturally the eurosceptics wanted a referendum because they believed that the electorate shared their scepticism about Europe but they acquired allies who were not opposed to Europe but were in favour of referendums, most notably the majority of the Liberal Democrats. However, a motion that a referendum must be held before the Act could take effect was defeated in the Commons on 8 March 1993 by 363 votes to 124. A similar motion in the House of Lords on 14 July 1993, for which Lady Thatcher and her friends pulled out all the stops, was defeated by 445 votes to 176; the highest number of peers voting in any division of the twentieth century.[26]

The issue of a referendum did not go away and dissident voices in the Conservative Party were calling for a referendum to be held before Britain accepted the idea of a single currency. The logical conclusion to this was the formation in 1996 of the Referendum Party by the late Sir James Goldsmith; the party being aimed at the failure of the Conservative government to allow a referendum on constitutional matters. To put pressure on the Tories to adopt a more sceptical approach, Goldsmith claimed that his party would fight 'every seat where the leading candidate has failed to defend your right to vote on the future of this nation'. Outwardly the Referendum Party was not anti-European – after all, Goldsmith was half French by birth, retained French nationality, lived for part of the year in France and was an MEP for a French constituency – but it claimed to want no more than to permit the British people a say through a referendum that had been denied them by the traditional parties.

As it happened the Referendum Party had little effect on the 1997 election, except being yet another nail in the coffin of the Major government. The official position of the Conservatives, as advocated by the chancellor, Kenneth Clarke, was to say that it was extremely doubtful that Britain would join EMU on the first wave in 1999, but it was nevertheless foolish to rule out the possibility while there was a chance of playing some part in the negotiating process by keeping Britain's options open. A policy of 'wait-and-see' was therefore adopted and maintained by John Major and the cabinet. A similar wait-and-see approach was also taken up by the Labour Party. Only the Liberal Democrats were willing to accept unqualified membership of EMU from the first, with or without a referendum.

That position remained after the election and Labour's victory. Official government policy was that Britain would join the single currency 'when the time was ripe', but both Blair and Brown agreed that the UK would only sign up to EMU and the euro after the public had been allowed their say in a referendum.

Collective responsibility

The referendum of 1975 was not the only breach of constitutional convention permitted by the Wilson government in the European cause. One of the oldest and most sacrosanct of conventions used to be that of collective responsibility, the premise of which is that all members of a government are collectively responsible for government policy. In the cabinet and elsewhere ministers might argue all they like about government proposals but once the cabinet has reached agreement, and the proposal becomes official policy, even dissenting ministers must support that policy. If they feel unable to do so they must resign from the government.

In 1975, when Harold Wilson was proposing the referendum on Europe and it was decided that official government policy was to campaign for a 'yes' vote, the prime minister was faced with the serious prospect of about a third of his government being so opposed in principle to European membership that they could not in conscience keep silent under the rules of collective responsibility. At the same time the prime minister could not afford to lose so many prominent members of his government if they obeyed the logic of the doctrine and resigned. On the basis that it was only a convention and not a statutory part of a written constitution, Wilson simply suspended the rules and stated that the doctrine of collective responsibility was inoperative for the duration of the referendum campaign. This enabled politicians such as Peter Shore and Tony Benn to campaign vigorously against government policy while remaining members of the Wilson government.

The suspension of the doctrine of collective responsibility was a pragmatic device to meet a specific dilemma, intended to be temporary. Once the referendum was over and the outcome decided, the rules of collective responsibility were re-asserted. However, the significance of conventions within an unwritten constitution is that, if they are ignored once, they can be ignored again if it is seen as expedient to do so. In theory all members of a government are bound by collective responsibility but, in fact, if a minister is in conflict with government policy over an issue of principle, particularly over European issues, then that minister no longer feels so bound to silence as was once the case. In the post-Maastricht period, eurosceptical members of the Major government, the most notable being Michael Portillo, felt free to make anti-European statements despite government policy. That acceptance of collective decisions being flaunted has followed the Conservatives into opposition under William Hague, with prominent Tory euroenthusiasts like Kenneth Clarke or Michael Heseltine quite ready to speak out against the party position on Europe, showing themselves as being perfectly ready to share a pro-Europe platform with Tony Blair and leading members of the Labour and Liberal Democrat parties.

Summary

There have been minor changes to the British Constitution as a result of EC membership, such as the use of the referendum and the abandonment of collective responsibility. But the major change has been the fundamental loss of at least theoretical sovereignty caused by British acceptance, through the Treaty of Accession, of the primacy of Community Law. Despite rearguard actions by the eurosceptics over issues such as the national veto, opting-out and variable geometry; the full and independent sovereignty of the British parliament has certainly been diminished. It has to be considered, however, how much that loss of sovereignty has to do with British membership of the European Union, or, rather, how far it is part of the inevitable inter-relatedness of modern economic life and the decline in the status of the nation-state. It is also a moot point as to whether some of the attitudes towards Europe adopted by British prime ministers – as was the case with John Major, and with Margaret Thatcher and Harold Wilson before him – are as a result of coherent policy decisions or whether they are adopted to appease the critics of Europe in their own party.

Notes

1 'Will sovereignty suffer?', *Guardian Education*, 17 May 1994.
2 Dicey quoted by Andrew Adonis in *Parliament Today*, Manchester University Press, Manchester, 1993, p. 8.
3 Aristotle, *Politics*, Sir Ernest Barker's edition, Clarendon Press, Oxford, 1946.
4 Duncan Watts, *Reluctant Europeans*, PAVIC Publications, Sheffield, 1994.
5 D. Judge, *The Parliamentary State*, Sage, London 1993.
6 D. Wincott, 'The Conservative Party and Europe', *Politics Review*, April 1992, pp. 14–16.
7 The Thatcher Bruges Speech and Nicholas Ridley's comments are quoted by Alan Watkins, *A Conservative Coup*, Duckworth, London, 1992.
8 Peter Alter, 'A giant leap into the unknown', in Victor Keegan and Martin Kettle, *The New Europe*, Fourth Estate, London, 1993.
9 John Major, 'William and Mary Lecture', University of Leiden, Holland, 7 September 1994.

10 David Marquand, 'Heart of the matter', in Keegan and Kettle, *The New Europe*.
11 Hugh, Lord Thomas of Swynnerton, in a lecture calling for a written constitution for the EU, delivered to the Menendez Pelayo Summer School, Santander, 3 July 1994.
12 All the quotations referring to Community law are taken from a publication of the European Commission, *The ABC of Community Law* (3rd edition), European Documentation Series, Luxembourg, 1991.
13 *Factorname v. Secretary of State for Transport (No. 2)* [1991], quoted in John Alder, *Constitutional and Administrative Law*, Macmillan, Basingstoke, 1994, p. 110.
14 *The ABC of Community Law*.
15 Harold Wilson's words quoted in Duncan Watts, *Reluctant Europeans*, p. 112.
16 Peter J. Anderson and Anthony Weymouth, *Insulting the Public? The British Press and the European Union*, Addison Wesley Longman, Harlow, 1999, p. 180.
17 Anderson and Weymouth, *Insulting the Public?*, p. 181.
18 Professor Juliet Lodge, of the Centre for European Studies, University of Hull, quoted in 'Party divisions over unity', *Guardian Education*, 7 June 1994.
19 Foreign and Commonwealth Office, *Britain in Europe, the European Community and Your Future*, HMSO Publications, London, 1992.
20 Philip Lynch, 'Europe's Post-Maastricht muddle', *Politics Review*, November 1993, p. 5.
21 John Major, 'William and Mary Lecture'.
22 TEU, Title II (Amendments to the Treaty of Rome), article 3b.
23 Perhaps a word is called for about the plural form of the word 'referendum'. Many people treat the word as a Latin noun of neuter gender, with the singular form '-um' becoming '-a' in the plural. However, the word is not a noun; it is the gerund form of the verb and as such does not naturally have a plural form in Latin. In English it is equally acceptable for the plural to be 'referendums', and this is the form I have used.
24 FCO, *Britain in Europe*.
25 Douglas Hurd, *Hansard*, 21 April 1993.
26 David McKie, *The Guardian Political Almanac 1993/4*, Fourth Estate, London, 1993.

5

Policy and the decision-making process

There are two categories of law in the European Union:

- **primary legislation**, which involves the body of law established by the founding treaties of the Communities, together with all later amendments and protocols attached to those treaties.
- **secondary legislation**, which encompasses all laws passed by the institutions of the Communities in order to fulfil the aims and purposes of the treaties.

It is important to recognise that all this law is applicable to the United Kingdom, and that the United Kingdom has its part to play in the formulation and implementation of that law.

Primary legislation

Community law in this respect is provided by the three treaties, with the various annexes and protocols attached to them, and their later additions and amendments: these are the founding acts ... Because the law contained in the treaties was created directly by the Member States themselves, it is known as primary Community legislation. This founding charter is mainly confined to setting out the objectives of the Community, establishing its mechanisms and setting up institutions with the task of filling out the constitutional skeleton and conferring on them legislative and administrative powers to do so.[1]

Primary law is therefore constitutional law, dealing largely with the relationship of the member states, both with Community institutions and with each other. On the other hand, primary law is the basis on which the European Court of Justice makes its judgments and, as in any legal system, the decisions made by judges and the precedents set by them form the basis for case law. And case law can apply to individual citizens, firms and organisations.

In the last chapter we established the primacy of Community law over national law. Even more important for the individual are the judgments referring to what is called 'direct applicability', which means that the rules laid down in the foundation treaties are applicable not only to the member states and institutions of the Community but directly impose obligations and confer rights on the citizens of the member countries, without those rules having to be adopted and amended by national law.

The first important judgment on this issue concerned Article 12 of the Treaty of Rome, limiting the ability of states belonging to the Common Market to impose or raise customs duties on goods circulating between members of the Common Market. A Dutch transport firm, Van Gend and Loos, were importers of chemical products from West Germany and, in 1962 they went to court in the Netherlands protesting that Dutch customs had increased customs duties on the goods they handled, in clear breach of article 12 of the EEC Treaty. At that time it was believed that laws contained in the Treaty applied only to states and institutions and could apply to firms and individuals only if adopted by national law. Now the Dutch court was being asked to rule that the Treaty of Rome conferred rights on individuals within member states. Feeling that it was not competent to rule on Community law, the Dutch court referred the case to the Court of Justice. Naturally, any such decision had major implications for national sovereignty and many member states made representations to the Court. However, judgment was given in favour of the firm, the judges stating, 'Community law not only imposes obligations on individuals but is also intended to confer upon them rights'.[2] This judgment was taken as the criterion for direct applicability and the case law thus established set a precedent for all subsequent cases of this nature.

In May 1973 a young Dutch woman, Miss Van Duyn, was engaged as a secretary by the Church of Scientology in the UK. The Church of Scientology was regarded by the authorities as highly dubious and was under investigation for practices by which young people were 'converted' and encouraged to join a community which took all their assets and forbade them to have any contact with family or friends. The church had therefore been declared 'socially harmful' by the British government, which was trying to shut it down. Because of her known association with an undesirable organisation, Miss Van Duyn was in effect declared *persona non grata*, barred from entry to the UK and refused a work permit. She immediately appealed to the British High Court on the grounds that Article 48 of the EEC Treaty guaranteed freedom of movement for all workers within the Community. The High Court referred the matter to the European Court of Justice and received the judgment that 'Article 48 has direct effect and hence confers on individuals rights that are enforceable before the courts of a Member State'.[3]

We can therefore say that the importance of primary law in the EU is as follows.

- Primary law, as established in the Treaties, has primacy over national law and, in these matters, the European Court of Justice has primacy over national courts.
- Its provisions are as binding on the citizens of member states as they are upon the states themselves.
- The foundation laws of the Community are to be enforced by the national courts of the member states in exactly the same way as they apply national law.

These decisions by the European Court of Justice have created a new role for national courts. In the past, British judges have enforced and interpreted the laws of the UK: it has never been within their remit to question the validity of those laws. Now, it is very much the duty of a UK judge to over-rule UK law if it conflicts with Community law. Quite early in Britain's membership, in 1974, a senior British judge wrote that Britain was now, 'part of a legal system which not only confers a right but imposes a duty on the Court in certain circumstances to invalidate legislation'.[4]

Secondary legislation

'Secondary legislation' means all those legal instruments devised and issued by the Community in order to administer policies laid down by the Community and achieve such aims and objectives of the Community as were established under primary legislation. Decisions made by institutions of the Community are passed to national governments for acceptance and implementation in the form of one of five different classes of legal instrument: regulations, directives, decisions, recommendations and opinions.

- **Regulations**: Once issued, regulations become immediately effective as law within the member states without the need for any national legislation to endorse them. For the UK the European Communities Act of 1972 gives authority for all subsequent EC regulations to have the same effect as UK domestic law approved by parliament. Although regulations become law in the form that was agreed in Brussels, sometimes additional legislation is required in the member countries to make them more effective.
- **Directives**: These are not as complete and detailed as regulations, but consist more of policy objectives. The results to be achieved are communicated to national governments and those objectives are binding on the governments. But the form and method in or by which those results are achieved is left to the discretion of the national governments.
- **Decisions**: Unlike regulations and directives, decisions are not directed at all member states but are specifically directed at one country; although it may equally be a firm, organisation or individual. Because these decisions are specific they are often administrative rather than legislative acts.

- **Recommendations** and **opinions:** These are little more than suggestions or tentative proposals put out by the Council or Commission and are not binding on the member states in any way. Strictly speaking they do not constitute Community legislation but are included here under secondary legislation because they may be taken into consideration by the Court of Justice when making a judgment about some other matter.

In any one year more than 12,000 legal instruments are issued. Two-thirds of these are non-political, being routine administration and dealing with matters such as price levels in the CAP. Of those instruments that can be considered legislative, 4,000 are regulations, 500 are decisions and 100 are directives.

There are basically two forms of Community legislation:

1 **Commission legislation** is made directly by the Commission and enacted under powers delegated by the Council. This legislation is largely made up of technical, trivial or routine administrative detail arising from legislation already agreed by the Council. However, the Commission can legislate without reference to the Council in certain areas, such as the granting of financial support from public funds.
2 **Council legislation** is described more fully below and involves consideration and consultation by the Council and European Parliament of proposals formulated by the Commission.

The policy, decision-making and legislative process

As stated above, most administrative or regulatory legislation coming from Brussels takes the form of Commission legislation, drafted by the relevant directorate-general with the assistance of an advisory or management committee. With such routine measures there is little need for scrutiny or decisions by ministers, commissioners or national officials.

On the other hand, when the regulations or directives to be issued are felt to be important or are likely to set a precedent or establish principles, then they are thought to need examination through the full Council legislative process. Traditionally described some time ago as, 'a dialogue between the Council, representing national cabinets, and the Commission ... acting ... in the "interests" of the Community as a whole',[5] the European Parliament acts in little more than an advisory capacity in this process. It is known as the consultative or single reading procedure.

The arrival of the Single European Act in 1987, followed by the Maastricht Treaty, together with a growing awareness of the 'democratic deficit', made it clear that there was a need for a greater involvement by the European Parliament in the legislative process. For a range of important measures, specifically those relating to matters arising from the implementation of the SEA, a three-way process involving Commission, Council and Parliament was evolved, known as the co-operative or two readings procedure. This was extended still further under Maastricht to give Parliament the right to a final veto in certain circumstances. This extension of the co-operation procedure is known as the co-decision procedure and, under the provisions of the Amsterdam Treaty has largely replaced the co-operation procedure in most matters relating to the single market.

The consultative procedure

1 Initiation: New policy initiatives are being put forward regularly and originate from a wide variety of sources. The suggestion may arise in the Commission, the Council of Ministers or in the European Parliament; it may be the proposal of a member state, either through the Council or through the state's permanent representatives; or it may come from an outside body such as a pressure group. Whatever the source a measure can only progress when it is adopted by the Commission, which is the only body with the power to draft legislation. Once a proposal is adopted by the Commission – a decision made at the highest level within the relevant directorate-general – that same DG is set to work in framing the first draft proposal.

2 Consultation: The first draft is treated rather like a Green Paper in the British system. It is circulated to experts, national governments, committees of the EP, the ESC and the Committee of the Regions, even pressure or interest groups if they are involved. The views of these various bodies may or may not be considered when the draft is framed into a formal proposal. This proposal is passed by the DG to the *cabinet* of the responsible commissioner, from there to the *chefs des cabinets* and then, ultimately, to the College of Commissioners. The commissioners may accept, reject or amend the proposal, or they could just as easily refer it back to the DG for re-drafting. The consultation process is very long-winded and it can take twelve months for the measure to move from draft to formal proposal.

3 Scrutiny: The formal proposal is passed to the Council of Ministers. It is also sent to the European Parliament, the ESC and, if relevant, the COR for their opinions. As has been said, the EP has no legislative role here, its opinion being purely advisory, which the Council is free to accept or reject as it chooses. The EP does, however, have the means to delay legislation if it wishes since the measure cannot proceed until the Parliament has given its opinion. If it wishes to delay matters until, for example, some change or amendment is made to the proposal, the EP can refuse to give its Opinion until such time as it gets its way over the amendment, or at least until such an amendment has been considered. Nevertheless, however effective the delaying process may be as a tool of negotiation, it has to be stressed that the EP has no veto in the consultative procedure.

4 The decision: The proposal from the Commission is passed to the Council for a decision; work on the proposal often beginning in the Council before the EP or ESC have given their Opinions. Preliminary work for the Council begins with a working party of national officials and representatives from the member states, who have the task of safeguarding national interests while reaching a common agreed text for the proposal. When the working party has gone as far as it can, the text of the proposal is passed on to COREPER who will attempt to reach final agreement. Any disagreements that COREPER cannot resolve can either be referred back to the working party for further negotiation, or it can be passed to the Ministers in Council for a political resolution.

Only the Ministers can make a legislative decision, either by unanimous agreement or by qualified majority voting. If no agreement can be reached at ministerial level the proposal can either be passed back to the Commission for the process to begin again, or the proposal can be referred to a future meeting in the hope that differences can be eliminated in the interim. In the event that agreement is reached in Council and the proposal adopted by the Ministers, that is the end of the consultative procedure.

The co-operative procedure

Brought in by implementation of the Single European Act, and extended by the TEU, this procedure was an extension of the consultative procedure that was introduced in an attempt to involve the EP in the legislative process, granting Parliament powers over legislation that previously it had only possessed over the budget. When the co-operation procedure is to be used has been prescribed by the relevant treaties and currently involves a large number of areas including the European Regional Development Fund, research, the environment and overseas cooperation and development. The alternative name for the co-operation procedure is the 'two readings procedure' because it involves the proposal being presented twice to both the Parliament and the Council.

1 First reading: The initial stages of this procedure are very similar to the consultative procedure. In this instance, however, asking the EP for its opinion is known as the *European Parliament First Reading* and the Parliament is free to suggest its own amendments to the proposal, which are then forwarded to the Council after having been incorporated in the text of the proposal by the Commission. Under the *Council First Reading*, the Council of Ministers does not reach a decision but comes instead to a Common Position, usually by qualified majority voting, although unanimity is needed if the Council does not agree with the Commission.

2 The European Parliament, second reading: The EP considers the Common Position of the Council over a maximum period of three months; although this can be extended to four months with the consent of the Council. At the end of this time they can act in one of three possible ways:

i   Parliament can approve the Council's Common Position
ii   Parliament can reject the Council's Common Position, as long as it is by an *absolute majority of all MEPs*
iii Parliament can amend the Council's Common Position, as long as it is by an *absolute majority of all MEPs*.

Whatever the decision by the EP, the matter is then sent back to the Council, except where the Parliament has proposed amendments. These must go first for further consideration by the Commission.

3 The Commission: Any amendments made to the Common Position by the EP must be considered by the Commission over a maximum period of one month, and one of two positions adopted.

i   The Commission can accept some or all the amendments made by the EP and incorporate them in the text of the Common Position. It is this amended text which is then sent to the Council.
ii   The Commission may not accept some or all of the EP amendments, in which case they are not incorporated in the text of the Common Position. However, the Commission must send to the Council of Ministers even those amendments it has rejected, together with the reasons for that rejection.

4 The Council second reading: The Council can follow a number of different courses of action depending on what has happened in the Parliament or with the Commission.

i   If the Parliament has approved the Common Position, it can be passed without further discussion, and becomes a legislative act of the Community.
ii   If Parliament rejected the Common Position by an absolute majority it can still be accepted by the Council, provided that action is taken within three months and that the Council decision is unanimous.
iii If amendments made by the Parliament have been incorporated in the Common Position by the Commission, the Council can accept the text by qualified majority voting.
iv   If amendments were not accepted by the Commission and not incorporated in the text, the Council can still over-ride the Commission's objections and accept the amendments, but only by unanimous decision.
v   If the Council fails to act on an amended proposal forwarded by the Commission within three months of receiving that proposal from the Commission, the proposal is judged to have lapsed.

vi If the Parliament failed to take any action during its second reading the Council can choose to adopt the first agreed Common Position without any further procedures.

The co-decision procedure

This process was developed by the IGC reporting at Maastricht and is the subject of Article 189b of the TEU. It is intended to share decision making equally between the Parliament and Council and is meant to temper the right to veto legislation that had been given to the EP by the cooperative procedure.

Under the co-decision procedure a **conciliation committee** is formed, made up of equal numbers of MEPs and ministers from the Council, with the mediating presence of the Commission. This is done in the case of one of two possible situations:

- if the Parliament has rejected an approved position of the Council
- if Parliament wishes to amend a Council proposal in a way unacceptable to the Council.

The conciliation committee will seek a compromise in the wording of the text that can be endorsed by both Council and Parliament. Because it comes after the second readings of the cooperation procedure the co-decision procedure is sometimes known as the 'third reading'.

The procedure applies to a wide range of issues but they specifically include: the free movement of labour, consumer protection, education, culture, health and trans-European networks. Under the terms of the Amsterdam Treaty the co-decision procedure largely replaces the co-operation procedure. It might be thought that the procedure would be long-winded but an early assessment of TEU provisions (in May 1995) noted that the average time for a decision to be taken under the co-decision procedure was less than 300 days.[6]

The assent procedure

This is not a legislative procedure but is nevertheless an important part of EU decision making. The requirement that the assent of the EP was needed for any proposed enlargement of the Union was extended under Article 228 of the Maastricht Treaty to include such other constitutional matters as association agreements with third world countries, the organisation and objectives of the Structural and Cohesion Funds and the tasks and powers of the European Central Bank.

Decision making – the budget

In Britain, where the English House of Commons has had control over the money supply since the fourteenth century, decisions taken about the Community budget are held to be very important. This was seen as especially true in the period 1979–84 when Mrs Thatcher was fighting hard to reduce Britain's budgetary contributions.

Yet the Community budget is remarkably small in comparison with the budgets of even medium-sized member states. However, the outgoings of the Community, especially on the Common Agricultural Policy, have always been heavy and that expenditure continues to increase, despite reforms to the CAP, to the dismay of net contributors such as Britain and, even more so, Germany.

The Community sets a ceiling on revenue and expenditure which is expressed as a percentage of the gross domestic product (GDP) of all member states combined. The ceiling for the period 1993 to 1997, which covers the implementation of the TEU, was fixed by the Delors Plan to 1.27 per cent of GDP. Any rise in expenditure was somewhat eased by reforms of the CAP which meant that the proportion of the Community budget spent on farming fell from 53 per cent in 1992 to 46 per cent in 1997, the first time that expenditure on the agricultural policy fell below 50 per cent of the Community budget.[7] By 1999 the EU budget was running at around 90 billion ECU, of which 45 per cent was given over to agriculture and 37 per cent to regional aid.[8]

Part of the eagerness for the enlargement of the Community in 1995 was that countries such as Austria and Finland would also be net contributors and would make a useful addition to swelling the hard-pressed budget. On the other hand, the prospect of the next generation of applicants, from Poland to Malta, is that all of them look likely to be net beneficiaries of the EU budget. Taken together, the ten former Soviet bloc countries plus Cyprus and Malta employ four times as many people in agriculture as the rest of the EU. 'The financial implications of extending even the current, semi-reformed CAP to these countries are huge – up to 12 billion ECU for the Visegrad four alone.'[9]

Revenue

Originally, the Community was financed by contributions levied on member states but this was found to be unsatisfactory and, since 1975, the budget has been financed through what are called 'own resources'. The components of these resources have changed over the years but there are three principal forms of contributions made by member countries, as determined under the Delors budget package introduced post-Maastricht in 1992. These components of Community revenue are:

- a levy on the customs duties, agricultural dues and other premiums charged on imports from non-member countries
- a proportion of national VAT revenue as the one consumer tax common to all EC member states
- a direct charge on a country's gross national product (GNP) as the best indication of what a country can afford to pay. This charge was raised from 1.2 per cent in 1994 to 1.21 per cent in 1995 and to 1.27 per cent in 1997.

These three components were first introduced in 1988 and the proportions of Community revenue represented then by the three were: VAT – 59 per cent; customs duties, including agricultural levies – 28 per cent; GNP charge – 10 per cent (there was also about 3 per cent in miscellaneous revenue outside the three main headings). As from 1993 the balance between the components was changed, with substantial reductions in the proportion represented by the VAT component, compensated for by increases in the GNP component. This change is because some of the poorer EC countries have a high consumption rate (and therefore pay more VAT) in relation to the size of their economies. In 1999, during arguments over funding of the CAP, Germany suggested that its own role as the largest net contributor to the EU budget could be ameliorated and made more equitable if the EU budget was exclusively funded by a simple levy on each country's GDP per head. Such a move would remove any need for the British rebate extracted by Lady Thatcher and would also reduce the disproportionate size of Germany's payments. Under such a system Italy and Belgium would stand to lose most when compared with the existing situation. The idea was shelved at the Berlin Council in 1999 but the issue remains on the table.[10]

It has to be noted that all the revenue of the Community comes from levies on the revenues of member states. The Community, unlike any other form of government, has no tax-raising powers of its own but is entirely at the mercy of the Council of Ministers, relying as it does on whatever levies the Council sees fit to grant, and out of which the Community must meet the expenditure commitments also fixed by the Council. It should also be noted that only the EC has a budget, the other two pillars of the European Union created by Maastricht being directly paid for by national governments.

Expenditure

The largest proportion of Community expenditure has always been devoted to the CAP, but reforms in the 1990s meant that this proportion was reduced to a figure below 50 per cent for the first time. This reduction, however, is balanced by a whole new range of expenditure created by the Maastricht agreement. This new spending is divided between three main areas:

- increased aid to the Social and Regional Development Funds, to provide help for the poorer regions of the EU and to assist convergence of economic standards prior to monetary union; after the CAP these funds are the largest recipient of EC expenditure, taking nearly 40 per cent of the budget
- money spent on increasing the competitiveness of European industry to reap the full benefit of the single market
- increased foreign aid to countries outside the EU, especially to states in eastern and southern Europe that were formerly part of the Soviet bloc and which are now working towards making themselves acceptable for EU membership.

The budgetary process

Each year's budget is different and there is therefore no typical format for the determination of the budget; yet it is possible to detect a standard pattern for the process.

1 The financial year of the Community corresponds to the calendar year and therefore begins on 1 January. During the previous spring and summer the Commission will begin preparing its estimates, these estimates being collected and collated by the directorate-general responsible for the budget, DGXIX. From these estimates DGXIX draws up a draft budget before 1 September at the very latest, and this is submitted to the Council of Ministers.
2 The Council of Ministers has previously, in consultation with the EP, drawn up what is known as the 'financial perspective', which is in effect the ceiling on expenditure mentioned earlier. Most of the Council's work at this stage is ensuring that the Commission's proposals do not exceed the spending limits fixed by the financial perspective. Within the Council the draft budget is scrutinised by the Budget Committee, often with the assistance of COREPER. The draft, with any amendments or revisions, is passed on to parliament. The deadline for this to happen is 5 October.
3 Some control over the budget has always been one of the few powers possessed by the European Parliament and MEPs are very jealous of their right to examine the proposed expenditure of Council and Commission. Most of the work is done by committees, most notably the EP's committee on budgets, but the revised version of the draft budget is approved by a plenary session of the Parliament. Up to 500 modifications or amendments are known to have been demanded for the draft budget, and it is only skilled negotiation by the chairs of the various EP committees that will succeed in producing a satisfactory unified text for approval by the plenary session.
4 In the second reading by the Council, during November, the Council may

modify, accept or reject EP amendments by means of qualified majority voting. The Council is bound by two conventions:

- the Council *may* reject Parliament amendments on issues that affect compulsory expenditures (as CAP expenditure is compulsory)
- the Council *must* accept Parliament amendments on discretionary expenditure (on foreign aid for example) as long as the required expenditure does not exceed the ceiling on total expenditure previously agreed.

5 The second reading by Parliament must take place before the end of December, by which time it is hoped that any disagreements between Parliament and Council will have been eliminated. If they have not been settled then the Parliament is within its rights to refuse to pass the budget. This, in fact, has been done quite often. For four years in the mid-1980s – 1984–88 inclusive – the budgets were rejected by the Parliament.

6 If the budget has not been adopted by 1 January, either because it has been rejected by the EP or because negotiations have become long drawn-out, the EC continues to function by means of 'twelfths'. Each month the Commission is allowed to spend up to one-twelfth of the agreed expenditure for the previous year. As a result some programmes may be delayed or put on hold, so it is in the interests of all to resolve any remaining differences before they get too far into the new year.

All matters relating to the budget are closely scrutinised by the Court of Auditors, within which there are groups dealing with specific budgetary questions such as the CAP or the Regional Fund. Since Maastricht the Court of Auditors has extended its activities from concern over financial rectitude to a wider monitoring of policy effectiveness. The Court not only checks that both revenue and expenditure observe legal regulations but also ensures that the Community is getting value for money by checking as to how far financial objectives have been met.

Scrutiny by the UK parliament

By accepting the terms of the Accession Treaty in 1972,[11] the British parliament accepted the primacy of EC legislation within the UK, with the exception of the need for some UK legislation to supplement Regulations and implement Directives. The Community legislation is not applied to the UK by any further UK legislation but is put into effect by way of statutory instruments or Orders in Council made under section 2 (2) of the European Communities Act 1972.

From the first the House of Commons sought to overcome this breach of parliamentary sovereignty by insisting that when a proposal passed from the Commission to the Council, the British minister concerned did not approve the measure until it had been scrutinised by the relevant parliamentary committee. This reservation was expressed in a series of resolutions of the House from 1980 onwards, but its application to all proposals of the Commission was only formalised in what is known as the Scrutiny Reserve Resolution on 24 October 1990.

The Maastricht Treaty which came into force in 1993 introduced the two new pillars of the European Union – Title V, dealing with defence and security, and Title VI, dealing with Justice and Internal Security. Since neither pillar involves legislation there was a period when both escaped scrutiny by national parliaments and there were calls for this to be rectified. Then there was the introduction of the co-decision procedure in Community legislation, which meant that a third reading stage was introduced into the legislative process that was not covered by the UK Scrutiny Reserve. The Amsterdam Treaty required an increased use of the co-decision procedure, while the same treaty included a *Protocol on National Parliaments* (Protocol 13) which imposed a six-week delay between the point when legislative proposals or proposals under the second or third pillars were sent by the Commission to EP and Council and the point when the decision was taken by the Council. This six-week period was ideal for scrutiny by national parliaments and it led to calls in the UK that the parliamentary scrutiny process be extended. This was duly done in a new Resolution of the House of Commons adopted on 17 November 1998.[12]

The new Resolution states that 'no Minister should give agreement to any legislative proposal or to any agreement under Titles V or VI which is still subject to scrutiny or awaiting consideration by the House'. Definitions of agreement include:

(a) agreement to a programme, plan or recommendation for European Community legislation
(b) political agreement
(c) in the case of a proposal on which the Council acts in accordance with the procedure referred to in Article 189b of the Treaty of Rome (co-decision), agreement to a common position, to a joint text, and to confirmation of the common position (with or without amendments proposed by the European Parliament)
(d) in the case of a proposal on which the Council acts in accordance with the procedure referred to in Article 189c of the Treaty of Rome (co-operation), agreement to a common position.

It has to be said that the scrutiny process can do nothing to prevent the implementation of Community legislation; the committees involved can only concern themselves with *prospective* legislation. Parliament can advise ministers on the line to take in negotiation, but they cannot amend or revise legislation once it has been through the relevant legislative procedure.

Scrutiny by the House of Lords

Ironically, the House of Lords has always been more concerned with the workings of Europe than the House of Commons, a general belief having been established that the Lords had the time and ability to deal with non-legislative matters for which the Commons did not have time in its busy timetable. What is more, the Lords not only have more time to discuss Community policies on the floor of the House but members of the Lords appear to be more willing to serve on European committees than their opposite numbers in the Commons. Their interest is probably aided by the fact that, unlike the rules pertaining to Westminster parliamentary elections, members of the Lords are permitted to stand for election to the European Parliament and several Tory peers, and more recently LibDem peeresses, have sat as MEPs over the years. Also in the Lords are many senior politicians who have served Europe in the past, such as Lord Jenkins, former president of the Commission.

With regard to the actual scrutiny process, a select committee, under the chairmanship of Lord Maybray-King, investigated possible procedures that could be adopted by the House of Lords and reported its conclusions in July 1973. Discussions arising from the Maybray-King Report finally resulted in the establishment of the Lords' European Communities Committee on 10 April 1974. In 1999 notice was taken of changes introduced by the treaties of Maastricht and Amsterdam and the committee changed its name to the European Union Committee. The Committee is appointed for each parliamentary session only, but its renewal has always been as good as automatic.[13]

The actual size of the Committee is not fixed, although it normally numbers about twenty. They are then divided up between six sub-committees, each of which has the power to co-opt members; so that, between permanent and co-opted members, about seventy peers are actively involved in the committee system. Add to these those peers with a special interest or expertise on a given subject who are invited to take part, and any lords who are MEPs who have an open invitation to attend, and it can be seen that there is considerable involvement by the Lords in the scrutiny of European legislation. To reflect the importance attached to this, the Chair of the European Union Committee is appointed to be Principal Deputy Chairman of Committees and is paid a salary as an official of the House of Lords.

The six permanent sub-committees are labelled A to F and are:

A Finance, Trade and External Relations
B Energy, Industry and Transport
C Common Foreign and Security Policy
D Environment, Agriculture, Public Health and Consumer Protection
E Law and Institutions
F Social Affairs, Education and Home Affairs.

Sub-committee E is very important because it reflects the former status of the House of Lords as Supreme Court of the UK, having the special task of considering the legal implications of Community law on UK law. The sub-committee is chaired by a Law Lord and has access to expert advice from a Counsel and a Legal Assistant. Sub-committee C is a fairly recent addition and was included after 1998 for the scrutiny of pillars two and three of the European Union. *Ad hoc* additional sub-committees can be set up at need as, for example, in the immediate aftermath of Maastricht a number of sub-committees were set up to examine the implications and problems of Monetary and Political Union.

The sub-committees meet once a week to hear and discuss evidence from which they draw up draft reports. The reports are passed on to the full committee which meets once a fortnight. If the draft is approved it is published as a Report of the Select Committee of the House. These reports also make recommendations as to whether there should be a debate on the report on the floor of the House.

Both committee and sub-committees have close relations with the EC Commission, the European Parliament and the British permanent representative in COREPER, with visits to Brussels, Strasbourg and Luxembourg by the chairs, representatives and clerks of the various sub-committees. Officials of the Commission may also come to London to join in deliberations of the sub-committees. The select committee receives regular reports on European developments from Foreign Office ministers, particularly after European Council summits. The committee is also active in the Conference of European Affairs Committees of National Parliaments (COSAC).

Scrutiny by the Lords begins with a memorandum from the relevant Ministry concerning the legal and political implications of a proposal submitted to the Council of Ministers. There are a large number of such memoranda since about 800 EC documents are submitted to national parliaments each year. The Chair of the Lords committee must sift through these memoranda and decide as to which are worth consideration and which represent mere routine detail. About a quarter of the proposals submitted are considered worth discussion and these are referred to the relevant sub-committee. Only about 10 per cent of these are sufficiently important as to merit a report and only about half of the reports are debated in the House. The committee may set out its views on a matter in a letter addressed to the relevant minister and government department and that letter included in the committee's correspondence which is periodically published in the form of a report to the House.

The scrutiny process is backed up by a 'scrutiny reserve' which states that the government cannot agree to any proposal in the Council of Ministers until it has been cleared by the committee. This arrangement was formalised in a Resolution of the House of Lords that was agreed on 6 December 1999 and allows the House of Lords the ability to influence the position the government will adopt in negotiating with the other member states of the European Community.

Scrutiny by the House of Commons

In the Commons the equivalent of the committee headed by Lord Maybray-King was the committee chaired by Sir John Foster, which reported in 1973 and which led to the formation of a select committee then known as the Committee on European Secondary Legislation etc., first appointed in May 1974. When Maastricht introduced two new pillars into the EU, both of them involved new categories of documents that the committee did not have the authority to scrutinise. The provisions of the Amsterdam Treaty, including Protocol 13, made for additional reasons for the scrutiny procedure to be reformed and modernised. Suggestions as to how this might be done were proposed in June 1998 and finally resolved in a Resolution of 17 November 1998.

Three changes were made to the scrutiny process in the Commons:

1 the name of the committee was changed to the European Scrutiny Committee
2 the remit of the committee included a new Scrutiny Reserve Resolution, discussed above
3 existing standing committees considering European legislation should be increased from two to five.

It was also recommended that:

• departmental select committees in the Commons should take an increased interest in European business
• there should be more links between Westminster MPs and MEPs
• a National Parliament Office should be established in Brussels.

New terms of reference for the committee included the scrutiny of documents which fell into one of six categories:

1 a proposal for legislation by the Council of Ministers, either alone or in co-operation with the European Parliament
2 any document which it is proposed should be submitted to the European Council, the Council of Ministers or the European Central Bank
3 any proposal for action under Title V of the TEU which is to be submitted to the Council of Ministers
4 any proposal for action under Title VI of the TEU which is to be submitted to the Council of Ministers

5 any other form of document which is published by one EU institution for submission to another EU institution
6 any other document relating to the EU, deposited in the House by a Minister of the Crown.

The committee has a membership of sixteen, with a quorum of five, but, unlike the session by session approach of the Lords, these are nominated for the term of a parliament. Like the Lords' committee, it receives copies of proposals made by the Commission to the Council of Ministers, together with an explanatory memorandum from the relevant government department. The committee meets once a week to consider the various matters laid before it, producing a report together with recommendations for any further discussion or debate within the Commons.

Parliament is informed of Community developments retrospectively by six-monthly reports prepared by the select committee and published as White Papers under the title *Developments in the European Community*. Originally debates on European matters took place late at night, with a one-hour limit on discussion, the whole heard before an empty and uninterested Commons chamber. However, in 1989, the whole system of scrutinising European legislation was examined by the Procedure Committee of the Commons and they recommended that debates should be more forward-looking. As a result, there are now regular twice-yearly debates on EC/EU matters, usually held just before the European Council meetings of June and December. Another recommendation of the Procedure Committee was that when the European Scrutiny Committee recommends that certain documents should be referred to the House for further discussion, discussion and debate should be moved from the floor of the House and into committee. The original proposal was for five standing committees which would differ from other standing committees in that, not only would they be permanent, but they would have no power to amend legislation.

In 1990 the Commons agreed to the setting up of the standing committees but modified the Procedure Committee's recommendation by saying that there should be just three. In the event insufficient interested MPs could be found to staff three committees and the system initiated in January 1991 provided for only two committees. However, the reforms of 1998 suggested that the system should revert to five standing committees and, in the event, a Commons Standing Order number 119 established three European Standing Committees, each with thirteen members nominated for the duration of a parliament. The chair is chosen from the Chairmen's Panel and may change for each sitting. The quorum is three, excluding the chair.

The three standing committees, with divided responsibilities, are:

A Agriculture, Fisheries, Forestry and Food; Environment and Transport Offices[14]

B Treasury, Social Security, Foreign and Commonwealth Office, Home Office, Lord Chancellor's Office
C Trade and Industry, Education and Employment, Health, Culture, Media and Sport.

The committees meet on a weekly basis and their programme consists of a ministerial statement followed by two-and-a-half hours' debate. Any resolution reached is reported to the House by the committee's chair. That resolution is put before the House as a motion which is moved in the House a few days later, although this recognition by the full House is merely a formality and no debate is allowed on the subject.

As has already been said, although scrutiny of European legislation has been tightened up since Maastricht and Amsterdam, the only power over European legislation possessed by either House of Parliament is the Resolution requiring ministers to await the scrutiny procedure before giving assent to measures coming before the Council of Ministers.

The role of the Civil Service

Unlike most other EC member states, Britain had neither a Ministry for European Affairs nor a specific minister charged with responsibility for European matters until the changes introduced by the Blair government in 1997. Before that the tendency was for British governments to treat European policy as a branch of foreign policy, thereby leaving the operational aspects in the hands of the Foreign and Commonwealth Office. Lady Thatcher tried to restrict the influence of the FCO, partly because she always distrusted the 'old-school-tie' type of links between the Foreign Office and what she called the 'Tory Grandees', and partly because she detected pro-European sentiments in the teams of officials provided by the FCO for European Councils and other meetings with EC fellow-members. During her premiership she actually contemplated the setting up of a separate Department of State but abandoned the idea when it was suggested to her that, since those Britons who had a close relationship with Europe – like Ted Heath or Leon Brittan – tended to 'go native', a European Affairs department could prove to be a Trojan horse of Europeanisation in Whitehall.

The nearest thing that the Conservative administration ever had to a minister of Europe was during the UK presidency in the second half of 1992. Tristan Garel-Jones, a minister of state at the FCO, was given the special task of co-ordinating the FCO's servicing of the many committees and working parties that Britain had to administer as president of the Community. In doing so he had the eager assistance of his Foreign Office civil servants because, as Duncan Watts has said, the FCO has always shown every sign of welcoming its work for Europe, 'Involvement in European policy has given the Foreign Office an interest in many areas of policy not usually associated with it; hence the powerful ... [role] ... of the Foreign Secretary ... [in pressing] ... for membership of the ERM'.[15]

Because the FCO has always claimed a leading role in anything to do with Europe it has within it two executive departments specifically designated to deal with European matters:

- the European Community Department (Internal), dealing with European matters in the UK
- the European Community Department (External) dealing with British interests in Europe.

These arrangements are based on the FCO's view that relations with the European Union are to be regarded first and foremost as facets of the UK's foreign policy, which should be dealt with exclusively by the Foreign Office. Nevertheless, over the years, the FCO has been forced to cede work on European issues to the Cabinet Office and other government departments until, according to Cabinet Office statistics issued in early 1999, there were no fewer than sixteen separate UK government departments dealing with specifically European policy issues.

A belief that the EU is essentially an aspect of British domestic policy rather than British foreign policy led government departments apart from the Foreign Office to set up an alternative to the two European Community Departments of the FCO. This they did by establishing an important European secretariat in the Cabinet Office.[16] Through a weekly meeting with the UK's Permanent Representative in Brussels this small secretariat, numbering no more than about twenty civil servants seconded from other departments, plays a major part in coordinating European matters:

- handling all those European matters likely to be included on Cabinet or Cabinet Committee agendas
- helping to frame agreements on common responsibilities between departments where European issues are involved
- briefing departmental civil servants on the present and future implications of British policy in Europe
- overseeing the scrutiny of European legislation by the European select committees of both Houses of Parliament, including the briefing of committee members on EU matters
- checking that the UK complies to the full with any requirements demanded by the European Commission in the implementation of EU legislation.

Within Whitehall departments there is a great deal of work for civil servants in supporting those ministers who are carrying out their European role as members of the Council of Ministers; something which becomes a particularly onerous task during the UK's presidency of the EU. When a minister attends a

Council meeting, he or she will be accompanied by a team of officials from the relevant department who act as advisers during meetings of the Council, as well as providing a secretariat to record the findings of the meeting and note the actions to be taken. This Council work for the Civil Service reaches far beyond actual Council meetings and includes regular contacts within and between national delegations over a period of several weeks in order to prepare the ground for the Council meetings. Council meetings are themselves so short that they rely on national delegations having reached a provisional conclusion as to the final form of any agreement before the actual meeting takes place. As a result ministers have comparatively little to do at Council meetings, merely concentrating on hammering out the final details while passing the main issues by the prior agreement established by the officials.

British civil servants in Brussels

British civil servants do a considerable amount of work for the European Union without losing their place in the domestic structure of the Home Civil Service. This is especially true of civil servants seconded to work in Europe while themselves remaining part of the British Home Civil Service. Typical of this are those civil servants appointed or seconded for service with the UK Permanent Representation on the Committee of Permanent Representatives.

At first a preparatory body set up to hammer out the details written into the 1957 Treaty of Rome, COREPER has developed into one of the most powerful groups of officials in the world. Over the years the committee has come to comprise literally hundreds of officials, which split for convenience into two bodies, COREPER I and II, as long ago as 1962. COREPER II is the senior, its core membership comprising the fifteen permanent representatives, while COREPER I acts as a forum for their deputies. The two committees are responsible for:

- keeping EU institutions and the governments and bureaucracies of the member states informed of each others' work
- ensuring that national and European policy are not at loggerheads
- finding compromises so as not to undermine core national positions.

In practice these different functions are difficult to separate and merge into the more general aim of keeping the Union working smoothly.[17]

The permanent representatives who make up COREPER are, of course, the equivalent of ambassadors to the Community and the British representatives are for the most part senior diplomats from the FCO, the UKREP having a regular staff of about forty officials plus ancillaries. The permanent representative in person is a career diplomat from the FCO, with the same status as a senior ambassador, ranking in seniority alongside the ambassadors to

Washington or Paris. The UKREP staff in its entirety, however, is only partially provided by either the FCO or the Diplomatic Service, with as much as two-thirds of the staff in fact being from other Whitehall departments, including the deputy permanent representative who is traditionally from the Department of Trade and Industry.

UKREP has three main functions:

1 UKREP officials provide advice, information and secretarial support in traditional Civil Service fashion for ministers and senior civil servants who are temporarily in Brussels or elsewhere in the Community on EU business.
2 The permanent representative and UKREP officials act to co-ordinate actions and liaise between the UK government and EU institutions. UKREP will lobby the Commission and European Parliament on behalf of British interests, while the British government will be kept in touch by means of the permanent representative attending meetings with the cabinet secretariat in London at least once a week.
3 As part of the EU legislative process, COREPER provides working parties which do developmental work on proposals put by the Commission to the Council of Ministers. These working parties are made up of officials and experts provided by national governments, either seconded directly or via the permanent representation. A member state such as Britain might have up to four of its nationals as members of any one working party and since there may be anything up to ten such working parties operating at any one time, the contribution made by the national delegations can be quite substantial and significant.

Civil servants working within UKREP are the only British representatives permanently based in Brussels, although there are many temporary secondments of national officials to Community institutions. One major European duty that can best be filled by a senior civil servant is by secondment to the support team of one of the two British commissioners since the members of a commissioner's *cabinet* are usually civil servants who have been seconded, either from the commissioner's own national civil service, or from another part of the EU bureaucracy. It is only natural that the convenience of familiarity means that it is not unusual for members of the *cabinet* to be fellow-nationals of the commissioner, even though convention expects at least one to be from another member state.

Joining the eurocrats

Around two-thirds of the administrative staff of the EU are employed by the Commission and as such are permanently employed and, for the most part, appointed on merit. In the case of senior or specialised staff, that merit is judged by means of highly competitive open examination. There is a career structure and most promotions are internal but the ever-present question of national jealousies prevents the organisation being truly meritocratic as something in the nature of a national quota system does exist, at least for those senior administrators who can initiate legislation.

The internal career structure of the Commission's secretariat is not very different from that of the British Civil Service. Members of the staff are divided into four categories:

- **Category A:** reserved for university graduates and represents the senior administrative staff and is the nearest equivalent in the EU structure to a senior civil servant in the open structure of the UK Home Civil Service. There is also a parallel **Category LA** for those administrative grade officials working as translators or interpreters in the Joint Interpretation and Conference Service
- **Category B:** executive grades
- **Category C:** secretarial and clerical officers
- **Category D:** manual and support service staff.

How to be a eurocrat

The Civil Service Management Code[18] states quite clearly, under the heading 'Service with the European Institutions':

> Departments and agencies should encourage staff with potential to consider service with the European institutions as part of their developmental training. Work in the institutions should normally be regarded as experience which will be valuable to the department or agency on the officer's return.

Recruitment for service with the EU bureaucracy is therefore encouraged by the Civil Service establishment and entry to service in Europe is by way of the normal recruitment channels of the Home Civil Service, even though success-ful candidates who are offered permanent service with the EU are required to retire from the UK Civil Service immediately upon appointment. There is a source of national pride for member countries in getting as large a number of their citizens as possible into service with the Community's institutions, competition for permanent places with the European institutions being very keen among would-be eurocrats from all fifteen member states.

However, permanent service is not necessarily the main aim of either the applicants in question nor the Civil Service establishment which has encour-aged their application. It is equally as likely that, rather than seeking a perma-nent position, British applicants are looking for long or short-term secondments to work in Europe, either for a specific purpose or simply to gain experience with European institutions as a career-building move, experience that can be useful both to the civil servants themselves and to the departments or agencies which employ them and to which they return after their time in Brussels or elsewhere in Europe.

There are basically three types of secondment available to British civil servants, as follows.

1 The *Stagiaire* schemes offered by the European Commission's *Bureau des Stages* in Brussels provide two five-month periods of in-service training, known in English as 'the Stage', which involve work experience in the Commission together with lectures and visits to other institutions. The two courses are open to university graduates and public service employees below the age of thirty and run from 1 March and 1 October each year. *Stagiaires* receive a cost of living allowance from the Commission.

2 The **Detached National Expert** schemes represent a specific form of secondment to the European Commission since here civil servants are recruited for their own particular expertise which is placed at the disposal of the European institution for periods of one, two or up to three years. The greatest number of such secondments lies in the field of science and scientific research, recruitment being through the Directorate General for Science, Research and Development (DGXII). The seconded specialists continue to be paid by their own departments but also receive a living allowance from the European Commission.

3 There are a number of schemes, such as the *Agent Temporaire* and *Auxiliaire* schemes, which offer temporary contracts for anything up to three years. These contracts are for specific employment within EU institutions such as the European Parliament, the European Court of Justice but most probably the Commission. The three factors that distinguish these people from permanent employees of the EU are:

- employment is for a fixed term, after which time the official returns to his or her own original employment in their home country
- those seconded to Europe need not resign from their own department; indeed their own departments are required to grant unpaid leave for the term of the secondment and to be prepared to re-employ them after their return from Europe
- staff on secondment will continue to be paid by their home department or agency, who will also be responsible for superannuation payments. There is also a responsibility for ensuring that their living conditions do not suffer and many of those on secondment will be paid a cost of living allowance under the particular rules that the department or agency has for those of its employees posted overseas.

A permanent transfer to work for the Commission is a career move open to any British civil servant, who can apply for transfer through the European Staffing Unit within the Cabinet Office or indeed by direct application to the Directorate General for Personnel and Administration (DGIX). However, since 1990 when the scheme was introduced, the normal method by which UK nationals qualify for employment as senior civil servants at category A of the EU bureaucracy is through an application for and acceptance onto the European Fast Stream programme which addresses two quite separate objectives in one single measure: the programme not only increases the number of UK nationals working within the EU, but also creates a substantial and influential section of the Home Civil Service which has considerable experience in dealing with European issues within a UK context.

Applicants for the Fast Stream programme need to be UK nationals, with a first or second class honours degree and aged no more than forty-one at the time of entering the programme. The age limit is fixed at forty-one because they aim to work in Europe after a couple of years' training and there is an age limit of forty-five for anyone applying to work for the Commission or other EU institutions. If accepted on the European Fast Stream the applicant becomes a full-time civil servant, working in a UK government department or agency but, 'the big difference is that their work has an emphasis on European policy issues, so they learn how the EU machinery works and how Brussels and Whitehall interact'.[19]

According to 1998 statistics issued by the Cabinet Office, thirty out of the eighty current European fast streamers were working on secondment in Brussels at any one time, most of the secondments being with the Commission. At regular intervals applicants will be invited through the Official Journal of the Commission to sit the highly competitive written and oral examinations that are the only possible way of entry into the EU recruitment schemes. If a candidate is successful they will take up their allocated post in Brussels or Luxembourg and will need to resign from the UK Civil Service since they will undertake upon taking up their new positions to place loyalty to the European Union above any national loyalties. There is a high level of success for UK Fast Stream applicants: the same 1998 report mentioned earlier had noted the names of eleven European fast streamers who had recently passed competitions for permanent posts with both the Council of Ministers secretariat and the European Commission. The training received on the Fast Stream programme will be invaluable in a career with the UK Civil Service, even those who fail the competitive examinations. As the Cabinet Office report says of unsuccessful candidates, '[they] could stay in the UK Civil Service and put [their] experience and training to good use there'.[20]

The role of pressure and interest groups in the community

One indication of the way in which an increased share of policy making has moved from national governments to the EC is the way in which pressure and interest groups are coming to focus their attention on the institutions of the Community in Brussels. The role of the Single European Act in removing the national veto from the Council of Ministers on all matters relating to the single market has meant a massive shift of influence over policy away from the Council to the Commission and, increasingly, the Parliament. 'Any British pressure group which continues to rely exclusively on lobbying Whitehall and Westminster is adopting a high-risk strategy, because on a large range of issues policies are now being determined in Brussels'.[21]

Recent years have seen a proliferation of interest groups operating in Brussels, sometimes with a permanent office and a large staff, at other times represented by a single lobbyist working on their behalf. These interest groups largely fall into one of four types.

1 Regional and local authorities. Some of these groups, from member countries which have a federal or semi-federal constitution, have offices in Brussels which act almost like embassies for the region concerned and have official backing. Other, less powerful, groups will be represented much less strongly and sometimes will work through their national delegation. The UK has tended not to be over-represented in this sphere but some regions, such as Wales, have long felt it worthwhile to maintain a promotions office in Europe and this has proved even more true – for Scotland as well as Wales – since the introduction of devolved government to both countries. Some local organisations feel that they can negotiate better directly rather than through national bodies. Merseyside, for example, had direct contact with Europe, over the heads of the UK government, in its campaign to get Objective One funding for the area. 'According to Harry Rimmer, Labour leader of Liverpool city council, Whitehall was never keen on the Objective One campaign because the status was gained over ministers' heads with a direct appeal to Brussels.'[22]

2 Multi-national companies and private or public corporations. EC directives can have an immense influence on business activities within the Community, either directly through tariff-control, taxation or competition legislation or indirectly through employment policy or measures of consumer protection. The Ford Corporation was one of the first to seek representation in Brussels in response to worries about competitiveness in the motor industry, but many other companies have followed their example, particularly those such as the major Japanese corporations who are looking for the most effective form of inward investment.

3 National interest groups. National groups probably still find it easiest to deal with their own national governments and civil services. But, increasingly, these groups find that it is worthwhile to have some representation in Europe, even if they cannot afford the expense of a permanent office in Brussels. The effectiveness of contact with the European decision-making process is particularly relevant for groups whose aims are not totally sympathetic to the government of the day, such as environmental groups or trade union and big business organisations. 'The EC decision-making process provides greater access to what in Britain would be considered "outsider groups", not normally influential in the inner circle of Whitehall-group contacts.'[23]

4 Euro-groups. These are interest groups that represent sectoral interests within several, if not all, the member states of the Community. These groups are obviously most active in areas that are seen to be of most concern to the Community; something like 150 different euro-groups being active in lobbying for agricultural interests. This reflects the fact that the growth of the CAP within the Community has meant that decisions on agricultural policy are increasingly taken in Brussels rather than at national level. As Nugent says, 'Pressure groups usually go where power goes.'[24]

The most important euro-groups are the umbrella organisations representing an entire sector of interest. Among the best known are:

- COPA, the Committee of Professional Agricultural Organisations
- UNICE, which is the employers' organisation, the Union of Industries of the European Community
- ETUC, the European Trade Union Confederation
- EEB, the European Environmental Bureau
- BEUC, the European Bureau of Consumers Organisations.

The umbrella groups suffer from two main disadvantages in the Brussels setting:

1 they represent such a range of interests that they can lack cohesion and fail to present a united front
2 they are often not specific to the EU but generally European, so that the ETUC, for example, represents over thirty trade union bodies in twenty different European countries.

Influence of the interest groups

The extension of lobbying interests within the Community has mushroomed in recent years. There are now estimated to be more than 500 euro-groups whose existence is officially or semi-officially recognised, over a thousand advisory committees working with the Commission, and over 3,000 full-time, professional lobbyists working in Brussels. In numbers, the lobbyists in existence probably match the numbers of Community officials involved in the policy-making process. What distinguishes the Community from most national governments is the apparent openness of Community institutions to those promoting sectional interests and the willingness of officials to talk to any lobbyist beyond just a few favoured groups. 'The very willingness of officials to talk to groups and individual firms means that the market for policy ideas is much more broad and fluid than in the UK.'[25]

Interest and pressure groups are involved with the European Parliament and committees such as the ESC and COR, but they deal mostly with the Commission, while pressure on the Council of Ministers is usually conducted at national level. The Commission above all, however, has formalised its relationship with the lobby groups by setting up recognised channels of communication:

- there are a large number of advisory committees specifically created so that they can brief and advise the Commission at the start of the policy-making process
- the so-called 'Social Dialogue' between the Commission and both sides of industry which involves regular meetings between the Commission, the European Trade Confederation (ETUC), the Union of Industries of the European Community (UNICE) and the European Centre of Public Enterprises (CEEP)
- commissioners and directors-general receive delegations and documentation from interest groups of all kinds and are in regular telephone communication
- representatives of the Commission attend meetings of the larger euro-groups
- Commission representatives will travel to member countries to meet national interest groups as well as national governments
- the Commission will participate fully in conferences and seminars set up by interest groups to investigate policy areas.

Summary

The Community has an established and complex procedure for the determination of policy making and legislation in which national representatives can take part and which involve all the institutions of the Community. Provisions of the SEA, TEU and Amsterdam Treaty are leading to a reduction in the democratic deficit through increased powers for the European Parliament in an extended legislative process. National involvement in the European process includes the scrutiny of European legislation by both Houses of Parliament and through the direction of civil servants to work in Europe. Possibly the greatest involvement of national interests is through pressure and interest groups and lobbyists of all kinds working in Brussels.

Notes

1 European Commission, *The ABC of Community Law*, 3rd edition, European Documentation Series, Luxembourg, 1991.
2 Case 26/62, *Van Gend & Loos* [1963] ECR 1 (Nature of Community law).
3 Case 41/74, *Van Duyn* [1974] ECR 359 (Direct applicability – freedom of movement).
4 Lord Scarman, quoted in Duncan Watts, *Reluctant Europeans*, PAVIC Publications, Sheffield, 1994, p. 94.
5 L.N. Lindberg and S.A. Scheingold, *Europe's Would-Be Polity*, Prentice-Hall, London, 1970.
6 Duncan Watts, *Introducing the European Union*, Sheffield Hallam University Press, Sheffield, 1996, pp. 180–1.
7 European Commission, *From Single Market to European Union*, Official Publications of the European Communities, Luxembourg, 1992.
8 Figures quoted by the London office of the European Parliament, January 2000.
9 Stuart Croft, John Redmond, G. Wyn Rees and Mark Webber, *The Enlargement of Europe*, Manchester University Press, Manchester, 1999, p. 73.
10 Martin Walker and Ian Traynor, 'EU splits along Paris-Bonn faultline', *Guardian*, 27 February 1999.
11 European Communities Act 1972, Section 2 (1).
12 Factsheet no. 56, *The House of Commons and European Communities Legislation*, Public Information Office of the House of Commons, London, originally published 1991 but amended and re-issued April 1999.
13 Information Sheet No. 4, *The House of Lords and the European Community*, Journal and Information Office, House of Lords, originally issued 1993 but amended and re-issued April 1999.
14 As far as European legislation is concerned, documents distributed to the three committees listed here are allocated according to the departmental responsibilities shown, even if those matters are also dealt with by the Scottish, Welsh or Northern Ireland Offices.
15 Watts, *Reluctant Europeans*, p. 100.
16 Robert Pyper, *The British Civil Service*, Harvester Wheatsheaf, Hemel Hempstead, 1995, pp. 176–7.
17 Details of COREPER are taken from an article by Alistair Keene in *Europa*, a discussion journal published by the European Commission, 1997.
18 Cabinet Office, *Civil Service Management Code*, Machinery of Government and Propriety Division of the Cabinet Office (OPS), London, 1996.
19 Cabinet Office, *Guide to Working in EU Institutions*, European Staffing Unit of the Cabinet Office (OPS), London, 1998 edition.
20 Much of the information on Civil Service involvement in Europe comes from Colin Pilkington, *The Civil Service in Britain Today*, Manchester University Press, Manchester, 1999.
21 Sonia Mazey and Jeremy Richardson, 'Pressure groups and the EC', *Politics Review*, September 1993, p. 20.
22 Peter Hetherington in the *Guardian*, 13 July 1994.
23 Mazey and Richardson, 'Pressure groups and the EC', p. 20.

24 Neill Nugent, *The Government and Politics of the European Community*, Macmillan, London, 1991, p. 111.

25 Mazey and Richardson, 'Pressure groups and the EC', p. 20.

6

The impact of European legislation on British policy issues

> The Europeans have gone too far. They are now threatening the British sausage. They want to standardise it – by which they mean they'll force the British people to eat salami and bratwurst and other garlic-ridden greasy foods that are totally alien to the British way of life. They've turned our pints into litres and our yards into metres, we gave up the tanner and the threepenny bit. But they cannot and will not destroy the British sausage!
>
> Jim Hacker in *Yes Prime Minister*[1]

In 'Party games', the episode of *Yes Minister* in which he becomes prime minister, Jim Hacker, as minister for administrative affairs, is given the task of implementing an EC directive whereby a sausage can only be so called if it contains 75 per cent of lean pork or beef. Since the humble British banger is composed largely of fat, gristle and head-meat it would not qualify under the Brussels criteria for the name of sausage. In discussions the European Commissioner concerned admits that it is only the name that is in question but, for political reasons affecting his own career, Hacker lets it be known that Brussels is seeking to abolish the British sausage and impose such alien products as salami and wurst. The tabloid press goes berserk at this latest European idiocy threatening the British way of life. Finally Hacker lets it be known that, after long and difficult negotiations, he has wrung a valuable concession from Brussels. As long as it is clearly labelled 'British sausage' the banger can continue as before. Jim Hacker is hero of the hour and saviour of British sovereignty. It is yet another instance of the way in which *Yes Minister* and *Yes Prime Minister*, while they were written as comedy to amuse and entertain, nevertheless were more than run-of-the-mill sitcoms because of an uncomfortable knack of being consistently close to the truth.

The truth behind this purely fictional dispute over the 'British sausage' has an uncanny echo in a twenty-seven-year argument over chocolate which relates to the fact that other EC members such as France and Belgium object to the fact that British chocolate contains vegetable fat rather than pure cocoa butter, and British milk chocolate contains rather more milk than is normal elsewhere. The dispute dates back to British accession in 1973 when Britain and Ireland refused to accept community standards requiring chocolate to contain 100 per cent cocoa ingredients.

For years Britain was unable to sell its chocolate in the EC and the tabloid press seized on this fact, going into overdrive when the suggestion was made that the British product should be re-named 'vegelate'. This was seen as a threat to the very core of the British way of life that was every bit as serious as any threat to the British sausage. It was only in October 1999 that the Commission worked out the necessary compromise, allowing British milk chocolate to be sold throughout the Community as long as it is clearly labelled '*family* milk chocolate'.

These two almost-farcical episodes, both the fictional and the factual, high-light a major factor in Britain's relations with Europe – the reaction of the British press to perfectly legitimate European legislation. The typical response of the tabloid newspapers to directives from Brussels that are otherwise perfectly innocuous has been to treat them as bureaucratic nonsenses that threaten to undermine the British constitution and overthrow our way of life. And when a compromise, that has always been on offer, is found, it is announced as though it were a success for British hard-headed common sense over the lunatic excesses of Brussels bureaucrats.

It is impossible to consider the impact of EC legislation on the British politi-cal and administrative structure without also considering the part played by a largely eurosceptical British press in mythologising the practices and inten-tions of the Commission and other EU institutions. For no other member country has the Commission felt constrained to publish a handbook de-mysti-fying the euromythology created by the British media.[2]

Euro-myths

Ever since 1973 it has seemed as though the British press can only present Europe in a negative light. This is overwhelmingly true of the tabloid press but can be equally as true for broadsheet newspapers such as *The Times* and the *Telegraph*. The hostile press began by criticising the CAP but rapidly extended to cover all directives and regulations emanating from the Commission. Positive benefits stemming from British membership are generally overlooked and the British public is left with the impression that the EC does nothing but dream up ridiculous regulations that at best involve ordinary people in bureaucratic nit-picking and at worst threaten the British way of life.

Most of these stories are untrue or, typically of myths, they contain a grain of truth onto which an exaggerated fiction has been constructed. Other stories are the result of misunderstandings or reports of proposed legislation that have been leaked before being properly drafted by the Commission. Occasionally the stories are true but have a rational explanation if their purpose is examined. Typical of such stories are the following.

- *'Get Netted. We won't play Ena Sharples, fishermen storm at Europrats.'* This story, possibly the most famous of the myths, was featured in the *Daily Star*, the *People* and the *Independent* during October 1992 and claimed that British fishermen, while at sea, were required by the European Commission to wear hairnets. The only truth in this story is that there is an EC directive in force – merely reinforcing an existing UK ruling – stating that workers in food processing plants should wear a suitable head-covering to prevent hairs from getting into the food. The EC directive pointed out that this rule not only applies to land-based plants but also to workers on board factory freezer ships, processing fish at sea.
- *'Brussels sprouts the curve-free cucumber.'* The *Sun*, *Daily Mirror*, *Daily Mail* and *Daily Express* all reported this story, claiming that EC regulations require all cucumbers to be straight. The EC had indeed laid down quality standards for cucumbers but this did not include a requirement for them to be straight. Any such rule is the work of the producers themselves who prefer straight cucumbers because then they can get more into the boxes in which they are marketed. Much the same sort of fuss sprang up in September 1994 over a Brussels directive on the length and curvature of bananas. The regulations were intended to prevent producers claiming EC subsidies for inferior products, stating that bananas should not be less than fourteen centimetres long and should not be 'abnormally' curved. The British tabloid press had a field day with banana jokes ('another banana skin for Europrats' ... 'Brussels goes bananas over bananas' and so on) but, finally, it transpired that Britain already had rules about the length and curvature of imported bananas that were far more stringent than those being applied by Brussels.
- *'Carrots are fruit, sprouts Brussels.'* This was made much of by the *Sun* and is, in fact, completely true, although without the implications suggested by the newspapers. Portugal, alone in the world, makes jam from carrots and enjoys a large export sale of the product. When Portugal applied to join the EC they became worried that EC regulations requiring jam to be made only from fruit would restrict their trade. In 1979 an EC directive classified carrots as fruit purely for the benefit of the Portuguese jam-making industry.

It will be noticed that many of the stories quoted above use words that ridicule the Community: an example being the constant use of the expression 'Brussels sprouts', or the replacement of the word 'eurocrats' with 'europrats'. This is typical of the way in which a hostile tabloid press uses derogatory words and images to convey an image of the EC as an over-fussy and faintly ridiculous bureaucracy. Always suspicious of Europe, the press has become increasingly more hostile in recent years as the right-wing in British politics in general, and the Conservative Party in particular, has moved from being merely euroscepti-cal to actually advocating withdrawal from the EU. Of nineteen national daily and Sunday newspapers, eleven are ideologically on the right and as such are more or less opposed to Europe.

The eurosceptic press, as typified by newspapers owned by Rupert Murdoch, from the *Sun* to *The Times*, has used a variety of techniques to manipulate British public opinion about Europe. These include the following.

- *Xenophobia* – this trades on an inherent British dislike of foreigners. Take, as a typical example, the statement included in a *Sun* editorial in February 1998: 'Would you buy a car from an Italian finance minister?' According to the tabloid press, foreigners are either corrupt, cruel to animals, incompe-tent, supported by the Mafia, fascists, international communists bent on re-introducing socialism into Britain or a mixture of all of these. In 1996 the arrest of a serial child-murderer in Belgium led the *Daily Mail* to point out the implications of the fact that Brussels is both the capital of a country perpetrating these horrific sex crimes and is also the city housing the European Commission and European Parliament.
- *Germanophobia* – hatred and distrust of Germany and the Germans is the driving force of many newspapers such as the *Daily Express*. According to this view the German desire for world domination pursued by Hitler, which failed when Germany lost the war, is now being realised by German domi-nation of the EU. In April 1997 the *Express* actually had a story headlined 'Germany is taking over the world' while, a few days later, an article on the Referendum Party included the sentence 'they all saw a plot, a conspiracy to put Britain under the heel of the Germans and we all know what sort of boots THEY wear'.[3]
- *Interference with British customs* – actions by the EU, taken for the sake of the individual and the good of the community, are denounced as interfering with the British way of life. A ban on the use by British fish and chip shops of diluted acetic acid instead of malt vinegar was depicted in the press as a move to ban Britain's favourite foods. An EC directive on the exploitation of child labour was described by the *Express* as a threat to the pocket money of two million British schoolchildren who have Saturday jobs or newspaper rounds!
- *Invocation of tradition and 'a thousand years of British history'* – this is used especially against the single currency and in defence of the pound; although that defence is often on very shaky grounds. In fact the traditional British monetary system of pounds, shillings and pence was swept away in 1971, without any major protests from the British public. Other protests as to the fact that the Queen's head would not appear on the euro notes ignored the fact that the royal portrait only appeared on British banknotes for the first time in 1964.

- *Ignore any positive contributions by the EU* – the tabloids in particular frequently fail to report significant European events and decisions, or if they do so it is a very short news item on an inside page. 'When ... the Blair government adopted the European Working Time Directive, it is significant that the importance of this European initiative, affecting as it will the lives of millions of Britons, was downplayed by all the eurosceptic broadsheets, ignored by the *Mail* on the day and relegated to less than 100 words of text in the *Sun* and the *Mirror* in low status locations in the papers'.[4]

Anderson and Weymouth call their study of the British Press and Europe *Insulting the Public?* because they claim that the attitude adopted by the press insults the newspaper-buying public in three ways:

1 the assumption is that the readers will not understand an item about Europe unless it is comprehensively simplified and trivialised, with any serious facts removed
2 it is further assumed that, even if the readers were able to understand the information, they would not want to know about it
3 on the basis of the first two points it is felt that the press has no obligation to provide the sort of serious facts that the public needs if it is to make up its own mind.

In 1994 the Commission set up a 'rapid-response' unit in the Information Division under a Danish director, Niels Thorgesen, to react immediately to distortions in the press, with the intention of nipping such stories in the bud before they could achieve mythological status. This unit has kept a watching brief on the eurosceptic British press since then, producing an occasional series of analytical papers called *Press Watch* which are distributed to key personnel in politics, the media and business. Unfortunately for the Commission it would seem that these reports have had little impact on the influential people they were intended for. Mythology seemed to flourish unchecked: in launching *Press Watch* number nine in April 2000, the director in charge of the Commission's London office, Geoffrey Martin, said that the distorted reporting of EU matters in the British press had created a deep-seated ignorance about Europe which had led in turn 'to a marked increase in support for British withdrawal' from the EU.[5]

The *Press Watch* report set out to name and shame the principal offenders in a bid to correct the bias. As it says, 'much of the British press, fuelled by the claims and counter-claims of domestic political campaigns, continues to obscure the substantive issues by sensationalising the trivial and presenting ill-informed opinion as fact. At the extremes, stories likening those implementing European child safety standards to Nazi collaborators (the *Mirror*) or suggesting that EU grants have funded IRA arms caches (*Daily Mail*) demonstrate nothing more than paranoia ... to the detriment of the public's understanding of what EU policies are trying to achieve.'[6]

The worst offender in the eyes of the Commission was the *Daily Mail*, with a total of eleven false or distorted stories recorded, but the paper was run close by the *Sunday Telegraph* with nine stories recorded. The stories are a mixture, as they were in the original euro-myth booklet, but once again they include a grain of truth wrapped up in such totally erroneous statements as the suggestion that Britain will have to give up the 999 emergency number; will have to give more leg room to theatre-goers; will have to give up Thomas Crapper's siphonic WC for the valve version; and will have to abandon the zero VAT rating.

Harmonisation and the single market

Although the bitterest arguments between eurosceptics and those in favour of European integration revolve around the issue of monetary union and the single currency, most misunderstandings about EC directives originate in the Single European Act and attempts that were made to apply the principles of the single market as from 1993. The problem initially was that each member country had its own national rules on health, safety and consumer standards, as a result of which a product which satisfied all the standards in one country may still offend the regulations of another and products made in one country might not be accepted for sale in another, negating the principles of the single market.

Originally the solution was seen to be the standardisation of rules, replacing many different national regulations with a single set of rules common to the whole Community. This, of course, gave rise to many anomalies such as the Portuguese carrot jam described above, and over the years a more realistic sense of what is practicable has meant that the emphasis has changed. Standardising or harmonisation has been replaced by a practice known as 'mutual recognition', meaning that whatever is legally produced in one member country is judged to be legally available for sale in any other member country; the consumer's interests being protected by stringent rules concerning labelling and consumer information.

The consumer in the EC is protected according to five fundamental rights:

1 The protection of consumers' health and safety – banning the sale of products that may endanger the health or safety of the consumer.
2 Protecting the consumer's economic interests – involving regulation of misleading advertising, unfair contractual agreements and unethical sales techniques such as those used in selling time-share.
3 Granting the right to full information about goods and services offered, including all directives on the labelling of food stuffs, textiles and medicines. Acceptable ingredients, additives and weights and measures are legitimised by e-numbers.

4 The right to redress – involving the rapid and affordable settlement of complaints by consumers who feel they have been injured or damaged by using certain goods or services.
5 Consumer representation in the decision-making process and usually meaning the Consumers Consultative Council, which is a committee made up of consumer associations from the various member states together with five EC advisory bodies – the European Bureau of Consumers Organisations (BEUC), the Confederation of Family Organisations in the EC (Coface), the EC Consumer Co-operatives (Eurocoop), the ETUC and the European Inter-regional Institute for Consumer Affairs (EIICA).[7]

Despite the flood of regulations and directives emanating from the Commission, most legislation on consumer affairs is the responsibility of national governments. Community legislation either fills in gaps left by national laws, or covers areas where the consumer in one member state has a complaint concerning another member state, as when a British consumer is the victim of dubious time-share sales in Spain. The guideline for Community legislation is 'As little regulation as possible, but as much as is necessary to protect consumers'.[8]

Since the EC's first consumer programme was issued in 1975 there have been EC directives requiring national action on:

- the safety of cosmetic products
- the labelling of foodstuffs
- misleading advertising and doorstep selling
- advertising aimed at children
- comparative advertising
- the selling of financial services
- consumer credit and unfair terms in sales and service contracts
- guarantees and after-sales service
- the safety of toys
- the safety of building and gas-burning materials
- an internal market in postal services.

One interesting facet of harmonisation suggested some years ago was that there should be a Single European Emergency Number, whereby EU citizens would be able to call on the police, fire and ambulance services by dialling exactly the same telephone number in all EU member states. This has now been done, the European number having been established in parallel with recognised national emergency numbers. In the UK the citizen can choose between dialling 999 and 112.

Aiding the harmonisation of products and services across Europe in the interests of the consumer is the European Standardisation Committee (CEN). This is a body made up of national standards agencies and affiliated producer and consumer organisations from nineteen European countries. It is not an EU body, although the EU often gets the blame for its more wayward decisions from the tabloid press. In fact, many proposals pilloried by the British press as 'Brussels madness' turn out actually to have been suggested by the CEN rather than the Commission.

The beef ban crisis

One area in which the EU's policy on the safety of the consumer has led to years of conflict and controversy between Britain and Europe concerns the disease of cattle known as BSE. Bovine spongiform encephalopathy (BSE, or 'mad cow disease'), is a terrible disease in which the cow's brain turns to a spongy jelly, leading inevitably to death since there is no known cure. Although BSE only came to light in 1986, spongiform diseases have been known for some time and the human form most closely related to BSE, Creutzfeldt-Jakob Disease (CJD), was first diagnosed in 1921.

For a long time no one suspected that a spongiform illness could be passed from one species to another, let alone that it could be passed from animals to humans. In 1988, however, a committee set up by the Ministry of Agriculture, Fisheries and Food (MAFF) discovered a link between BSE in cows and scrapie in sheep. As a result a selective cull of BSE-affected cows began in 1989. Unfortunately most farmers failed to declare the full extent of the disease in their herds for fear of losing money and the effectiveness of the cull was weakened. In early 1989, first Germany and then the United States banned the import of British beef.

In March 1996 a government research team in Edinburgh discovered a link between BSE and a more virulent form of CJD which had been reported as affecting ten young people whose average age was twenty-seven. The connection between these worryingly early deaths and BSE was admitted by the then health secretary, Stephen Dorrell, in a statement to the public made on 20 March. The result could well be described as panic-stricken:

- beef sales to the public collapsed
- the European Union imposed a worldwide ban on the sale of British beef
- while the EU agreed to provide 70 per cent of compensation for the slaughter of infected beasts, this 70 per cent was offset against the British rebate from the EU and the true value of the compensation payments was probably nearer 25 per cent.

The government's strategy was to argue that there was nothing wrong and they summoned up teams of veterinary experts to argue with the European Commission for agreement to lift the ban. When that was refused 'the government decided to attempt to shift the blame for what had happened on to the

European Union'.[9] The British government announced a programme of non-cooperation in decisions of the Council of Ministers until the EU agreed to withdraw the ban: as a result, European business was disrupted for three weeks and eighty different European measures were blocked by a British veto. The anti-European actions of the government may have helped John Major with his own party but it did nothing for Britain's status in Europe and it finally destroyed any willingness on the part of the Europeans to help Britain, 'The residue of ill feeling left by the British tactics was everywhere apparent ... as they look to Europe's future, others have decided they can no longer accommodate their awkward island neighbours'.[10] Europe remained adamant in its refusal to lift the ban and there were many advisers who told the government that, whether or not the threat from BSE was real, the public worldwide had lost confidence in British beef.

Early in 1997 the relevant committee of the European Parliament produced a report that was extremely critical of the British government's handling of the situation and the BSE crisis stumbled on to the end of the Conservative government and beyond. The more conciliatory attitude towards Europe exhibited by the Blair government had its impact and there was talk of a relaxation of the ban, certainly as it related to the beef cattle of Scotland and Northern Ireland. Then, in December 1997, the situation worsened again when a ban was introduced within Britain on the sale of beef on the bone.

In the same month a new inquiry into the whole BSE affair was announced, the inquiry beginning its work in March 1998. Within a year the inquiry had made its report, giving British beef a clean bill of health, a conclusion shortly afterwards endorsed by the scientific committee of the EU which pronounced British beef to be as safe as any in Europe. After a vote by the Council of Ministers, in which the French abstained, the EU lifted its ban on the export of British beef as of 1 August 1999. Unfortunately both Germany and France refused to lift the ban, although France's refusal was because the French food agency did not accept the safety of British beef, whereas the German ban was technically a procedural matter concerning the autonomy of the German *Länder*.

On 30 October 1999 the European scientific committee rejected the French case and the Commission instructed the French that they must lift the ban or be held as being in breach of EU law. France not only refused but retaliated by threatening to take legal action against the Commission for failing to protect consumer health. In the first week of the year 2000 the European Commission duly began legal action against France in the European Court. The food safety commissioner, David Byrne, who was spearheading the action against the French, also contemplated action against the Germans, but in the event Germany lifted their ban on 18 March 2000.

Agriculture

The impact of European agricultural policy upon the UK is measured more in terms of the controversy surrounding the policy than in its implementation. From the very first days of Britain's membership the Common Agricultural Policy epitomised just what it was that the British people thought of as being wrong with the Community.

In its conception the CAP had the worthiest of aims and objectives in attempting to make the Community self-sufficient in food, while guaranteeing a good standard of living for those involved in agriculture. In the implementation of the CAP, however, some of the worthiness of purpose disappeared. Encouraged by the French, with an essentially peasant agricultural economy, the CAP provided a guaranteed intervention price for all agricultural products, significantly without any limit being put on production.

As a result the CAP could be claimed as both a success and a failure. By 1973 the Community had become self-sufficient in cereals, beef, dairy products, poultry and vegetables. In the years that followed, however, despite the increase in population brought by enlargement, production increased into ever greater surpluses. By 1990 the countries of the Community were producing 20 per cent more cereals than they could consume, but continuing to pay the farmers more than the world price for all the cereal crops they could produce. The costs of the CAP increased at an even faster rate than production, since there was not only the cost of the support price to farmers but also the cost of storing the vast food surpluses.

By 1990 the cost of the CAP to the EC, in terms of the taxes and higher prices needed to pay for it, had reached around £92 billion, or £270 per head for each man, woman or child.[11] There was also the non-financial cost, both in terms of the dubious morality that laid out expenditure of that extent for the benefit of the mere 7 per cent of the EC population actually engaged in agriculture, and in the righteous indignation of the rest of the world which saw EC surplus production sold off at rock-bottom prices with what amounted to a massive subsidy. The repercussions of this last point nearly destroyed agreement on the Uruguay round of talks on the international agreement that was due to replace GATT.

For Britain the problem was that the CAP was devised before Britain was a member and the ground rules laid down bore no relation to the needs of British agriculture. Britain's farmers were both fewer in number and more efficient than, say, France's farmers and the feeling was that Britain was paying heavily to support inefficiency elsewhere. There was also a question of national taste. British farmers can produce large quantities of wheat for which the farmers are paid large sums under the CAP. But British taste does not like flour produced by British wheat, preferring hard wheat imported from Canada and elsewhere outside the Community; on which Britain has to pay the levy raised on all non-Community food imports. Figures produced by the Treasury in 1993 suggested that an average family of two adults and two children in Britain paid an extra £14 a year in food bills, simply as a result of the CAP.[12]

Reform of the CAP became inevitable in the 1980s as the Community repeatedly failed to agree a budget and teetered on the brink of bankruptcy. In 1991 reforms began under the then commissioner for agriculture, Ray MacSharry, and switched the whole emphasis of the CAP away from support payments for unlimited production onto topping-up payments for farmers who restricted their production within strict quotas. At the heart of this reform was a 'set-aside' policy by which farmers withdrew 15 per cent of their land from food production and for which they were then compensated. For poorer farmers such as the hill farmers of Wales, Scotland and the Pennines, the emphasis of support moved out of the CAP and transferred to the 'Leader' programme of regional aid.

The impact of the reforms on the UK environment was quickly seen in the extent of 'set-aside' land on British farms and the disappearance of the bright yellow of rape from the British landscape. But, in its own way, the new policy was just as controversial since farmers were now seen as being paid large sums of money to do nothing. The dangers of this were pointed out by Professor Howard Newby, head of the Economic and Social Research Council, who pointed out that, with set-aside likely to take 30 per cent of farmland out of agricultural use by the end of 1996, subsidies as great as £4–£5 billion from the EC and UK government might well be paid to around 30,000 landowners, merely to keep the land out of production.[13]

The reforms of 1992 were judged to be successful in that they cut the product surpluses held by the Community without jeopardising a 4.5 per cent increase in farmers' incomes. Further reform was, however, rendered necessary by the potential impact of the enlargement of the EU eastwards, which could mean an increase of 50 per cent in the extent of agricultural land, not to mention a doubling in the size of the agricultural workforce. There was general agreement, however, that the main thrust of reform should be to move away from subsidising over-production and turn instead to selective aid programmes.

Three areas where it was declared that reform was required were:

1 *cereals*: where it was projected that surpluses could rise to 58 million tonnes by 2005
2 *beef*: where, despite BSE, stocks of surplus meat were due to reach 1.5 million tonnes by 2005 unless there was a change of policy
3 *dairy prices*.

These were the problems tackled by Franz Fischler, the new agriculture commissioner, as soon as he took office in January 1999. Under the German presidency of the Council of Ministers the solutions arrived at were:

1 intervention prices for cereals would be progressively reduced by 20 per cent, with farmers receiving compensation payments for about half the drop in prices
2 subsidies to beef farmers would be cut by 20 per cent in three stages over seven years
3 there is to be a 15 per cent cut in support for dairy prices but implementation is delayed for three years and, although milk quotas are set to rise, no reform is to be expected in this sector until 2003.

These reforms were rather less than the Commission had sought: 30 per cent cuts in both cereal and beef having been proposed. Provisional estimates suggest that by the year 2006 the CAP will be costing between £1 billion and £5 billion more than the Commission wanted. On the other hand, Nick Brown, the British agriculture minister, estimated that changes to the CAP would cut consumer bills in Britain by over £1 billion a year: an annual saving of £70 for the average family of four.

Regional aid

For Britain, this is the reverse side of the CAP coin. Where the UK is a net loser over agriculture, it is a major beneficiary of Europe's policy towards regions in need of regeneration and development, especially since, out of the 50 million Europeans living in run-down industrial areas, some 20 million of them live in the United Kingdom.[14]

There are significant inequalities not only between the economies of Europe's member countries but also between different regions of the same country. In some countries the GDP for the country as a whole may equal or even exceed the EC average, but there will still be regions which fall below that 75 per cent figure. In Italy, for example, the GDP for the region around Milan is 137 per cent of the EC average, but that for Sicily is 68 per cent.[15] In 1990 a survey was conducted so that these differences in wealth between one member country and another, and between one region within a country and another region of the same country, were redressed ahead of the single market. The structural funds of the Community were reformed in 1989 and five priority areas identified as objectives for financial aid; three of those five being purely regional in scope.

The United Kingdom as a whole was judged to have a standard of living 100.7 per cent that of the EC average, but that figure conceals a significant difference between the 121 per cent enjoyed by south-east England and a figure of 74 per cent for Northern Ireland; only south-east England and East Anglia had a standard of living higher than the EC average at that time. Large areas in the regions of the UK were able to lay claim to support from the regional funds of the EC, under one of three out of the seven different types of regional aid.

Objective 5b regions

Objective 5 as a whole deals with rural areas. Objective 5a is given over to the modernisation of farms and has little relevance to much of Britain except for a few hill farms. Objective 5b is meant to make up for the decline in the importance of agriculture; replacing employment and income in areas where farming has been rationalised; and counter-acting the drift of population away from rural areas. The objective is therefore to re-train and re-employ former agricultural workers, replacing an economy dependent on farming with a new economy based on small businesses or tourism. Regions of the UK most affected by Objective 5b at the time were Dumfries and Galloway, North, Mid and West Wales (bar Clwyd) and Cornwall.

Objective 2 regions

This objective has the aim of providing economic diversification for areas formerly dependent on traditional heavy industries such as coal, steel or ship-building. Help is needed in these areas to attract alternative industries, to re-train the work force and regenerate the environment. These regions have always received EC funds, especially areas which were badly hit when a dominant industry closed down: as with Consett in County Durham, a former steel town which was devastated by the closure of the steel works.

This assistance under Objective 2 has possibly increased under the reformed Structural Funds, because Britain, as the first industrialised country in the world, is suffering disproportionately in the post-industrial world. About 40 per cent of the total EC population living in Objective 2 regions are to be found in the UK. The regions concerned are the Central Lowlands of Scotland, West Cumbria, the north-east including Tyne and Wear, Tees-side and Cleveland, most of Yorkshire and Humberside, Greater Manchester, West Midlands and South Wales.

Objective 1

These are the weakest areas of the Community, countries or regions where the GDP is lower than 75 per cent of the EC average. Three countries are Objective 1 in their entirety – Greece, Portugal and Ireland, while so is most of Spain and the southern half of Italy. The problem of saying which regions qualify for Objective 1 status begins with EU officials who identify those regions whose economic output per head is less than 75 per cent of the average. The amount due to each region is calculated by a formula which matches the extent by which their performance falls below the 75 per cent mark with a number of other factors such as unemployment levels. Five sorts of projects are eligible for Objective 1 funding: business support, infrastructure, training, community development, and agriculture and fisheries.

Originally, the situation in the United Kingdom was judged to be less serious than elsewhere in the Community and it was only Northern Ireland which qualified for Objective 1 status for many years. But this was the fault of the UK government, which was reluctant to apply for this status on behalf of any British region, 'because they thought it would be interpreted as a signal of Britain's economic decline'.[16] Another handicap was the reluctance of the UK government to put up any of its own money, despite it being a requirement that national governments should exactly match EC funds before Brussels loosens the purse-strings. Not that any money is ever actually received from Brussels: as a net contributor Britain simply subtracts the amount of funding due from Brussels from the amount the UK is due to pay into EU coffers.

In the summer of 1994 two regions of Britain, which had previously been treated as parts of larger regions, emerged as regions in their own right and recipients of Objective 1 funding. They were the Highlands and Islands of Scotland and Merseyside. The award of this status to Merseyside was delayed by the failure of the British government to satisfy Brussels that the Treasury would not take advantage of European money to withdraw British state funding for the area, the Merseyside Task Force bidding for European funds having to appeal to Europe directly over the heads of the British government. Apparently the Major government had wanted to use 40 per cent of the European money on schemes that would have manipulated the unemployment figures. Their plan was rejected by Brussels who require the Objective 1 funding to be additional money; it is not to be regarded as replacing national funding and saving the money of national governments.

The reluctance of central government to provide money to match EU investment in the regions has continued even after the 1997 election and the accession of a Labour government. In 1999 it was announced that Wales, Merseyside, South Yorkshire and Cornwall would qualify for £3.2 billion of Objective 1 funding in the six years between 2000 and 2006. At this point, however, problems arose because central government was reluctant to use money from the Regional Selective Assistance budget to match EU funds, even though the Brussels contribution doubled the annual £150 million of the regional budget to £300 million. The national government prefers to use these funds as sweeteners to encourage foreign companies to make any inward investment in certain areas.

Richard Caborn, a minister at the DTI with the task of sorting out the English regional claims, announced that the government was unwilling to match the entire £3.2 billion and that there would be a shortfall of £534 million. As a result, South Yorkshire, due to receive £780 million from the EU, was £300 million, or 38 per cent short in UK funding; Merseyside, due £844 million, was £150 million or 17 per cent short; and Cornwall missed out on £84 million, or 26 per cent of its expected funding. And, since the UK must hand back to Brussels any moneys which are not matched by national funding, that shortfall of £534 million can be doubled into a loss of more than a billion pounds. The situation was considerably worse in Wales, where the first secretary, Alun Michael, only raised £25 million of a potential £1.2 billion total. In January 2000 the Liverpool MP Peter Gilfoyle resigned as a defence minister in order to speak out on the backbenches about what he saw as a government failure to secure European funding for north-west England. In early February his loss was followed by Alun Michael who was forced to resign from leadership of the Welsh Assembly.[17]

In developing Agenda 2000 there was considerable concern that these problems should be resolved and the structural funds made more effective ahead of enlargement, because the average income in the applicant countries is only one-third of the EU average and it could well be that the entire new entry might qualify for Objective 1 under existing criteria. The Commission has therefore proposed the following:

- the seven existing objectives should be reduced to three – Objective 1, concerned with improving competitiveness; Objective 2, promoting economic diversity; and a new Objective 3 for areas not covered by Objectives 1 and 2 but which need help in order to adapt and modernise their systems of education, training and employment
- management of regional funds should be simplified and decentralised by a new partnership involving the direct involvement of the regions with the Commission, possibly through the Committee of the Regions.

The environment

At the Dublin Council of June 1990 the Community's commitment to environmental issues was confirmed in a declaration signed by all twelve heads of state or government.

> The environment is dependent on our collective actions; tomorrow's environment depends on how we act today... We intend that action by the Community and the Member States will be developed on a co-ordinated basis and on the principles of sustainable development and preventive and precautionary action.[18]

The EC was late in becoming involved with the environment. The Treaty of Rome contained a commitment to improve the quality of life for member states but the possibility that this commitment might apply to the environment was not accepted until the late 1960s and it was 1973 before the first action programme on the environment was announced.

In the 1980s came the realisation that the environment, and specifically the pollution of the environment, is very much a Community matter, because pollution pays no heed to national boundaries. Pollute the upper reaches of the Rhine and the pollution will affect France, Germany, the Netherlands and ultimately the seaboard of the North Sea. Air pollution in Britain can create acid rain over wide stretches of Northern Europe.

Concerns such as these led the Community to undertake an intensive programme of preventative measures, leading to a total of 280 environmental legislative measures, 200 directives, and four action programmes approved between 1973 and 1991. There was a change of emphasis in 1987 due to the work involved in setting up the Single European Act. Environmental requirements on factories and industrial plants, if it were left to national governments to administer them, could lead to differential costs and a loss of competitiveness in some national industries compared with others. There was therefore the need for a co-ordinated approach by all governments so as to provide a level playing field for the various member states involved in the single market.

Also in 1987 the World Commission on Environment and Development (WCED) produced what is known as the Brundtland Report, drawing attention to the way in which economic growth was leading to the destruction of finite resources. The WCED called for 'sustainable' growth. This, together with the institution of the single market, produced the communiqué of the Dublin Summit, the establishment of a European Environmental Agency in 1990 and the introduction of a fifth action programme, named 'Towards Sustainability' to run from 1993 to the year 2000.[19]

The main targets of EC environmental legislation have been pollution of the air, water and soil, together with the problem of waste, particularly toxic waste. Since the emphasis shifted to sustainability the Community laid great emphasis on issues such as the conservation of finite energy sources such as fossil fuels, saving energy through insulation and other means and the generation of energy from renewable sources like wind, sun and tide. There has also been a growing interest in the protection of wildlife, both flora and fauna, and the EC has ruled that in future any major new engineering project must take into account its effect on the environment, particularly on the habitat of wildlife, before it is allowed to start.

Community directives have laid down emission standards for the release of pollutants into the air and water. Directives have concerned the release of sulphur dioxide (1980), lead in exhaust gases (1982), nitrogen dioxide (1985) and ozone levels (1992). There has also been a continuing programme curbing the emission of carbon dioxide, held responsible for global warming. Key directives have also been issued concerning the quality of drinking water, the pollution of rivers and waterways and the quality of bathing water at seaside resorts.[20]

A major environmental initiative was the 1992 habitat directive, based on a 1979 directive for the protection of birds and intended to preserve or restore the habitat for species of flora and fauna whose existence is threatened by intensive farming or pollution. In legislating for this directive the British government joined proposals for wildlife habitat with the 'set-aside' provisions of the reformed CAP to produce the Habitat Scheme. This scheme, launched by the then agriculture minister, Gillian Shepherd, sought to persuade farmers to restore the natural environment in three areas.

1 Any set-aside land which is managed for the nurture of endangered species of plants, butterflies, birds and so on would receive an extra subsidy.
2 Along the fringes of certain key waterways farmers would be paid to maintain a strip twenty metres wide from the water's edge within which farmers would not use artificial fertilisers and pesticides. This will allow safe areas for the colonisation by wildlife while preventing the pollution of the water by nitrates and other toxic substances, with their consequent effects upon fish life and the food chain of water-birds.
3 Certain areas of land reclaimed from the sea or marsh and maintained by expensive and potentially damaging coastal defence or drainage schemes will be allowed to revert to natural water-meadows, marsh or wetlands with a subsidy being paid to farmers if the land in question is withdrawn from crop production.[21]

Environmental schemes are expensive and therefore unpopular with governments and industry. As a result there have been many disputes between national governments and the Commission about non-compliance with Community directives on the environment. In one major upset the British government's first attempts to privatise the water industry had to be abandoned because the Community refused to accept the suggestion that the privatised water companies should regulate themselves. It was only after the institution of the National Rivers Authority to police the activities of the water companies that privatisation could go ahead.

A long-standing dispute has been about the standard of bathing water on British beaches. This dates back to a directive of 1975 which demanded that national governments should designate bathing beaches which would be required to meet strict guidelines on water quality by 1985. The British government was first in trouble because they wanted to designate no more than twenty-seven beaches for this purpose: after discussion this number was raised to 446. The British government then pleaded for more time to comply with the set standards and was granted an extension until 1995. Yet a report by the National Rivers Authority in 1994 showed that fifty-five beaches in Britain could well fail to meet the required standards by the 1995 deadline and might still have waters unsafe for bathing because of raw sewage and other pollutants.[22] Progress has tended to be up and down, and there are bad years as well as good, but the turn of the century was beginning to see a real improvement in the number of British bathing beaches judged to be safe for bathing.

Another high-profile dispute between Britain and Europe has been over the directive requiring civil engineering projects to have regard to the environment. In 1991 the then commissioner for the environment, Carlo Ripa di Meana, officially warned the UK government that it was in breach of Community regulations in seven engineering projects, the most famous of which was the building of the M3 motorway across Twyford Down, an area of natural beauty and of historical and scientific interest near Winchester. The

Commission withdrew its objections to Twyford Down in 1992, but disputes over the government's road-building programme continued with major arguments over the Newbury by-pass and proposals to widen the M25 across the Runnymede meadows where Magna Carta was signed.

Disputes between the Community and Britain have a high profile because environmental pressure groups such as Friends of the Earth learned very early that the open nature of European legislation allowed for greater involvement of interest groups in the decision-making process. And, while the Commission would not normally intervene on its own initiative, it was much more ready than national governments to respond to complaints. Over the years the Commission has received more complaints about Britain than any other member state: in 1990 for example there were no fewer than 125 complaints registered.[23] And it is not only interest and pressure groups who intervene in this way. Local authorities who have to implement environmental legislation have begun direct contact with the Community. In July 1993 Lancashire County Council took the British government to the European Court of Justice for failing to clean up bathing beaches at Blackpool, Southport and Morecambe.

However, it should not be assumed that Britain is the worst offender. Typically, in 1991, in terms of non-compliance with Community directives the UK, with twenty-three offences, was the fourth most compliant; only Denmark, Luxembourg and the Netherlands having a better record. That twenty-three compares favourably with Greece's fifty, Italy's fifty-three and Spain's sixty-six.[24]

Social issues

Most directives and regulations emanating from Brussels relate to economic issues and concern some aspect of the single market. The TEU introduced a comparatively new element in the emphasis it placed on social issues, specifically as they concerned employment policy. This was the so-called Social Chapter of the Maastricht Agreement which regulated matters such as workers' health and safety, working hours and conditions, a minimum wage, rights to consultation through Works Councils and the rights of women in the workplace. The social dimension in the Maastricht Treaty was against the instincts of Mrs Thatcher and her successors, as was expressed in the words of one MP, Michael Portillo: 'The government will not tolerate unwarranted interference in people's lives from Brussels which would put extra costs on employers, make firms less competitive and reduce the number of jobs. We have decided not to be part of the Social Chapter and that position will not change.'[25]

As a result of British objections, the Social Chapter was not integrated within the text agreed at Maastricht but was added as a protocol subscribed to, at the time, by eleven members, in other words by all members apart from the

United Kingdom. The procedure demanded by this protocol meant that Commission proposals for social legislation would be vetoed by the UK but later re-introduced under the protocol as a measure applicable only to the Community minus Britain. This, for example, was the procedure adopted in September 1994 when Michael Portillo, as employment secretary, vetoed a proposal before the Council of Ministers to permit men to take three months unpaid paternity leave on the birth or adoption of a child. At the same Council meeting Portillo gave notice that Britain would treat proposed legislation on the rights of part-time workers in the same way.

Three years later the Labour government under Tony Blair accepted all the terms of the Social Chapter, including the minimum wage, shorter working hours and paternity leave provisions. And in 1999 Michael Portillo himself was forced to acknowledge that the dire consequences that had been forecast if Britain accepted the EU's social legislation had just not happened. Even the minimum wage was accepted and almost welcomed, even by those employers who had previously been the most hostile. Portillo announced that if the Conservatives got back into power they would accept the Social Chapter as a given fact and he could see no reason why any future Conservative government should make any sort of attempt to overturn the legislation.

Nevertheless, it is interesting to consider those elements of social legislation that did escape the system and which became enforceable in the UK, despite the disapproval and opposition of the British government at the time.

Trade union rights

In March 1994 the European Court reversed British anti-union legislation by finding that, in the privatisation of health service and local government services, the government had ignored a directive of 1977 concerning workers' rights when public enterprises are transferred to new ownership. Under the terms of the Court's ruling the British government could be fined if it did not introduce legislation to re-impose collective bargaining on those privatised companies that had set up non-union agreements.

Equality for pensioners

Again in March 1994 the Commission took action against the British Treasury which was proposing to issue grants for home insulation to old-age pensioners in order to offset the effects of VAT on heating bills. The Commission took action under sexual equality rules because, in Britain, men and women could not apply for these grants at the same age. The government was obliged to accept that sixty would be the age at which application for the grants could be made, even though men would not be pensioners until they were sixty-five. Later that same year a decision by the European Court against the Dutch government, but applicable to all member states, ruled that part-time workers

should have equal pension rights to full-time employees, back-dated if necessary. However, in order to gain that equality, British pensions for part-timers
would be payable only at the age of sixty-five, for women as well as for men.

The real success for British pensioners, however, came when a case before
the European Court ruled that it was unfair that men should have to wait
until they were sixty-five before they qualified for free prescriptions, when
women could receive free prescriptions at sixty. The British government had to
concede the point and grant free prescriptions to all men and women over the
age of sixty.

Women's rights

Perhaps the greatest beneficiaries of European social legislation or judgments
are women. 'All the most progressive legislation on women's rights is coming
from Europe. The British government is continually being pushed to act by
European directives and court decisions.'[26] The cases with the highest profiles
were women who were dismissed from the armed services when they became
pregnant. As a result of a ruling from Europe the British courts had to award
substantial damages to the women affected, who could number in excess of
5,500.

These rulings over sexual equality have little to do with the Social Chapter of
the TEU. Most are as a result of Article 119 of the Treaty of Rome which states
the principle that men and women should receive equal pay for equal work. In
1984 the European Court ordered the British government to amend the Equal
Pay Act so as to read 'equal pay for work of equal value', which meant that
employers could no longer justify inequalities in pay by claiming that men and
women were doing different jobs. In one case a female speech therapist claimed
equality with a male pharmacist because they had a similar health service
grade, although he earned very much more than she did.

European rules have also helped women in cases of equality of retirement,
maternity benefits, compensation to pregnant women for unfair dismissal,
invalid care allowances, sexual harassment in the work place and so on. It is
through actions such as these, from the Commission and the European Court,
that some measure of social legislation was forced onto the UK government
even during the years of Conservative hostility and before British acceptance of
the Social Chapter.

Economic policy

The Intergovernmental Conference at Maastricht agreed a timetable for
achieving economic and monetary union. This was to include economic
convergence on inflation, interest rates and currency stability, the introduction
of a single currency and the setting up of a Central European Bank. The

programme set out at Maastricht saw a Stage 2 in this process that would begin in 1994 and end with the final Stage 3 of complete union in 1999. Britain had originally intended to be part of the EMU, albeit reluctantly on the part of many Conservative ministers. In September 1992, however, the events which culminated in the so-called 'Black Wednesday' led to the UK's withdrawal from the ERM and a negotiated opt-out for Britain from the EMU timetable.

Thereafter the timetable had no formal regulatory position in the UK. Thanks to the opt-out negotiated at Maastricht the British government of the time chose to adopt the position that Britain would be free to join or not join the EMU according to what would be best for British interests. In the run up to EMU and the single currency British economic policy was naturally constrained by European factors such as the single market and the strength of the deutschmark but otherwise did not feel obliged to heed what the rest of the 'euroland' countries were doing. As the then chancellor, Kenneth Clarke, said about the Commission's convergence statement in 1994, 'I'll wait to see what the Commission recommends. I'll follow it if I agree with it and not if I don't.'[27]

That position, of waiting to see what would happen while remaining on the sidelines outside the single currency, became official Conservative Party policy for the 1997 general election. And, after the election, something very similar was adopted as policy by the Labour government. It was no secret that Gordon Brown as chancellor was very keen to join EMU and the single currency but, in support of Tony Blair's stated aim, he argued for Britain to wait until it was absolutely clear that Britain had satisfied the five criteria laid down by the Treasury for British entry (see Appendix 6 for a list of the five criteria). Because of this policy decision British policy is not directly affected by European monetary measures, just as Britain has ruled itself out from having any effect on EU policy. One irony of the situation when the currency union was formed on 1 May 1998 was that, with Britain holding the EU presidency at the time, Gordon Brown had to take the chair for the actual ceremony creating monetary union but then had to withdraw from the room while the ESCB members of ECOFIN discussed matters related to the euro, which the UK is barred from discussing.

Yet, it would be naive to think that Britain is totally unaffected by the policies followed by the monetary union. Once the euro became a reality on 1 January 1999, there was a sense in which British involvement became inevitable. Europhobes may well believe that Britain has won a great victory in preserving its own currency and refusing to have anything to do with the euro, and may believe, equally sincerely, that these are the outcomes most ardently desired by the people. But,

- Britain inevitably has to use and trade in the common currency and the London financial markets conduct an ever-increasing share of their business in the euro
- the eleven members of the eurozone represent a trading bloc with which Britain conducts 60 per cent of its trade

- even before the euro was introduced, firms such as British Steel, ICI and Marks and Spencer announced that they were ready to bill and be billed in euros by their suppliers
- even the apparent failure of the euro, which steadily lost value against the pound and dollar, to the delight of those eursosceptics who felt that this failure justified their own hostility, has had an impact on the British economy. One result of the falling value of the euro was to make the pound over-valued in a market where Britain does 60 per cent of its export business. When BMW pulled out of the Rover car company two reasons given for Rover's poor performance were the over-valued pound and Britain's failure to join the euro.

Competition policy

European legislation on competition in industry and commerce has been in existence for some time but gained greater importance after the establishment of the single market. As a former commissioner for competition policy has said, 'The continuing integration of the Community and the ever-present need for the protection of the consumer from competitive abuses, ensures that competition policy will always play a vital role in Europe'.[28] Competition legislation in Europe has had its effect on Britain in a number of spheres, including anti-monopoly and cartel legislation, selective distribution systems and action against restrictive nationalised industries.

Cartels

The aim of European legislation here is to prevent companies in various countries getting together to fix prices or rigging the market against the interests of the consumer. One area that has concerned Europe for years is the high fare structure on European airlines, where routes are assigned to specific companies and on which competing airlines are not permitted to fly. Prices have notably fallen on routes where competition from economy airlines like easyJet or Ryan Air has been introduced.

Selective distribution

This is where multi-national companies prevent customers in one Community country from buying a product in another where the price is cheaper. The most noticeable example of this is in the car industry where the same model of car can be many times cheaper in another EC country. At one point, when British buyers had discovered that they could get a car in Belgium at anything up to 40 per cent less than they would have to pay in Britain, the Ford was taken to the European Court because it was refusing to supply right-hand drive models for British use to Belgian dealers.

Removing national monopolies

The Community is interested in opening up national monopolies to competition when it is suspected that the monopoly is protecting inefficient practices. A principal target is the large state monopolies in the telecommunications field like Deutsche Bundespost Telekom or France Télécom. These cannot affect Britain domestically as the privatisation of British Telecom took place some time ago, but the removal of the state monopoly in the mainland EC does open up opportunities to British telecommunications companies. In the reverse direction, the Dutch post office among others is acting competitively to secure international mail services that the post office in Britain has been prevented from offering by the conditions applicable to the Royal Mail's monopoly position.

Internal security

One of the three pillars of the European Union instituted at Maastricht was a new deal on the policing of internal security through the Europol system, which would mean the abolition of border checks within the boundaries of the EU. The main advocate for the removal of internal borders was the Schengen Group, of France, Germany and the Benelux countries, so-called because of a meeting at the small Luxembourg town of Schengen in 1985. The five countries came to a formal agreement in 1990 and were joined by Italy (1990), Spain and Portugal (1991), Greece (1992) and Austria (1995). Occasionally the Scandinavian countries are reported to be thinking seriously about joining, but the United Kingdom and the Republic of Ireland resolutely remain outside the Schengen Agreement.

The reluctance of Britain and Ireland to agree to the removal of immigration controls for visitors entering one of the two countries from another EU country has a great deal to do with the problem of terrorism and the need to control the movement of terrorists and their weapons. But it has also a great deal to do with the insular nature of both the UK and Ireland and the two countries' lack of land frontiers. Both countries prefer to check thoroughly at the point of entry and then allow the visitor to move freely and unchecked within the country. In this way the UK can avoid the system of identity cards and residency permits demanded by most countries in the mainland EU.

This drawing back from the removal of border controls is not unique to the British Isles. Many more states began to express doubts at the growing number of illegal immigrants, swollen by gypsies and others seeking political asylum; an influx which reached new levels in 1999 and 2000. Estimates made in the summer of 1999 put the numbers of illegal immigrants smuggled into the EU every year as 400,000, with the EU already containing nearly a million displaced persons, the highest level of stateless migrants since the post-war diaspora of 1945.[29] The Amsterdam Treaty, which came into force in August

1999, took note of the growing concern and made dealing with immigration an EU-wide responsibility rather than leaving it to individual countries. In October 1999 a summit at Tampere in Finland established the first moves towards creating a system of fingerprinting immigrants and maintaining an EU-wide computer database, as well as proposing measures such as repatriation, which could lead to problems with civil rights groups.

In January 2000 the principle of the Schengen Agreement was undermined when both Belgium and Luxembourg reimposed border controls to counter an expected increase in the number of illegal immigrants. The Belgian interior minister, Antoine Duquesne, insisted that it was a temporary measure lasting only a few weeks 'to dissuade illegal arrivals in our country and to combat effectively the mafia-style networks that exploit these people'. He also made it clear that a clause of the Schengen Agreement allowed member countries to opt out for short periods in the light of special circumstances. For British eurosceptics, however, the actions of Belgium and Luxembourg were final proof that the Schengen policy of a common EU external border had failed to control illegal immigration at a time when the sheer number of immigrants and asylum seekers was causing major concern in the UK.[30]

As far as asylum seekers are concerned, however, the EU member countries do not have as much freedom of action as might be thought and adjustments to the Schengen Agreement are a very minor factor in the equation. A statement by a British government minister in February 2000 made it clear that Britain's response to the refugee crisis had very little to do with directives from Brussels, stating that, 'far from being a European treaty, it is the 1951 United Nations Convention on Refugees – signed by more than 120 countries – that obliges the United Kingdom to assess every asylum claim on its merits'.[31]

The disharmonies of harmonisation

Earlier in this chapter we discussed the concept of harmonisation and the extent to which the Community is willing to allow for national variations to avoid over-regulation. This does lead to certain anomalies where British practice differs from the European standard.

- *Non-approved additives.* Certain colouring agents and flavourings in food are not approved by the EC but are nevertheless accepted as legal in British foodstuffs because of traditional practice. Examples are the green colouring added to mushy peas, the yellow employed on smoked haddock and the red dye added to Red Leicester cheese.
- *American programmes on TV.* The Commission laid down a directive for television broadcasting which states that at least 50 per cent of the material broadcast within the EU must be of European origin. Britain, however, issues two types of licence to television companies; one to domestic broad-

casters using terrestrial stations on a frequency assigned to the UK; and another to non-domestic satellite broadcasters using international frequencies. The former are bound by the European-content rules but the latter are not, and can broadcast material which is 100 per cent American, even if the television company is British-owned, based in Britain and aimed at a British audience.

- *Metrication.* For a long time Britain has been adjusting to the metric system in weights and measures and the UK has accepted for most purposes the standard metre or litre as laid down by the EC. For some time now the temperature has been quoted in Celsius, motorists have appeared willing to buy petrol sold and priced in litres, while products in the supermarket have been sold in grams. Yet, for traditional reasons certain measures remain unaltered instead of, or alongside, the metric equivalent. Milk in bottles on the doorstep and draught beer in pubs are still sold by the pint even though their equivalents in the shops are sold by the litre. Athletes may now run the 1,500 metres but distance by road is still measured in miles. And small shopkeepers and market stallholders are usually prepared to sell in pounds and ounces even when, strictly speaking, they are breaking the law in so doing. In one other respect the UK is unusual even when using the metric system. The British practice appears to be to divide metres and litres into thousandths as millimetres and millilitres, while the continental practice is to divide into hundredths, as with centimetres and centilitres.

- *Taxation.* Another area that is supposedly subject to harmonisation is taxation. However, each member country is left free as to the extent and severity of the tax. In this way there is a Community ruling that the principal tax on goods and services should be VAT but the UK is free to set its own rate of 17.5 per cent and to allow certain goods such as children's clothes to be zero rated. However, the Community does issue directives on VAT from time to time and, whether the nation-states adopt the directive as it stands or not, they have to adjust their national policies accordingly. For example, the Sixth VAT Directive referred to financial services, as a result of which the UK government imposed VAT on insurance premiums and considered its applicability to the purchases of shares and on bank transactions. One development, however, is that a proposal from the Commission to the IGC reporting at Nice in December 2000 recommended that in future all decisions on VAT should be made by qualified majority voting rather than leave taxation matters vulnerable to the national veto.

In another sphere, the UK's individual application of excise duties is creating difficulties, particularly after the abolition of duty-free shops on cross-Channel ferries. The duty on drink and tobacco in the UK is far higher than it is in the rest of the EC. For example, the British duty on a pint of British beer was around thirty pence at the time the single market was introduced, as against about eight pence for the equivalent in France. The difference in duty on spirits was even greater. Since the single market removed many of the restrictions on the personal import of beer and other alcoholic drinks, it has become commonplace for consumers to cross to France to purchase their drink. The trade became so regular that Sainsbury and Tesco have set up their own outlets in Calais to cash in on the trade. British brewers, distillers and, of course, the Treasury have been losing millions of pounds in profits and lost duties each year.

Summary

The rulings of the EC have had their effect on all aspects of life in Britain, even though some of the horror stories about interference from Brussels are little more than modern mythology. The impact of the Common Agricultural Policy on both British farming and the British economy may not always have been beneficial, but there have been benefits for the consumer and taxpayer, if not necessarily for the farmer. For many economically depressed parts of the country considerable assistance has come from regional aid.

The impact of environmental legislation has been most marked and environmental groups operating in Britain have found their causes considerably helped by the accessibility of the EC's legislative process and by the support of the European Court. It is true that Britain has, or has had, opt-outs on social, security and monetary issues, but one lesson that has emerged from the Community as it has developed is that it has become a community in all senses of the word and no member can be totally isolated from community actions.

Notes

1 Jonathan Lynn and Antony Jay, 'Party games', *Yes Prime Minister*, Volume 1, BBC Enterprises Ltd, London 1986.
2 The European Commission in the United Kingdom, *Do You Believe All You Read in the Newspapers? The Euro-myths*, London, February 1994.
3 The examples of euroscepticism in the press are taken from Peter J. Anderson and Anthony Weymouth, *Insulting the Public? The British Press and the European Union*, Addison Wesley Longman, Harlow, 1999.
4 Anderson and Weymouth, *Insulting the Public?*, p. 183.
5 Report by Nicholas Watt, *Guardian*, 13 April 2000, p. 2.
6 The European Commission Representation in the United Kingdom, *Press Watch 00/09*, London, April 2000. Available as a nine-page booklet and from http://europa.eu.int
7 European Commission, *Consumer Rights in the Single Market*, European File Series, Luxembourg, 1993.
8 Christiane Scrivener, former EC Commissioner for Consumer Affairs, in European Commission, *Consumer Rights in the Single Market*.

9   P. Dunleavy, A. Gamble, I. Halliday and G. Peele G. (eds), *Developments in British Politics*, vol. 5, Macmillan, London, 1997, p. 340.

10   Report in the *Financial Times*, 24 June 1996.

11   Figures quoted are those for 1993 and are the subject of an article by Larry Elliott, 'Year of living dangerously', in Victor Keegan and Martin Kettle, *The New Europe*, Fourth Estate, London, 1993.

12   Elliott, 'Year of living dangerously'.

13   Richard Norton-Taylor and Kevin Cahill, 'This land is their land', *Guardian*, 13 August 1994.

14   European Commission, *Helping Europe's Regions*, European File Series, Luxembourg, 1992.

15   Figures produced by the European Commission in 1990. The GDP is expressed in PPS (purchasing power standard) which is a cost of living index based on a common 'shopping basket' of goods and services.

16   John Carvel, 'Merseyside wins record Euro-grants', *Guardian*, 13 July 1994.

17   Objective 1 figures for 2000–06 are taken from an article by Oliver Morgan, 'Parsimony and red tape mean UK regions miss out on EU aid', *Observer*, 13 February 2000.

18   European Commission, *Protecting our Environment*, European File Series, Luxembourg 1992.

19   Stephen C. Young, 'Environmental politics and the EC', *Politics Review*, February 1993, pp. 6–8.

20   Department of the Environment, *Protecting Europe's Environment*, HMSO, London, 1992.

21   Paul Brown, Environment Correspondent, *Guardian*, 16 May 1994.

22   Reported in the *Guardian*, 16 May 1994.

23   Young, *Environmental Politics and the EC*.

24   *The Economist*, 'The dirty dozen', 20 July 1991.

25   Michael Portillo, Employment Secretary, commenting on the issue by the Commission of a six-year social programme, 27 July 1994.

26   Jane Grant of the National Alliance of Women's Organisations, reported by Sarah Rutherford, 'Europe, my Europe', *Guardian*, 17 May 1994.

27   Kenneth Clarke, at an informal council of EU finance ministers, Lindau, Germany, September 1994.

28   Sir Leon Brittan, then commissioner for competition policy, in *Competition Policy in the European Community*, European File Series, Luxembourg, 1992.

29   Figures quoted by Ian Black, 'Refugees in Britain: special report', *Guardian*, 27 March 2000.

30   Ewen MacAskill, 'Belgium restores frontier curbs', *Guardian*, 10 January 2000.

31   Barbara Roche, junior minister at the Home Office, 17 February 2000, reported in the *Guardian*.

Part III

Participation

7

Representation – elections and the European Parliament

Article 138 of the EEC Treaty included the following provision: 'The Assembly shall draw up proposals for elections by direct universal suffrage in accordance with a uniform procedure in all Member States'. The Assembly approved such proposals as early as 1960, but found itself frustrated by yet another requirement of Article 138 which gave the deciding voice to the Council of Ministers with the words: 'The Council shall, acting unanimously, lay down the appropriate provisions ...'[1]

From this it can be seen that, although it had been the intention from the first for the Community to have its own democratically elected parliament, this objective was thwarted for twenty-two years by the more intergovernmental members of the Council of Ministers, represented by France originally but by Britain and Denmark thereafter. The reason for these delaying tactics was the knowledge that direct elections would give increased legitimacy and credibility to the deliberations of the European Parliament; that such increased legitimacy would confer an improved status and authority on the EP; and that such an improvement could only be at the expense of the stature and authority of national parliaments. Those who valued parliamentary sovereignty wanted to ensure that the EP could be dismissed as being no more than an empty discussion chamber with no constitutional purpose, legitimacy or authority.

After British entry in 1973, the UK was allocated thirty-six seats in the European Parliament, with members of the British Parliament, both Commons and Lords, being nominated as MEPs and with the thirty-six seats distributed between political parties in proportion to those parties' representation at Westminster. This meant that all members of the European Parliament had what is known as the 'dual mandate' in that they were, at one and the same time, members of both the European Parliament and their own national parliaments. The main disadvantage of the dual mandate was that parties not represented in the national parliaments could not get representation in Europe, however large their support. In addition, critics of the EC were not represented in the Parliament because only euroenthusiasts tended to put their names forward for nomination. There was also the question of how effective members holding the dual mandate could be in either capacity, given the pressure of work the dual role laid upon them.

The dual mandate largely disappeared after 1979 and the introduction of direct elections. Indeed, in a number of countries such as Belgium or Germany the dual mandate is no longer permitted and many member countries – or parties within those countries – have rules restricting it. Indeed, this is the case for the British Labour Party which does not allow its MPs to stand for the European Parliament. However, even if the dual mandate is permitted, there is another factor which inhibits members of national parliaments from seeking election to Europe, and that is a ruling which says that ministerial office is incompatible with membership of the EP – any national member of parliament who was also an MEP would thereby rule themselves out of consideration for promotion to ministerial rank.

The one area within the UK where the dual mandate still finds favour is Northern Ireland, where John Hume and Ian Paisley have both been MEPs since 1979, as well as being members of the Westminster parliament. However, there is a history of the dual mandate in Northern Ireland: Ian Paisley was a member of the Northern Ireland parliament at Stormont between 1970 and 1973, despite being the Westminster MP for North Antrim at the same time. The Conservative Party has no members of the House of Commons holding the dual mandate, but it is not uncommon for members of the House of Lords to stand for election to the European Parliament, and to be elected. In 1999 there was a feeling on the part of Conservative peers that forthcoming reforms of the House of Lords could mean a reduction in their political role in Britain and that they should now look to Europe for new fields of activity. In the European elections of June 1999 three Conservative peers, Lords Bethel, Inglewood and Stockton, were elected as MEPs; Lord Bethel becoming deputy leader of the PPE-ED, the right-wing political grouping in the EP. June 1999 also saw the election of two Liberal Democrat baronesses, Sarah Ludford and Emma Nicholson.

Electoral systems

Although the Council of Ministers was forced to concede direct elections to the European Parliament in 1979, the Council proved unwilling to grant the other provisions laid down in the Treaty of Rome which were meant to create a uniform procedure in all member states. For example, there is no uniform eligibility for candidature as an MEP; the age qualification in the various member countries ranging from eighteen to twenty-five, and with some countries barring the dual mandate as mentioned above, while other countries actually welcome it. It is only since the 1994 elections that the EU's citizenship rules laid down at Maastricht made it possible to stand and vote in one's country of residence rather than one's country of national origin. Even here there is no uniformity since Luxembourg, which has a very high proportion of non-nationals in its resident population, demands a five-year residency before allowing access to the electoral system.

EU countries cannot even agree on the day on which European elections should be held. The UK chooses to stick with Thursday, which is the day normally used for Westminster or local elections, and this practice has been followed by other countries such as Denmark, Ireland and the Netherlands. Most European countries, however, vote on Sundays, in both national and European elections. Since election results are declared simultaneously in all member countries this divided practice means that voters in those countries which vote on Thursday have to wait until Sunday evening to find out whom they have elected, while officials have the problem of keeping ballot papers securely locked away for the best part of three days.

The most serious failure in standardising the procedure for European elections was in the choice of electoral system to be used. It was originally envisaged that all member countries would choose a common electoral system: by which a form of proportional representation was obviously intended. However, the UK resisted the arguments and insisted on retaining the British 'first-past-the-post' electoral system for constituencies in Great Britain, the system remaining in use from 1979 until the elections of 1994. The Blair government, on assuming power in 1997 promised that, in line with other constitutional reforms, they would have a proportional system in place by the time of the 1999 elections. In accordance with that promise, the European Parliamentary Elections Act of January 1999 established an electoral system based on regional lists which was first used in the elections of June 1999.

Even after the introduction of proportional voting, the UK does not have a uniform system. Back in 1979, even the most diehard supporters of first-past-the-post recognised that the sectarian nature of Northern Ireland politics would cause considerable problems if a majority system of voting failed to give representation to the Catholic minority. The Province of Northern Ireland, entitled to three MEPs, was not divided into the three constituencies to which it was entitled, according to the pattern in Great Britain, but was established as a single three-member constituency with its three representatives elected by the single transferable vote system of proportional representation. That variation has continued in force despite the 1999 act.

All member states are therefore united in using a proportional system of voting of some kind. Yet, because the UK set a precedent by breaking ranks in 1979, there has been a consequent general failure among the other states to agree on a common system of proportional representation. Most countries use straightforward list systems but Belgium, Denmark, Italy and the Netherlands have a preferential vote element built in to their systems. The Republic of Ireland, like Northern Ireland, uses the single transferable vote and Luxembourg, with six MEPs, has a system whereby each voter is entitled to six votes which they can split between the candidates as they wish.[2] In a number of countries employing a list system of proportional representation there is a threshold, usually 5 per cent of the vote, which parties have to reach before they are granted representation.

There is a significant difference in the populations represented by MEPs in the various member states. As with qualified majority voting in the Council of Ministers, seats in the EP are allocated to member states for political reasons as much as for strict proportionality. Before 1994 Germany had the same number of MEPs (eighty-one) as France, Italy and the UK, despite having a much larger population. As from 1994, when the rise in population caused by German re-unification made an increase in the number of EP seats necessary, the new distribution of seats meant that larger member states had one MEP for each 500,000 electors. At the other end of the scale, the smaller member states are probably over-represented in an attempt to prevent them being overwhelmed by the larger states in the decision-making process. For example, compared with the larger states' average allocation of one seat per 500,000, medium-sized states like Denmark have an MEP for approximately each 250,000 registered electors, while the smallest member country, Luxembourg, has an MEP for every 37,000 electors.[3]

The new British system

There was a prolonged argument over the type of electoral system that should be put into place for Great Britain when proportional representation was finally introduced. There were many who supported the single transferable vote as it was used in Northern Ireland, while others wanted a suitable variation on the additional member system similar to that used for elections to the Scottish parliament. However, it was decided that, since the constituency link is so weak in European elections because of the numbers involved, the simplicity of the list system as it is generally used in Europe was preferable. As a result, the provisions of the European Parliamentary Elections Act are:

- the United Kingdom is divided into electoral regions
- England is divided into nine electoral regions
- Scotland, Wales and Northern Ireland each constitute a single electoral region
- there are 87 MEPs elected in the United Kingdom, of whom
  - 71 are for England
  - 8 are for Scotland
  - 5 are for Wales
  - 3 are for Northern Ireland.

The electoral regions in England and the number of MEPs elected for each are:

North East (four), North West (ten), Yorkshire and the Humber (seven), West Midlands (eight), East Midlands (six), Eastern (eight), South West (seven), South East (eleven) and London (ten).

The system of election chosen for Great Britain was a regional list system with the following characteristics:

- votes may be cast either for a registered party or for an individual candidate, but votes can only be given if a party or candidate is named on the ballot paper
- the first seat is allocated to the party or candidate getting most votes
- the second and subsequent seats are allocated as to the numbers of votes given, but parties who have already been allocated seats have the votes given to their party divided by the number of seats allocated plus one
- for second or subsequent seats, a party which has already been allocated a number of seats equal to the number of names on the party's list will be disregarded
- for second or subsequent seats, an individual candidate who has already been allocated a seat from the party list will be disregarded
- seats allocated to a party are filled by names on the party's list in the order in which they appear on that list.

As has already been mentioned, the single transferable vote system of voting is used in Northern Ireland.[4]

The party list method of elections created a great deal of controversy, and it almost had to be imposed by force on sections of the Labour party. There is a strong argument that the system can be regarded as undemocratic. Not only is the choice of candidates for the list entirely the responsibility of the party hierarchy, but the very same people also choose the order in which candidates' names are listed on the ballot paper, thus determining the chances that named candidates have of being elected or not being elected. In other words the party has complete control of the process, allowing not even party grassroot workers to have a say, let alone the electors. Alternative systems that have been suggested include party primaries by means of which it would be the party membership who would choose whose names went onto the lists. This was rejected on the grounds that, with local elections, European elections and elections in devolved Scotland and Wales, the electorate had already suffered a voting overload in 1999 without becoming involved in primary elections as well. A more serious suggestion was made that electors should be allowed to indicate preferences on the lists of candidates rather than simply vote for the list as a whole. The case for this was argued hard and long but was finally rejected, leaving many critics able to say that the European elections did nothing to reduce the Community's democratic deficit but represented yet another example of the party leader's patronage at work.

Turnout and apathy

One aspect of European elections that has always attracted a great deal of attention is the low level of voter participation. In three countries, Belgium, Luxembourg and Greece, voting is compulsory and their turnout figures can be regarded as respectable, with Belgium and Luxembourg managing a turnout of around 90 per cent, while Greece averages out at about 70 per cent. In most other countries of the Community the turnout is little more than 50 per cent, while three countries in 1999 had turnouts that were less than a third of the electorate. Of those three, a mere 24 per cent of the UK electorate could be bothered to vote: not only the lowest turnout that the UK has ever managed in the European elections but a record low figure for anything other than a local election. The other two countries with low turnouts were Finland and the Netherlands: Finland dropping to 30.1 per cent from the 60.3 per cent who turned out for Finland's first European election in 1996, while the Netherlands merely maintained its record for UK-like low figures, with 29.9 per cent in 1999 compared with 35.6 per cent in 1994 (see Appendix 2 for turnout figures 1979–99).

There has always been a Europe-wide apathy towards the European elections, with turnouts in the past ranging from a low of 56.8 per cent in 1994 to a high of 62.5 per cent in 1979. In 1999, however, the elections hit a new low of 49.4 per cent, meaning that less than half the EU electorate felt ready to vote for the European Parliament, despite the increased powers given to the EP and the parliament's heightened profile as a result of its disciplining of Santer's Commission. It does mean that the EU faces a crisis of legitimacy in that it has been saying for years that something must be done to correct the democratic deficit; only to find that when something is done about it the outcome is spurned by the electorate.[5]

There were many explanations given for this apathy, the three most significant being as follows.

1 It is suggested that it was a protest against national governments and even more specifically national left-wing governments. Across Europe, eleven of the EU's fifteen national governments are allied to the European Socialist Group and fought the election on a common manifesto, and it was certainly the left-of-centre parties that lost ground to parties of the right in all countries.
2 The electorate might be seen to be voting or abstaining in protest at the introduction of the single currency. Throughout the election period the press was reporting a steady decline in the value and prestige of the euro on the world's money markets.
3 The election was fought while the EU was fully involved in the war in Kosovo, an intervention that was very unpopular with many countries, but especially in Italy and Greece.

As for the UK, it has always had a poor turnout record for anything other than Westminster elections and the level of voting in European elections is very much in line with the turnout for local elections. In this connection it is worth noting that the abysmally low figures for the European elections in June 1999 followed closely on a fairly disastrous round of local elections in May. The two events are not unconnected. No matter what other reasons there may be for voting for one's Westminster MP, the main motivating factor for the voter is the chance to choose the government that will rule the country for the next four to five years: that vote matters. If even the important responsibilities of local councils are seen as being of no great matter in comparison with this, how much more irrelevant is an election which does not form a government, which does not select a legislature and which does not affect policy decisions? The British public does not understand the European Parliament, does not see that it has any relevance to their lives, and therefore sees no reason why they should vote for it.

Thanks to the indifference of the British electorate to European elections, the people who ought to be working hard to overcome that apathy – the politicians, parties and the media – are equally indifferent. The media are only interested in what interests their readers, listeners or viewers and therefore cannot be bothered with what apparently leaves the public cold. The parties are not going to devote precious resources to European politics when their resources are already limited for the more important field of national politics. And, with a few notable exceptions, politicians of ability and public appeal are not going to become involved in an activity so far removed from influence and power in the national arena.

The role played by European elections in the UK political process is very similar to that assumed by local elections. The electorate does not look on European or local elections in isolation but more as a reflection of national politics; the reasons for people voting as they do being founded on national rather than European politics. And this is not only true of the UK. Throughout Europe in 1999 there was evidence that the movement of votes from left to right in those member countries with a governing party of the left was very much to do with a general disillusionment with those governing parties. As was said after the 1994 elections, 'In effect the elections were fought as twelve different national votes with distinct domestic flavours, rather than on common issues or programmes'.[6]

The role of an MEP

Among the many aspects of the European Parliament that are unknown to the average British citizen is any conception as to what an MEP actually does. As is the case with the British parliament, one obvious assumption is that members spend most of their time in the debating chamber: but if this is far from the case at Westminster, it is even less true of Strasbourg or Brussels. Even when commissioners are summoned before Parliament to answer for their area of responsibility or to make a policy statement, very few bother to listen or question them. A wonderful example of this is provided by Matthew Engel's description of Sir Leon Brittan's appearance before the Parliament in 1994 to announce the new world trade agreement that would replace GATT, 'In the whole vast near-circular debating chamber there were, officials and flunkeys aside, only a dozen people. The press gallery was almost empty ... This was not a particular comment on Sir Leon or his subject ... It is always like this. No one goes to debates, except to speak. No one listens except the interpreters.'[7]

The point about interpreters is important since there are eleven official languages in the Community and it is very hard to make an impact with a speech when one's words cannot be understood directly by most of the people present: even the finest speech-making cannot survive the neutral intermediary of an interpreter. As Engel says, 'oratory, rhetoric and invective all fall flat'.[8]

In the European Parliament all the real work is done in committee, even more so than at Westminster. All MEPs serve on at least one of the seventeen committees, the membership of which is proportional not to national representation but to the political groupings in the Parliament. The committees are very much bound up with the Community legislative process, spending up to nine months on items of legislation entrusted to them and ensuring that about one-third of all legislation originates from the Parliament. Maastricht gave MEPs a considerable say in certain policy areas related to the Single European Act, such as education, culture, public health, consumer protection and action programmes on the environment, and that involvement was increased by the Amsterdam Treaty.

There are seventeen specialist committees within the EP:

- Culture, Youth, Education, the Media and Sport
- Citizen's Liberties and Rights, Justice and Home Affairs: dealing with all aspects of human rights and also concerned with the internal security pillar of the EU, including Europol
- Legal Affairs and the Internal Market: covering both Community Law and co-ordinating aspects of national legislation
- Agriculture and Rural Development
- Fisheries
- Budgets: including not only the annual Community budget but all aspects of the financial framework of the Community
- Industry, External Trade, Research and Energy
- Women's Rights and Equal Opportunities
- Regional Policy, Transport and Tourism
- Environment, Public Health and Consumer Policy
- Development and Co-operation: largely concerning help for the Third World, including the Lomé Convention

- Budgetary Control: which basically means auditing Community expenditure
- Employment and Social Affairs
- Constitutional Affairs: now largely concerned with enlargement
- Foreign Affairs, Human Rights, Common Security and Defence Policy
- Economic and Monetary Affairs
- Petitions: to receive and analyse petitions received from EU citizens.[9]

As a result of the Maastricht Treaty, ad hoc, temporary committees of inquiry may also be set up by a vote of the parliament (the BSE crisis is a typical example of the sort of issue calling for an ad hoc committee).

MEPs are paid the same salary as is paid to members of their own national parliaments, although they can choose the currency and country in which to receive that salary. These salaries are constantly changing but the lowest paid are the Finns and the Spanish, who receive less than one-third of the salary paid to the Italians, by far the best rewarded. British MEPs come pretty well exactly in the middle; those elected in 1999 having a salary of £47,008. Any MP enjoying the dual mandate as a member of a national parliament as well as the EP receives their normal parliamentary salary for their work at home, plus one-third of that salary for their work as an MEP. Because there are such wide variations in salary between MEPs of different nationalities, the Amsterdam Treaty laid down the aim of moving towards a common statute for all MEPs in order to remove such disparities. The accountancy firm Pricewaterhouse-Coopers was asked to assess the 'relative position of a national MP's salary in each member state vis-à-vis the remuneration for other political offices'. Due to report in May 2000 it is anticipated that a figure around that currently paid to British MPs will eventually form the uniform European rate.[10]

Expenses and allowances are the same for all MEPs and are often very much better than national allowances. Subsistence and travel allowances are particularly favourable since they have to cater for the considerable amount of travelling MEPs must do, not only between Brussels, Strasbourg and Luxembourg but also between the EP and their home country. The figures agreed, as of 1 January 1998 (converted into sterling), are:

- *general expenditure* (office and communication costs etc): £2,215 per month
- *travel allowance:* 52p per km for the first 400 km and 26p per km thereafter – for journeys to EP meetings within the Community
- *travel allowance* (including hotel costs) for travel throughout the world when on parliamentary business: maximum of £2,037
- *subsistence allowance:* £157 for attending meetings within the Community (covers both accommodation and meals); £78 per day on top of actual bed and breakfast costs for attending meetings outside the Community
- *secretarial assistance:* maximum of £6,388 per month.[11]

There are frequent complaints about the amount of money paid out to MEPs and the comfortable lifestyle they are said to enjoy; the tabloids making great play of the 'Brussels gravy-train'. The pressure of complaints has led to the introduction of sanctions by which MEPs may have their allowances cut by half if they do not attend at least 50 per cent of plenary sittings of the EP. Despite any such sanctions, however, it has been claimed that a perfectly honest MEP can, without fiddling the system, bank a six-figure sum for every session they spend as a member of the EP. And yet, for all the complaints and accusations, it has to be said that the costs of the European Parliament, even with its heavy expenditure on interpreters and translation, are less than half of what is spent in the USA on the House of Representatives.

One area where some suspicion lingers after the corruption scandals in the Brussels Commission, as well as in various national parliaments, concerns the extent of payments that are made to MEPs by lobbyists and interest groups. In order to counter this there is a register of interests on the British pattern that is supposedly completed by MEPs, copies of which are kept in Brussels and Luxembourg. But the register is not kept very assiduously and very few MEPs are particularly scrupulous in declaring their interests: only Dutch and British MEPs seem to make any serious attempt to declare all their external interests and allowances.

Political groupings

Members of the European Parliament do not sit or associate as national groups but as members of a variety of political groupings based on an approximation of ideological similarity. The largest of these groupings form transnational federations for mutual assistance at election time, creating propaganda and campaigning material based on an agreed manifesto. None of these federations and few of the other groups have the cohesiveness or discipline of national political parties, but there is certain feeling of common interest. The groups have more influence than individuals or small national groupings would have and they receive financial support from the Parliament for administrative and research purposes, dependent on their size. According to the EP rules of procedure a group has to have a minimum of twenty-six MEPs if all the members come from a single state, but the minimum number of members required changes according to the number of countries involved, so that a minimum of just thirteen members is required if four or more states of origin are involved, sixteen if from three states or twenty-one if from two.

There are two major groupings or party federations in the EP which have at least one MEP from each member country in their ranks. What was originally the larger and more cohesive of the two is the Party of European Socialists (PSE), which is still the more cohesive, although its position as largest grouping was lost in the elections of June 1999 when only 180 PSE members were elected, as against 224 for the conservative parties. Representing the broad left in European politics, the PSE group ideologically ranges from the 'hard-left' of state interventionists to the more moderate 'centre-left'. The majority, however, belong to the latter category, being more social democrats than pure socialists and almost uniformly advocating a version of the 'third way' professed by Tony Blair and New Labour. In the 1999 elections electors on the left seemed to want a move back to a more traditional socialism, as exhibited by the French and Spanish parties, at the expense of the more moderate centre-left policies advocated by Tony Blair or Gerhard Schröder. One result of the decline in the number of British Labour MEPs from sixty-two to twenty-nine meant that Pauline Green lost the leadership of the PSE to Enrique Baron Crespo of Spain, although the new leader of British Labour MEPs, Alan Donnelly, was elected vice president of the group.

On the centre-right, the European People's Party and European Democrats (PPE-ED) replaced the PSE as largest grouping by gaining 224 members in the elections of June 1999. In origin this group was made up of Christian Democrats and the full title of the group still contains the words 'Christian Democrat' in parentheses, but the great days of Christian democracy seem to have been replaced by a wider centre-right approach. UK Conservatives and the sole Ulster Unionist MEP are associated with the PPE, but very loosely since the British parties find the strongly pro-federal approach of the party hard to live with. After the June 1999 elections there were weeks of negotiations before the Conservatives announced that they would only join the PPE on the basis of a deal which had been arranged whereby the PPE would drop all federalist references from its constitution, replacing the word 'federalism' with the words 'decentralisation and subsidiarity' wherever it appears. The PPE also added the name of the European Democratic group to its own. Until 1992 this had been a group of almost exclusively British Conservative MEPs, together with two anti-Europe Danish MEPs. It was only after the departure of Mrs Thatcher in 1990 that the Conservatives felt able to join the PPE, finally affiliating in May 1992.

All other political groupings in the EP are smaller and do not have representatives in all the member countries. The largest of these groups is the European Liberal, Democrat and Reform Party (ELDR), which elected fifty-one members in June 1999, including ten British Liberal Democrats. Despite the presence of some Liberal members with leftish tendencies the Liberal parties of mainland Europe are still very much rooted in the laissez-faire liberalism of the nineteenth century and the ELDR as a whole is much more a party of the right than its British component.

Firmly on the left of the EP is the Confederal Group of the European United Left/Nordic Green Left (GUE/NLG) whose forty-two MEPs elected in June 1999 largely represent the remnants of former Communist parties. Also affiliated to the left are the Greens (VERTS). Until 1989 the various Green parties formed part of the so-called Rainbow Group but an upsurge of support for green politics in 1989 produced sufficient representation for them to create a group of their own with increasingly successful results. After this split the remainder of the Rainbow Group formed themselves into the European Radical Alliance, which elected nineteen members in 1994, most of them members of the French radical party known as the 'Tapie List' after its leader Bernard Tapie. In 1999 this group renamed itself the European Free Alliance (ALE) and, in the negotiations which followed the June elections decided to rejoin their old Rainbow allies in the Greens, forming the fourth largest group in the EP with 48 members acting together under the general title Group of the Greens/European Free Alliance (Verts/ALE).

On the right is the Group for a Europe of Nations (UEdN), a grouping created out of a dislike for the Maastricht Agreement and originally led by Philippe de Villiers and the late Sir James Goldsmith. It was rather more successful in 1999 than it had been in 1994 but Goldsmith's death and the rival attraction of the EDD group has led to a serious decline in its influence. Appearing for the first time in 1999, the Europe of Democracies and Diversities (EDD) brought together groups hostile to any further integration in Europe. It elected representatives in only four countries – Belgium, France, the Netherlands and the UK, in the last of which the group is represented by the UK Independence Party, who had intended to join the UEdN but changed their minds as a result of internal disagreements.

The remaining twenty-six MEPs are regarded as independents and are largely not attached to any of the foregoing groupings because those groupings fight shy of association with parties that are too openly on the far right. Of the independents, eighteen have formed a group under the EP's rules, the Technical Group of Independent Members (TGI) with members from Le Pen's Front National of France and the Alleanza Nazionale of Italy. Eight independent MEPs with little in common are unable to form a grouping under the rules, but these include the totally independent Ian Paisley of the Democratic Unionist Party from Northern Ireland and a group that was to cause even more controversy after the Austrian national elections in early 2000: the neo-fascist group of five Austrian MEPs belonging to Jörg Haider's Freedom Party (see Appendix 1 for a breakdown of party groupings in the 1999 European Parliament[12]).

The European elections of 1999

The 1999 elections were obviously of importance for a number of reasons.

- They were the first elections since the Maastricht and Amsterdam treaties had come fully into force, both of which had granted extensive powers to the European Parliament including a share in the co-decision process for all EU legislation except that relating to agriculture and fisheries.

- The elections came shortly after the European Parliament had really flexed its muscles for the first time in exposing the controversial points which ultimately forced the resignation of the Santer Commission. Taken in conjunction with the preceding point it can be said that these were the first elections to be held since the EP had benefited from a diminution in the democratic deficit through the acquisition of new powers.
- The elections were the first to be held since the majority of member countries had joined the single currency. The vote could therefore be treated as either a censure motion or a motion of confidence on the performance of the euro.
- The elections took place at a time when the EU was much involved in attempting to settle the conflict in Kosovo. The elections could therefore be seen as a sort of referendum on the EU's role in defence and foreign affairs.

Opinion polls before the election were not optimistic that the electorate would respond to this supposed importance and, in the event, the election results seemed to bear out the poll findings. The UK was particularly badly affected in recording the lowest turnout in a national election ever, at a mere 24 per cent. But this only reflected an apathy that was Europewide: with the total turnout figure at 49.4 per cent, falling below 50 per cent for the first time ever. This figure compares with a total turnout of 56.8 per cent in 1994, 57.2 per cent in 1989, 59 per cent in 1984 and 62.5 per cent in 1979 (see Appendix 2 for the turnout figures for the six European elections since 1979).

Of the three major party groupings in the EP, the PPE made striking gains at the expense of the PSE, the new parliament being dominated by the centre-right. As the outgoing leader of the PPE, the Belgian Wilfried Martens said, 'This is a historic victory, the first time in 20 years we have more MEPs than the socialists'.[13] But the centre-right did not have an overall majority and could therefore not dominate the new Parliament, not even after negotiations led to the PPE being joined by the British Conservatives and their allies in the ED. To counter the still potent left, the PPE would have to come to an arrangement with the liberal parties of the ELDR or with a number of splinter groups on the right, most of them being openly anti-federal, anti-Maastricht in their policy platforms. Everything seemed to point to a considerable degree of confusion on the part of voters as to just what the EU stands for: an interesting example being Dana, the former Eurovision song contest winner, who was elected MEP by the Republic of Ireland despite the fact that she lives in Alabama and ran on an anti-abortion platform, an issue over which the EU has no control. These various factors lead inevitably to the conclusion that the electors of the EU are far more eurosceptical than their leaders. 'Voters also delivered more members than ever before opposed to the whole idea of the EU, such as those from the UK Independence party'.[14]

Another thing that became very clear was that, however much the propagandists might have hailed these elections as truly European and fought on pan-European issues, the fact is that, as was said about the 1994 elections, 'the elections were fought as twelve different national votes with distinct domestic flavours, rather than on common issues or programmes'.[15] There are now fifteen different nations involved rather then twelve but that only makes the point even more true that party preferences and swings of opinion are not uniform across the Community but differ from one country to the next, as the following shows.

Austria: twenty-one seats and turnout of 49 per cent. The largest group elected were from the Social Democrats, the party of the Austrian chancellor, Viktor Klima (31 per cent); running very close were his coalition allies, the People's Party (30 per cent). Both these parties are from the centre in politics but the extreme right got a substantial toehold in European politics with the 23 per cent of the vote given to Jörg Haider's Freedom Party. The critical issue in the campaign was that of retaining Austria's much prized neutrality at a time when the EU was involved militarily in the former Yugoslavia and a common defence force was being discussed.

Belgium: twenty-five seats, divided into fourteen seats for Flanders, ten for francophone Wallonia and one for the German-speaking area around Malmédy. All the major parties have French and Flemish divisions and there is one party exclusively for German speakers. Flanders tends to be more right-wing than the old mining districts of Wallonia. Voting in elections is compulsory and the Belgians also hold their European elections on the same day as the general election, resulting in a turnout of 90 per cent.

Belgium was suffering the aftermath of a scandal in which the governing Christian Democrat/Socialist coalition had covered up for more than a month one of Europe's worst food contamination stories since BSE, with cancer-causing dioxins found in eggs, milk, chicken, pork and beef. The voters punished the ruling politicians by throwing out the government politicians in the general election and by voting largely for francophone and Flemish-speaking green parties in the European elections, giving the PPE and PSE together a mere eleven of Belgium's twenty-five seats.

Denmark: sixteen seats and a turnout of 50.4 per cent. Anti-Europeanism, which was seen as a significant trend in 1994, continued to be successful in attracting voters. The two anti-European parties won five seats (one for the UEdN and four for EDD) one more than the two government parties. These results seem to confirm that Denmark is the most eurosceptical of all the member states, sometimes even more so than Britain.

Finland: this is only the second time that Finland has elected MEPs. The first European elections after the country's 1995 accession took place in 1996 when a total of 60.3 per cent voted to fill Finland's sixteen seats. This time the turnout was almost exactly halved to 30.1 per cent, the third lowest turnout in the EU. There was a swing to the Conservatives of 5 per cent, although they did not win an extra seat, even though the party of prime minister Paavo Lipponen lost one seat. Blame for the poor turnout was credited to extremely hot weather on polling day, a bitter argument about MEPs' expenses and a media campaign which ignored the issues involved so as to concentrate on celebrities standing for the conservatives like the rally-driving champion Ari Vatanen.

France: eighty-seven seats and a turnout of 47 per cent, France's worst ever. The prime minister's Socialists were the winners but only by one seat, the PSE having twenty-two seats against the PPE's twenty-one. Gains were made by the anti-EU 'Rally for France', led by the former interior minister Charles Pasqua which beat the Gaullist party of president Jacques Chirac, 'Rally for the Republic'. The green party, led by Danny Cohn-Bendit, picked up 9 per cent to become the fifth largest French grouping. The right-wing National Front under Jean-Marie le Pen did rather badly, only receiving 5 per cent of the vote and, in fact being beaten by the pro-countryside 'hunters and fishers' party.

Germany: ninety-nine seats and a turnout of what Chancellor Gerhard Schröder called a catastrophic 45.2 per cent. Schröder regarded the figures as catastrophic because his party, the Social Democrats, were faced with a 10 per cent swing to the Christian Democrats, despite widespread disillusionment with former Chancellor Kohl. The CD took fifty-three seats against the SD's thirty-three. The greens also suffered for entering into a coalition agreement with the Social Democrats, dropping from twelve seats in the 1994 parliament to nine in 1999. The anti-government vote was motivated by a poor economic performance by German industry and commerce in the recent past; a disappointment in the performance of the deutschmark as a mainstay of the euro; and the backing given by the German government to NATO actions in Kosovo. Only one smaller grouping, former communists allied to the GUE/NGL, gained any seats in the EP. The liberal Free Democrats and the far-right Republicans both fell below the 5 per cent threshold and failed to gain representation.

Greece: with twenty-five seats Greece had a turnout of 70.2 per cent, down yet again on the figures for 1994 and 1989, and a fairly low figure given that Greece is one of the three member states where voting is compulsory. There was little change in the overall position of the parties, although the conservative opposition party, New Democracy, gained slightly over the Pasok party of prime minister Costas Simitis, with the communists in third place. EU issues played virtually no part in the campaign. The electorate was more concerned about two unpopular government actions, first in supporting NATO in Kosovo and second in handing over the Kurdish leader Ocalan to the Turks.

Ireland: fifteen seats and an average turnout in the country at large of 50.5 per cent, although the percentage turning out to vote in Dublin was as low as 25 per cent. Nevertheless, the Republic of Ireland was one of the very few countries to show a significant increase in turnout compared with 1994. As always the elections were ostensibly about Europe but were very much influenced by the situation in the North and the Good Friday peace agreement. Bertie Ahern's governing Fianna Fail party increased its share of the vote, but then so also did Sinn Fein, despite the fact that the police north and south of the border spent the election campaign period digging for the bodies of those 'disappeared' by the IRA. As previously mentioned, one unusual Irish result was the election for Connacht of the singer Dana, who stood on an independent anti-abortion platform, despite the fact that the EU has no say in any member country's policy on abortion.

Italy: eighty-seven seats with a turnout of 70.8 per cent, a very high figure for this election but the lowest figure yet recorded for Italy where a turnout of more than 80 per cent was the rule until 1994. The Socialists belonging to prime minister Massimo d'Alema's governing party got the largest share of the vote with 41 per cent, but they were run very close by Silvio Berlusconi's Forza Italia party which got 38 per cent, and ultimately the swing to the right was quite significant if Forza is counted alongside the smaller parties. Since Italy imposes no threshold on its regional list system a huge number of parties represent Italy in the EP, often by single representatives whose election is based on less than 1 per cent of the vote nationwide.

Luxembourg: as the smallest Community member state Luxembourg has six seats in the EP for an electorate of less than 250,000. Turnout was 85.8 per cent, a high figure largely due to the fact that voting is compulsory, as it is in Belgium. Luxembourg was the country most affected by the Maastricht provision that all EU citizens can vote in whichever country they inhabit: 30 per cent of Luxembourg residents being non-native EU citizens. One interesting result in the Grand Duchy was that the former Luxembourg prime minister and disgraced president of the Commission, Jacques Santer, was elected as one of the Christian Democrat MEPs.

Netherlands: thirty-one seats and a turnout of 20.9 per cent is by far the lowest turnout the Netherlands has ever recorded for a European election and lower than any other turnout except Britain's. The ruling left-liberal coalition parties under prime minister Wim Kok lost out, mainly to the greens who increased their representation from one to four MEPs. The opposition Christian Democrat party remained the largest individual party to be represented, the party's nine seats comparing with eight for the ELDR and six for the PSE.

Portugal: twenty-five seats and a turnout of 40.4 per cent, which may have been low but which is at least better than the previous turnout of 35.5 per cent. The centre-left socialists remained the largest party, taking 43 per cent of the vote for twelve seats, while the right wing Liberal Social Democrats got nine seats, on 31 per cent of the vote.

Spain: sixty-four seats and a turnout of 64.4 per cent, which bucked the trend by increasing its turnout figure by almost 5 per cent since 1994. The conservative Popular Party of prime minister Jose Maria Aznar held on to being the largest party with twenty-eight seats. The socialists held on to second place with twenty-two seats only because the former prime minister Felipe Gonzales came out of retirement to rally the falling vote.

Sweden: twenty-two seats and a turnout of 38.3 per cent. The Social Democrats under the prime minister Goran Persson held on to the largest number of seats on a much reduced vote. The biggest success belonged to the opposition liberals led by the charismatic figure of Marit Paulsen, the mother of ten children. Her party tripled its vote and representation in comparison with the initial election in 1996.

United Kingdom: eighty-seven seats and a turnout of less than 25 per cent, by far the lowest turnout in the whole Community and easily the lowest turnout for any British election fought at a national level. The Conservatives made sweeping gains – from a 32 per cent general election share of the vote to 38 per cent – as the Labour vote collapsed, falling from 44 per cent to a mere 28 per cent. On a bad night for pro-Europeans, electors voted against the left and for euroscepticism, the Liberal Democrat vote also falling to 13 per cent although the introduction of proportional representation means that the number of seats won by the LibDems actually rose from two to ten. Contesting the elections for the first time was the UK Independence Party, which is so anti-European that there was doubt as to whether any of those elected would be able to bring themselves to take their seats in Strasbourg. In the event the UK Independence Party gained 8 per cent of the vote and thus were awarded three MEPs. Proportional representation also helped the green and nationalist parties to a total of six seats: two each for the Green Party, the SNP and Plaid Cymru, all six sitting with the VERTS/EFA grouping. The SNP has had MEPs in the past but this was a first-time breakthrough for the greens and the Welsh nationalists. In Northern Ireland the single transferable voting system ensured that the three seats were neatly distributed between one MEP each for the Ulster Unionist Party, the Democratic Unionist Party and the SDLP.[16]

Summary and the question of referendums

Despite the growing democratic powers of the European Parliament, the elections of 1999, just like those of 1994, seem to show that the people of the

Community as a whole are less enthusiastic about Europe than many of their leaders. Turnout in European elections has always been poor in the UK but it was never so poor as it is now, representing as it does less than a quarter of the electorate. Turnout is, however, also showing signs of a serious decline in other member states. Even when people do vote they are hardly acting out of any sense of belonging to Europe, tending to vote on domestic rather than European issues, mostly in order to show their displeasure with national governing parties. Because of the personal factors involved the electorate of the Community tends to show more interest in referendums than in elections for the European Parliament.

In two countries, Ireland and Denmark, it is a requirement of the constitution that constitutional changes should be put to the people in a referendum. Both countries referred the question of accession to the EC in 1972, 71 per cent of the Irish voting and a massive 90 per cent of the Danes. Twenty years later, both countries held referendums on the ratification of the Maastricht Treaty, the Danes most famously having to hold a second referendum in May 1993, after having voted 'No' the first time. The Irish voted in much the same numbers as in 1972, 69 per cent voting in this referendum. The Danes, however, dropped back a little, 82 per cent voting in the first Maastricht referendum and much the same in the second.

Britain has only had one referendum on European matters and that is the one called by Harold Wilson's government in 1975. As is the case in European elections, the UK showed itself the most apathetic member state with 64 per cent voting: although that represented almost twice the number who now vote in European elections. The future is likely to see the question of referendums becoming a much more important part of British relations with Europe since both major parties, in their own different ways, are committed to putting the issue of a single currency to the electorate before any decision on participation is taken.

France has also had just one referendum, on the Maastricht Treaty in September 1992. Then the turnout was 70 per cent, a low figure compared with Denmark but comparing well with the 50 per cent normal to French European elections.[17]

The difference in participation between referendums and elections for the EP shows that people appear to be more willing to vote in referendums over a matter that they can see as being important to themselves than they are to vote in elections to a parliament that seems to have no direct effect on their lives.

Notes

1 Neill Nugent, *The Government and Politics of the European Community*, Macmillan, London, 1991, p. 142.
2 The source of this information is the Directorate-General for Information and Public Relations, Central Press Division of the European Parliament, as circulated

through their UK Office, 2 Queen Anne's Gate, London SW1H 9AA, now also to be found on the Internet at http://www.europarl.eu.int/uk

3   Figures taken from *Facts Through Figures*, Eurostat, Luxembourg, 1994. Note that the figures relating to the numbers represented by MEPs refer to qualified voters, not to total populations. In terms of population, Germany, with ninety-nine seats, has one MEP for every 818,000 people while Luxembourg, with its six seats, has one MEP for every 66,000 people.

4   The European Elections Act (14 January 1999), the full text is available from the website of the UK parliament: www.parliament.uk/

5   Martin Walker, 'Voters indifferent to MEPs' new powers', *Guardian*, 14 June 1999.

6   Philip Lynch and Stephen Hopkins, 'Europe decides', *Politics Review*, September 1994, pp. 9–11.

7   Matthew Engel, 'Parliament of snoozers', *Guardian*, 25 January 1994.

8   Engel, 'Parliament of snoozers'.

9   Details of the committees and party groupings are available from the European Parliament's UK office, as in note 2.

10   Discussion on the future of MEPs' salaries and expenses comes from an article by Francis Elliott in the newspaper *Scotland on Sunday*, 9 April 2000.

11   Figures quoted for MEPs' allowances were provided by the College of Quaestors of the European Parliament. The figures quoted here are those applicable as of 1 January 1998.

12   Party groupings are listed by the European Parliament's UK office, as above.

13   From a press conference, as reported in the press 14–15 June 1999.

14   Stephen Bates, 'The Euro-order changeth', *Guardian*, 14 June 1999.

15   Lynch and Hopkins, 'Europe decides', pp. 9–11.

16   The review of the results across Europe is very largely based on an article by Stephen Bates, 'Strasbourg's winners and losers', *Guardian*, 15 June 1999.

17   Figures quoted are taken from *Keesings Contemporary Archive*, various dates.

8

British political parties and Europe

The area of British political life which has been most affected by membership of the European Union lies, without doubt, in its impact on the policies of the political parties. The Labour Party split over the the question of Europe in the 1980s, while the Conservatives followed suit in the 1990s, having lost a leader over the issue in the process. In the development of British political parties the argument over Europe and European integration has assumed the same importance as the Repeal of the Corn Laws or Home Rule for Ireland did in the nineteenth century: as a contentious issue which has dominated the political agenda and re-drawn the political map.

The Liberal Party and its successors

Of all the parties, the Liberals, followed by the Liberal-SDP Alliance and, latterly, the Liberal Democratic Party, have been the most consistent in their attitude to Europe. Membership of what was then still known simply as the Common Market was the policy of the Liberal Party in the early 1960s and they remained consistently supportive of a pro-European policy throughout the successive applications and rejections of the 1960s, even while the Conservative and Labour parties blew hot and cold over the matter.

The 'Gang of Four' who formed the SDP broke away from the Labour Party over a number of issues, but it was Labour's policy on Europe that was the match to the powder keg and the SDP was solidly pro-European from the first. It could hardly be anything else since one of the four – who became the SDP's first leader – was Roy Jenkins, who had been president of the European Commission between 1979 and 1981, leader of the Britain in Europe campaign during the 1975 referendum, and who had resigned from the Deputy Leadership of the Labour Party in protest at Labour's stance on Europe. Indeed, the formation of the SDP and its alliance with the Liberals was the product of ideas first put forward in the Reith Lecture given by Roy

Jenkins on his return from the Commission presidency, a lecture which advocated not only a strategy that would 'break the mould' of bi-partisan British politics but one which would involve increasingly closer integration with Europe.

The Liberal Democrats, in deference to its antecedents, are wholeheartedly pro-European. Indeed it is often said that the LibDems are too uncritical in their attitude towards Europe. In this view the party will accept without question those policies emanating from Europe which perhaps ought to be questioned. Most criticised of all is the attitude that will ignore possible tactical advantage in the British political arena if, by adopting those tactics, they compromise their pro-European status. On 5 November 1992 there was a vote in the House of Commons on a Labour amendment to the 'paving motion' for the Maastricht Ratification Bill. With a substantial number of Tory rebels ready to vote with Labour there was a real prospect of defeating the government and possibly forcing the resignation of the Major administration. But a vote against the Maastricht provisions could be interpreted as a vote against Europe and the LibDems were unwilling to risk that. As a commentator wrote, 'The Liberal Democrats, though opponents warned them that they might save the life of an unpopular government, declared that the cause of Europe ought to come first, and voted with the Conservatives'.[1]

The Liberal Democrats were heavily criticised by the Labour Party and others for their part in that critical vote, but the point made by Paddy Ashdown at the time was that sufficient damage had already been done to Britain's place in Europe by the actions of the two major parties. Britain could no longer afford to send ambiguous messages to Europe by appearing to reject a pro-European measure.

The Nationalist parties

The Scottish National Party was once bitterly opposed to Europe, campaigning vigorously against membership during the 1975 referendum. Their position then was basically that a party campaigning for independence for Scotland could hardly advocate yet another level of government to which the people of Scotland would be subject. Since 1983, however, the position of the SNP has changed to one of advocating a strong and federal European Union. The reasoning now is that it would make sense for an independent Scotland to be a full member of a federal European Union, thus eliminating any control of Scotland from Westminster, replacing domination by London with direct relations between Brussels and Edinburgh, in the true spirit of John Major's advocacy of subsidiarity. The European dimension also helps to reduce the doubts about economic viability which used to be advanced against full Scottish independence.

'An independent Scotland within Europe' has been the slogan of the SNP in recent years. After all, the SNP claims, with an electorate of 3.9 million, Scotland is many times the size of Luxembourg, a third as large again as Ireland and about the same size as Denmark. The SNP has been helped in coming to this conclusion by being the only minor party in mainland Great Britain to have had a representative in the European Parliament since the start of direct elections; Winnie Ewing won the Highlands and Islands constituency in 1979 and held it until she retired in 1999.

The position adopted by the Welsh nationalists, Plaid Cymru, mirrors that of the SNP, from initial hostility to current enthusiasm for Welsh independence within Europe. As was the case with the Scottish party, the Welsh position on Europe was reinforced by seeing the favoured position accorded in Brussels to the regions of other member states. Wales had set up its own office in Brussels to promote the interests of the Principality even before the establishment of the Welsh assembly opened up direct links between Wales and the Committee of the Regions.

In Northern Ireland the Unionist parties are largely hostile to Europe, Ian Paisley's Democratic Unionists more so than the official Unionist Party. This has not stopped the Unionists from campaigning vigorously in the interests of the Province, most notably in pursuit of a special dispensation from the beef ban for Northern Irish cattle. The Social and Democratic Labour Party has been more supportive of Europe than the unionist parties because it offers a way in which republican Northern Ireland politicians can work alongside those of the Republic of Ireland within the European context.

All these minor parties have maintained a united policy front on Europe throughout, even if that policy has changed over the years, as it has done with the SNP or PC. When we turn to the two major parties, however, it is a very different story. For both parties the relationship with Europe has been turbulent, with major and potentially fatal divisions in both parties over their European policy.

The Labour Party – the hostile phase

Historically the Labour Party was opposed to Britain's membership of the European Community. Originally the attitude of the Labour Party was governed by the 1945 Labour government's attempts to make major changes to British society through a programme of nationalisation and the introduction of the Welfare State. To bring about what they saw as necessary changes, the government needed to be in full control of the British economy and social legislation; a true reforming government being unable to dilute its programme through the need to co-operate with other countries. For many on the left of the party, the EEC, as it was established in the mid-1950s as a business-orientated Common Market, was little more than a capitalist club, membership of which was inimical to socialist principles.

A Marxist, Tom Nairn, writing about Europe at the time of Britain's accession to the Community, pointed out that Labour's opposition to membership was not solely ideological. There is, in fact, an old-fashioned strain of British nationalism in grass-roots Labour thinking and a strongly xenophobic, vaguely jingoistic, attitude underlying working-class values.[2] It was that nationalistic thread which split the party over what their attitude should be towards the Macmillan government's first application to join the EEC in 1961. Most of the party was bitterly opposed to the idea but no one could be certain as to the attitude of the leadership. In the summer of 1962 the Labour leader, Hugh Gaitskell, seemed to define his own stance, claiming that to join Europe would mean that Britain had to throw out 'a thousand years of history for the sake of a marginal advantage on the price of a washing machine in Düsseldorf'. Yet, only a few weeks later, in replying on television to a talk by the prime minister, Gaitskell seemed to hedge his bets, saying that he would wait to see the terms of entry before he committed himself. Macmillan had great fun at Labour's expense, telling the 1962 Conservative Party Conference that Labour's policy on Europe reminded him of the old popular song:

> She didn't say 'yes', she didn't say 'no',
> She didn't say 'stay', she didn't say 'go',
> She wanted to climb but dreaded to fall,
> So she bided her time and clung to the wall.[3]

Shortly after this Macmillan's application was rejected by De Gaulle and Labour's scepticism seemed to be vindicated.

It was Gaitskell's successor, Harold Wilson, who initiated Britain's second application to join the Community in 1966. Wilson was always a pragmatist and he weighed the ideological and nationalistic objections to Community membership against the penalties of being excluded from the then economic success of the six EC members, concluding that membership was desirable. The second rejection of Britain by De Gaulle dented Wilson's confidence and publicly he reverted to a position critical of Europe. However, he had become convinced of the need for Britain to be involved in the development of the Community, and this would inform his thinking after Labour's re-election in 1974.

The Labour Party – re-negotiation and referendum

When the Heath government negotiated the terms for Britain's entry into the Community in 1971 it was decided that Labour would oppose the government in the motion accepting the principle of EC membership. But Wilson was still playing it canny by avoiding outright condemnation of membership itself. The Labour stance was that the terms negotiated by Heath's team were wrong for

Britain and would have to be re-negotiated before Labour could accept them. In a free vote of the House of Commons the principle of EC membership was passed by 356 votes to 244. Significantly, in the light of future divisions, thirty-nine Conservatives voted against the government motion, and all of sixty-nine Labour MPs went against party advice to vote with the government.

Wilson's main concern was to keep his party united despite the deep divisions that had opened up over Europe and, in order to avoid giving offence to anyone, gave no clear guidance as to the leadership's stance on Europe. The party entered the first general election of 1974 with senior members of the party advocating at least three different approaches:

1 those who believed the party should accept membership now that Britain was in the Community and that the party's energies should be devoted to getting the best possible deal for Britain out of the Community (Wilson's private position)
2 those who wanted immediate withdrawal from the Community and the full restoration of British parliamentary sovereignty
3 those who believed that Britain should probably stay within the Community but that the terms needed to be re-negotiated (Wilson's public position).

The party made no attempt to paper over these cracks, but rather chose to flaunt them, as when they decided to devote their last party political broadcast before polling day to the issue of Europe. 'About half the team then talked about the Common Market. Michael Foot claimed British housewives were paying high prices in the shops to subsidise French farmers; Shirley Williams said Labour would re-negotiate the terms of Britain's entry and Denis Healey added 'we can get out altogether if we don't get what we want'.[4]

Between the February and October elections of 1974 Harold Wilson, at the head of his minority government, determined his strategy for dealing with divisions within the party. The device adopted by Wilson to keep all shades of opinion in his party sweet, was to fight the October election with the manifesto promise that membership terms would be re-negotiated and that the government would take no further action until the public had given their verdict in a referendum.

At a European Council meeting in Dublin in March 1975 the British government formally requested a revision of the terms agreed in 1971. By June 1975 Jim Callaghan was able to announce changes in the terms that were cosmetic rather than substantive, but which were sufficient for Wilson and Callaghan to be able to endorse them when placing the matter before the electorate in the referendum. The referendum itself was so worded as to encourage a yes vote, the question put being 'Do you think the United Kingdom should stay in the European Community (the Common Market)?'

The referendum campaign was not fought by the political parties but by two all-party umbrella groups – Britain in Europe supporting a yes vote and the

National Referendum Campaign in favour of a no vote. Wilson wanted to remain aloof from the campaign but he was left with the problem of a deeply divided cabinet, all eager to take part in the campaign but with sixteen ministers wanting to support a yes vote and seven wanting to advocate a no. To escape his dilemma, Wilson took the unusual step of suspending the convention of collective responsibility so that prominent ministers such as Barbara Castle, Peter Shore, Tony Benn and Michael Foot could campaign against government policy while remaining members of the government.

At first Wilson tried to prevent cabinet ministers on opposing sides from appearing on the same platform or on the same television programme. But this was relaxed towards the end and the *Panorama* television programme was allowed to screen a head-to-head confrontation between Roy Jenkins and Tony Benn. Wilson maintained his neutrality but his preference for a yes vote was known and may have been influential in persuading 66 per cent of the electorate to vote in favour of membership. Certainly Tony Benn thought so when he said 'I regard it as the third election in which the Labour Party was defeated and Wilson won'.[5]

The Labour Party – renewed hostility

The defeat of Labour in 1979 led to a resurgence of anti-European thinking in the party. The left, as exemplified by Tony Benn, blamed the Conservative victory on a lukewarm attitude towards socialism in the Labour leadership, and advocacy of European policies was seen as one of the hallmarks of that lukewarm attitude. With the hard left in control of many constituencies and exercising their influence on Conference, Labour policy began to move leftwards towards an uncompromisingly anti-European stance.

In 1981 the party finally split, with David Owen, Shirley Williams and Bill Rodgers joining Roy Jenkins to form the Gang of Four which issued the Limehouse Declaration and brought the SDP into existence as a party which felt very strongly about Europe: the Labour MPs who followed the Gang of Four into the SDP comprised the most pro-European sections of the Labour Party. Their departure, combined with the leftward drift of the party led to a renewed rejection of and sustained opposition to European integration.

In the run-up to the 1983 general election under Michael Foot the Labour Party adopted the alternative economic strategy (AES):

> The AES assumed that it was possible to revitalise the ailing British economy through a programme of socialist economic expansion which would include domestic reflation and the use of import controls. An essential prerequisite was full economic sovereignty. In other words, a potential Labour government would need to have full control of the British economy. This was not deemed to be possible with continued membership of the EC.[6]

The Labour Party fought the 1983 election committed to a policy of complete withdrawal from Community membership, which was the most extreme position ever to be adopted by Labour in opposition to Europe. At the time it seemed that Labour had rooted itself in an anti-EC position and that nothing was likely to change. About sixteen years ago two of our more distinguished political commentators could write, 'It is quite possible that a future Labour government will want to take Britain out of the EEC, or demand such fundamental structural changes as the price of staying in, that withdrawal becomes inevitable'.[7]

The Labour Party – the change of direction

Since those words were written the Labour Party changed so fundamentally that it could be described at the start of the 1990s as 'the more European of the two major parties'.[8] Yet the change was slow in coming, only really beginning in 1987, when Neil Kinnock set up a review of the party's policy following the election defeat of that year. There are those cynics who say that Labour's change of direction was little more than a political device to counter the direction taken by the Conservatives, but Labour's change of heart was more deep-seated than a mere search for electoral advantage. It was based on a number of premises that needed rethinking after Labour's third successive general election defeat.

- The economists in the party recognised the interdependence of economic processes in the modern world and came to doubt the viability of the AES in isolation from the powerful economic blocs such as the EC.
- There was a realisation that the continued success of Mrs Thatcher and the Conservatives meant that, while there was no scope in Britain for advancing the policies of the left, those policies were still prominent in Europe and that it was possible to introduce social policies into Britain via the Commission – what Mrs Thatcher called 'Socialism by the back door'.
- Exposure of the faults in the British political system by groups such as Charter 88 made advocacy of parliamentary sovereignty less acceptable, removing one of the props from the nationalistic arguments against Europe.

The real turning point was the visit to Britain in 1988 of the president of the Commission, Jacques Delors. Delors came to Britain to address the Trades Union Congress and received a standing ovation for a speech in which he laid out his thinking on a social charter for Europe, which guaranteed certain minimum standards for pay, working conditions and social benefits across the whole Community. This was so much in line with Labour thinking that the party enthusiastically endorsed the direction being taken by Delors and the Commission. Labour's change from an anti-European to a pro-European stance is therefore due to a change in the nature of the European Union. When the Community was seen as little more than a trading area for the benefit of commercial interests, the Labour Party felt obliged to oppose it; when the Community was seen as promoting improved social and environmental standards, then it became natural for Labour to support it. It is, in many ways, a mirror image of the change in Conservative attitudes to Europe.

To a Labour Party denied any hope of power in Britain since 1979, Europe seemed a logical way by which the social policies desired by Labour could be introduced into Britain, despite even a Conservative government, and the acceptance of a pro-European stance was adopted successively by Neil Kinnock, John Smith and Tony Blair. The modernising tendency in the party associated with the rise of Tony Blair and known as New Labour were virtually all pro-Europeans. It was ironic for Labour to see Neil Kinnock, who had campaigned against Europe in 1983, accept the post of European commissioner in 1994, be promoted to deputy president of the Commission in 1999, and all in a Brussels where his wife was a prominent MEP.

The Conservative Party – the decline of support

In the same decade which has seen the Labour Party move from antagonism to support in its attitude to Europe, the Conservatives have moved in the opposite direction, from support to a situation where leading members of the party can advocate withdrawal from the Union. The trigger for this change is the same for both parties and is the belief that Europe should be something more than just a mere club of trading partners. But, whereas the Common Market aspect of Europe was the thing which Labour found most objectionable, for many Conservatives that remained the sole justifiable reason for membership. Once the single market was established the European Community had served its purpose and senior Conservative politicians became determined not to let the movement towards European integration proceed any further.

During the 1960s and 70s the Conservatives were dedicated to British membership of the Community. Ted Heath, as the prime minister who took Britain into the EC, became and has remained an enthusiast for European integration. While Heath remained leader, opposition to Europe within the Conservative Party was muted, the only prominent party member to raise his voice against the policy being Enoch Powell, who urged fellow-Tories to vote Labour in 1974 as an anti-European gesture.

Margaret Thatcher was critical of Europe from the first, but her criticisms were more to do with operational matters such as the Common Agricultural Policy rather than the basic principle of membership. She was particularly concerned about the influence of the Commission, which she referred to dismissively as the 'Eurocracy', with what she saw as its tendency to over-regulate economic activity through devices such as the CAP, at the expense of the free operation of market forces.

Up until the creation of the Single Market the prime minister was seen by her European colleagues as being bloody-minded and confrontational but working in her own idiosyncratic way towards some vision of Europe. That this was not the case and that Mrs Thatcher was going to lead an increasingly vocal eurosceptical movement within the Conservative Party only became clear as a result of the same event that caused Labour to change – the advent of Jacques Delors as president of the Commission.

The impression created by Lady Thatcher has always been one of single-minded dedication and undeviating steadfastness of purpose. In reality her views were an uncomfortable marriage of two contradictory nineteenth-century ideologies – nationalistic conservatism and economic liberalism. The economic liberal could take pride in the creation of the single market but the nationalist in her reacted against the consequences of that act, namely against the imposition of a single currency and a European Central Bank and at the whole social dimension which formed part of the Delors Plan.

> Mrs Thatcher seems to believe that the Community will introduce socialism by the back door. She has been particularly vitriolic in her attacks on the 'social dimension' of the Community, whether in the form of the social charter or the social chapter discussed at Maastricht. At her 1988 speech in Bruges Mrs Thatcher argued that she would not allow the frontiers of the state to be rolled forward by the EC when she had spent nine years rolling them back in the UK.[9]

The Bruges speech led to the formation of the Bruges Group and an identifiable faction within the Conservative Party opposed to any suggestion of European federalism, political or monetary union or any measure which might lead to any further diminution of British sovereignty. As has been reported in an earlier chapter, the attitude towards Europe adopted by Mrs Thatcher was one of the major factors in her downfall and resignation. Once out of office and freed from the restrictions of her position, Lady Thatcher, as she had become, became the leading voice and propagandist of the Euro-sceptical tendency; that tendency rapidly assuming the characteristics of a party within a party. In parliament there was a number of Conservatives of ministerial rank who were unable to criticise Europe too openly because of the constraints of office but a sizeable group of backbenchers grew up under the unofficial leadership of Bill Cash, MP for Stafford.

The Conservative Party – Maastricht and after

From the moment John Major became prime minister he was plagued by trouble from his backbenchers as the eurosceptics in the party shifted their position. Until then Conservative attacks on Europe had centred on centralism in the Community, or were directed against 'creeping socialism'. Now the main line of attack switched to one of outright nationalism in defence of British sovereignty. 'Federalism' became the 'f-word' that was not to be mentioned in polite society.

In negotiations leading to the Maastricht treaty John Major succeeded in cutting out the word 'federal' where it had appeared in the draft treaty as well as negotiating opt-outs for Britain on both EMU and the social chapter. Major may therefore have felt he had done enough to satisfy the eurosceptics with the deal he had negotiated but in fact the most bitter debate within the party was about to follow, in which the prime minister suffered from one major disadvantage. In the 1992 election the overall government majority had been reduced to twenty-one, while there were known to be at least thirty eurosceptics ready to vote against the party line. The government had become very vulnerable to any backbench rebellion.

The European Communities Amendment Bill 1992 began its passage through parliament on 7 May 1992, reaching its second reading on the 21st and 22nd of that month. Contrary to popular opinion it was not intended to ratify the Maastricht Agreement; as a treaty that could be ratified by the government without reference to parliament. The bill was for the purpose of absorbing the Maastricht provisions into British law. This the rebels were determined to prevent, while the government were equally as determined to put down any dissent. Prior to the vote on the second reading the party whips did everything to persuade reluctant Tory backbenchers to vote with the government, from persuasive talk about how subsidiarity had removed the threat of federalism on one hand, to outright threats on the other. Those threats in turn ranged from reminders that rebels could forget any hopes of promotion, to hints that scandalous details of the rebel MPs' private lives might be leaked to the press. Even so, twenty-two Conservatives voted against the government on the second reading, although the decision by Labour to abstain led to the government having a comfortable majority of 336 votes to 92.

At that moment, when the bill was about to move into its Committee Stage, its progress was halted by the Danish referendum which rejected Maastricht. Suspended until the position of Denmark had been resolved, the bill remained in limbo until after the summer recess. In the intervening period any eurosceptics were reinforced in their thinking both by the anti-Europe feeling revealed in Denmark and France and by the setback to monetary integration provided by Black Wednesday and the collapse of the ERM. As the confidence of the rebels increased the government gave a hostage to fortune by agreeing to a Labour suggestion that they should subject the suspended bill to a paving motion which would give the Commons' permission for the bill to proceed. Constitutionally there was no requirement for such a motion and there had been no precedent in the passage of other controversial measures.

When the Commons voted on the paving motion on 5 November, twenty-six Conservatives voted against the government, and another sixteen abstained. The government would almost certainly have been defeated if the Liberal Democrats had not voted with them. Even so, the bill went into Committee

Stage with the most vigorous opposition to the Conservative government coming from the Conservative backbenches: there were now forty or more identified Tory rebels who declared that they were ready to bring down the government rather than see an extension of Brussels' influence.

The bill received its third reading on 20 May 1993, exactly one year after its second reading. Labour abstained again and the government received 229 votes in favour, with 112 against, 41 of whom were Tory rebels. The bill then passed to the Lords where another struggle was foreseen, largely because two of Europe's most vocal opponents were now members of the Upper House – Lord Tebbit and Lady Thatcher. Yet the expected struggle did not actually happen and the bill made rapid progress. The showpiece debate and vote was over the issue of a referendum, with Lady Thatcher espousing a course that she was once the first to condemn. As it happens the government packed the Lords with its supporters, loyal backwoodsmen being drafted in from the remotest of locations. The referendum amendment was lost by 445 votes to 176, the largest vote in the Lords during the twentieth century.

The bill received the Royal Assent on 20 July 1993 but the Commons immediately moved to a Labour amendment which stated that Britain must accept the Social Chapter before ratifying Maastricht. The debate was fixed for Thursday 22 July and all the attentions of the whips were concentrated on winning over the rebels. It is during this time that feelings within the Conservative Party became particularly bitter. 'These people are going to be hated for all time', said Edward Heath about the rebels. Some of the eurosceptics came back into the fold but others became even more entrenched in their position by the pressure being brought to bear on them.

There were two votes on the question of the Social Chapter. On the first, which was on the Labour amendment for acceptance of European social policies, eighteen rebels proved willing to vote against the government, resulting in an apparently tied vote of 317 to 317, resolved by the Speaker's traditional casting vote for the government. But on the second vote, on a simple government statement, the number of rebels rose to twenty-five and the government was defeated by 324 votes to 316. The government had to re-present the motion on the following day, this time making it a vote of confidence which would have required the government to resign if defeated. Despite the rebels' earlier promise to bring down the government if necessary they gave way at this point and the government had a majority of forty.

The government were then free to ratify Maastricht, but it was only after incalculable damage had been done to relations within the Tory Party.[10]

The Conservative Party after Maastricht

In March 1994, Martin Kettle wrote an article in the *Guardian*[11] bemoaning the fact that the common terminology employed by the media tended to divide opinion on the issue of Europe into just two groups, the euroenthusiasts and the eurosceptics, whereas he claimed that he could distinguish at least four different attitudes.

- *Euroenthusiasts* are those who welcome membership of the Community and moves towards integration. They are somewhat uncritical of European measures and are typified by the Liberal Democrats or Ted Heath and his supporters.
- *Europhobes* is the more accurate term for those commonly labelled as eurosceptics, such as Bill Cash, who are rather more than merely sceptical and who would quite gladly welcome a British withdrawal from Europe.
- *Eurosceptics*, in the true sense of the term, are what Kettle describes as people 'who doubt the wisdom of the European project but who are prepared to go cautiously along with it'. They accept that in a few areas such as the single market the European Union has its uses but are highly sceptical about any European involvement in areas like social policy, defence or internal security.
- *Europrogressives* or *Europositives*: the group no one mentions but who, according to Kettle, probably form the majority, not only in Britain but throughout the Community. They are people who 'are basically in favour of the Euro-project but who don't want to endorse change indiscriminately'. These are the people who voted two to one to remain in the Common Market in the referendum of 1975 and who would probably vote in the same proportions today.

The point Kettle was making in his article was that John Major, at the time he took over from Lady Thatcher, was a europositive, eager to put Britain 'at the heart of Europe' and able to say at the European Council in Edinburgh, 'the majority of people in this country want us to make a success of our membership'. The conflicts of the debate forced Major to change in order to accommodate the europhobes in his party by adopting a highly critical attitude in European Council meetings, blocking measures not for the sake of Britain or Europe but in order to keep the favour of his party at home.

This move by party leaders from a positive to a sceptical perspective did not seem to appease the europhobes in the party. Instead, they became more and more openly phobic as Major changed his position. Originally a backbench movement, the europhobes began to attract government ministers and even members of the cabinet into their ranks. Prominent cabinet ministers of the time, including Michael Portillo, Peter Lilley, Michael Howard and John Redwood, not only spoke out critically about aspects of the Community but used the increasingly phobic reactions of the Tory grassroots to form a power-base for their own ambitions and career prospects. Major recognised this fifth column in the Cabinet and, in a famous aside to Michael Brunson with an ITN camera team, was overheard to refer to high-ranking members of his own government as 'bastards'.

The Conservatives and Europe in the 1997 general election

The issue of European Union membership came to dominate the 1997 general election to the detriment of most other issues and not necessarily to the benefit of those members of the Conservative Party who insisted in bringing the matter to the fore. The subject of debate and controversy was the question of European Monetary Union and the acceptance of a common currency, but, for many of those involved, arguments over EMU were just a coded way of opposing European unity and advocating British withdrawal from the EU.

The Maastricht Treaty laid down a timetable for monetary union, with the first wave of members joining on 1 January 1999, as well as establishing the convergence criteria, which are the measures of unemployment, inflation, national debt and other economic indicators which member countries would have to satisfy before being allowed to join the common currency. At the time of Maastricht the UK won an opt-out clause in the treaty which meant that Britain did not have to join if it did not want to. Since at the time the opt-out was granted the economic recession in Britain suggested that the UK would never satisfy the convergence criteria, no one worried overmuch about an issue like EMU. As the economy improved, however, and it looked as though Britain might easily satisfy those criteria, there were those – even in the Tory government – who began to contemplate the possibility of the UK joining EMU in the first wave. The mere prospect made the eurosceptical wing of the Conservative Party ever more strident in their demands that government and party must rule out membership of EMU at any time and under any conditions.

Even beyond the Conservatives there was a growing opposition to Europe, manifested in 1996 by the formation of the Referendum Party by the late Sir James Goldsmith, formed so as to demand a referendum on constitutional matters such as any deepening of the European Union. To put pressure on the Tories to adopt a more sceptical approach, Goldsmith claimed in his election material that his party would fight 'every seat where the leading candidate has failed to defend your right to vote on the future of this nation'. Outwardly the Referendum Party was not anti-European – after all, Goldsmith was half French by birth, retained French nationality, lived for part of the year in France and was an MEP for a French constituency – but it claimed to want no more than to permit the British people a say through a referendum that had been denied them by the traditional parties. As Goldsmith said, 'we are not politicians and our only aim is to secure a Referendum'. Yet his election literature was openly opposed to the European Union, with statements such as 'unelected Brussels bureaucrats will soon be handed almost total control of our lives'. The explicit aim of the party was the referendum but its implicit purpose, hardly hidden and understood by the electorate, was to achieve Britain's withdrawal from Europe.

Although the stated reason for the Referendum Party's existence was that no other party would allow a referendum, this was quite clearly untrue, as even the most perfunctory reading of the relevant party manifestos would show. In speaking of entry into EMU the Conservatives stated that 'no such decision would be implemented unless the British people gave their express approval in a referendum'; Labour said, 'the people would have to say "Yes" in a referendum'; while the Liberal Democrats had always held the opinion that 'the British people must give their consent through a referendum'.

It is hard to see what the Referendum Party hoped to gain from participation in the general election. The only possible explanation of their strategy was that the Conservative Party would adopt a far more eurosceptical position in order to avoid opposition from a Referendum Party candidate who would split the right-wing vote.

The official position of the Conservative Party, as advocated by the chancellor, Kenneth Clarke, was to say that it was extremely doubtful that Britain would join EMU on the first wave in 1999, but it was nevertheless foolish to rule out the possibility while there was a chance of playing some part in the negotiating process by keeping Britain's options open. A policy of 'wait-and-see' was therefore adopted and maintained by John Major and the cabinet. A similar wait-and-see approach was also taken up by the Labour Party. Only the Liberal Democrats were willing to accept unqualified membership of EMU from the first.

Opposition to the official Conservative position came from the Referendum Party, Dr Alan Sked's UK Independence Party and many Tory backbenchers. Even before the election campaign began, the europhobic Tory MP, Sir George Gardiner, was deselected by his Reigate constituency for making disloyal statements and ultimately fought the election as a Referendum Party candidate – losing his deposit by so doing. A multi-millionaire right-wing businessman, Paul Sykes, offered up to £2,500 in election expenses to any Tory candidate who was willing to campaign against the introduction of a single currency.

As many as 232 candidates accepted Paul Sykes's offer and included opposition to Europe in the personal election messages to their constituents. This was significant enough when only backbenchers were involved but, towards the end of the campaign, even government ministers like John Horam and Angela Rumbold were breaking collective responsibility by campaigning against EMU membership. Kenneth Clarke, as the only europhile of any substance in the government, was increasingly isolated as other ministers remained strangely silent on the subject, or made studiously equivocal statements with one eye on future contests for the Tory Party leadership. Even left-of-centre Tories like Stephen Dorrell moved to a eurosceptic approach, 'Dorrelling away pretending to hold views that they don't', as one senior Tory was quoted as saying.

Europe therefore became a major issue in the 1997 general election but not in the way that anyone might have expected.

- The final three weeks of the election campaign were dominated by Europe to the exclusion of virtually every other issue.
- Discussions concerning Europe were almost exclusively about whether the candidates would rule out British entry into the single currency and other matters like fish quotas and beef bans, which were of some concern to the electorate, were largely ignored.
- There is no evidence that the British people are as europhobic as the right wing of the Conservative Party think they are. The British are sceptical in the true meaning of the term; they dislike foreigners, particularly the Germans; they do not like the idea of 'losing the pound' and they can get very annoyed with the more futile bureaucratic measures from Brussels. However, abstract arguments over concepts such as national sovereignty come a poor second to bread and butter issues like taxation or education.
- The arguments over Europe were very clearly not about Europe itself but far more about internal arguments and divisions within the Conservative Party. As one prominent Tory politician, Lord Whitelaw, said, 'The reason they got into trouble was over Europe. If they can't work together they won't achieve anything'.

The divided parties

As we have seen, Martin Kettle proposed a typology of divisions in John Major's Tory Party before the 1997 election. Alistair Jones of De Montfort University did much the same exercise for the party led by William Hague into the 1999 European elections.[12] In his survey he identified six different groupings within the party on just the European issue.

- **Anti-marketeers:** these make up a group who are totally opposed to membership of the European Union. Some, like Teddy Taylor, have been opposed from the days before British entry: Taylor resigned from the government in 1971 because of Heath's pro-European stance. These long-term opponents have been joined by those like Norman Lamont who merely started by a sceptical approach over certain issues but ended in complete opposition and calls for withdrawal.
- **Gaullists:** this group claims to be pro-European but it is a Europe in which all the member states preserve their national identities in what De Gaulle used to call a Europe des Nations. This is the group favoured by Lady Thatcher who was proudly patriotic and claimed she did not wish to see British, French or German characteristics submerged so as to become what she called 'identikit Europeans'.
- **Tory modernisers:** largely those involved in trade or commerce like Michael Heseltine, this group wish to protect British interests by taking a more active role. On the euro, for example, they believe that Britain should belong, if

only so as to have a voice on the committees developing and regulating the single currency.

- **Free market neo-liberals:** this group is proudest of all of the single market. They are pragmatists in that they want what is best for Britain and are willing to sacrifice some aspects of sovereignty in return for the triumph of market forces. John Major typified their attitude.
- **Federalists:** the goal of a united Europe was once a common belief in the Tory party but it is now definitely a view held be a small minority. The one group who have remained true to this view of Europe is made up of the Tory MEPs who have 'gone native', to use Lady Thatcher's expression, under the federalist influence of the PPE.
- **Common-sense Europeans:** these are the group that Kettle called europositives, labelling them with the description 'people who are basically in favour of the Euro-project but who do not want to endorse change indiscriminately'. Once a majority in the Conservative Party it is a group that it shrinking rapidly in the face of the scepticism and hostility exhibited by William Hague and many party activists.

This is not to say that Labour is united on this issue. They too have their anti-European campaigners still, as typified by Tony Benn and Dennis Skinner. But New Labour as led by Tony Blair, and with a whole host of spin doctors to manipulate opinion, has been a lot better at masking dissent within the party than the Conservatives and European issues do not figure very prominently in Labour's strategy. Only the Tories have seized on Europe and the single currency as issues they believe will win them the next election. From the moment he was elected leader, William Hague became more and more antagonistic towards the EU, ruling out even thinking about joining the euro for at least ten years. He managed to antagonise the pro-Europeans in his own party to such an extent that some europhiles broke loose and the 1999 European elections actually saw a pro-European Conservative Party fighting an anti-European Conservative Party. As it happens the pro-European Tories did very badly but it was a warning that the risk of a divided party is very real; a risk made even more manifest in August 1999 when it was decided to discipline some pro-European Tories and prominent figure such as Julian Critchley and Ian Gilmour were expelled from the party. The anti-European Tories have grown steadily more extreme and more opposed to Europe than ever, invoking memories of the hard left of the Labour Party in the early 1980s; even down to the factional in-fighting common to extremist wings of parties.

Summary

Any hope that there may be a consensus between the parties on European matters is more than ever a pipedream that will never be realised. Labour, the

Liberal Democrats and the nationalist parties are all more or less supportive of Europe, even if they all have their anti-European dissidents. In the Conservative Party opposition to Europe has gained strength but it appears much stronger than it is because it is supported by a generally europhobic press. The party hierarchy are convinced that an anti-European stance will win them the next election and they point to their successes in the 1999 European elections. However, it is worth bearing in mind that with apathy keeping the UK turnout down to less than 25 per cent of the electorate, and with the Conservative share of the vote standing at 35.77 per cent, then support for the Tories was actually little more than 8 per cent of the electorate; hardly as hefty an endorsement of euroscepticism as many party faithful believe.[13]

Notes

1 David McKie (ed.), *The Guardian Political Almanac 1993/4*, Fourth Estate, London, 1993.

2 Tom Nairn, *The Left Against Europe?*, Penguin, London 1973.

3 The exchanges between Gaitskell and Macmillan are quoted in Michael Cockerell's excellent book about relations between television and politicians, *Live from Number 10*, Faber and Faber, London, 1988.

4 Cockerell, *Live from Number 10*, p. 202.

5 Cockerell, *Live from Number 10*, p. 222

6 Ben Rosamond, 'The Labour Party and European integration', *Politics Review*, April 1994, p. 21.

7 Bill Jones and Dennis Kavanagh, *British Politics Today*, 2nd edition, Manchester University Press, Manchester, 1984.

8 Stephen George, *Britain and European Integration Since 1945*, Basil Blackwell, Oxford, 1991.

9 Daniel Wincott, 'The Conservative Party and Europe', *Politics Review*, April 1992, p. 12.

10 A full account of the Maastricht debate, with analysis of the various divisions and the voting record of all MPs, is to be found in McKie (ed.) *The Guardian Political Almanac 1993/4*, pp. 199–224.

11 Martin Kettle, 'A leader lost amid the phobes and sceptics', *Guardian*, 19 March 1994.

12 Alistair Jones, 'UK relations with the EU and did you notice the elections?', *Talking Politics*, Vol. 12, no. 2, Winter 2000, p. 312.

13 Election results quoted by Jones, 'UK relations with the EU'.

9

The citizen of the European Union

The EU does not noticeably appeal directly to the individual, although euro-enthusiasts are always ready to quote opinion polls conducted by the statistical offices of the Community claiming majority support for the EU among the public in all member-countries. In 1991, for example, a Eurobarometer opinion poll found that 53 per cent of the population, across the twelve member states, claimed to feel a sense of belonging to Europe, 'sometimes' or 'often'.[1] In 1994, only 22 per cent of the British population questioned by Eurobarometer wished to see an end to the Union, while 25 per cent claimed they would feel 'profound regret' at such an end; and an incredible 41 per cent actually said that they felt that European integration was 'too slow'. Even in 1999, in the wake of the most apathetic European elections ever and with the Conservatives under William Hague in full voice against the EU, as many as 46 per cent of Britons thought that by the year 2020 the European Parliament would be of more importance to them than the Westminster parliament.[2] Yet, although it is probably true that a majority of British electors would still vote for continued membership in a rerun of the 1975 referendum, it would be an apathetic form of support, basically meaning little more than that people think that now we are in we might as well stay in, and that it would be less of an upheaval to remain in the Community than to leave it. When it comes to European integration it is hard to find any real enthusiasm among the general public and that does not only apply to Britain. 'European integration has been promoted by political élites rather than by the electorate as a whole ... Elite-led advances in European integration may not correspond to popular wishes, as the 1992 Danish referendum demonstrated.'[3]

One reason for public indifference to Europe is ignorance. Most people are unaware of the benefits of Community membership and they have not been enlightened, either by a sceptical Tory government that did not wish people to know just how much they may have benefited from EU membership, nor by a more europhile Labour government which suspects that public opinion might be eurosceptical and do not wish to risk electoral displeasure by showing too much enthusiasm. And any governmental reticence is heavily reinforced by a media which is far more interested in publicising the faults of the Commission and pouring scorn on the advantages of membership than it is in singing its praises. A small proportion of the population have direct contact with European action, and acquire strong attitudes for or against Europe as a result: those working in agriculture or the fishing industry are examples of citizens who have been angered or frustrated by Community actions. Others, living in depressed areas which are in receipt of Community funding, might also be aware of Community influence thanks to the placards announcing European funding for some improvement in the infrastructure such as the building of new roads. The majority of people, however, remain unaware of any benefits or penalties of EU membership except for such peripheral benefits as being able to buy unlimited quantities of cheap drink on a day trip to Calais.

Nevertheless, aware of it or not, all British citizens have been affected to some extent by the UK's membership of the Community. Apart from the influences on British policy noted in Chapter Six, there are two main areas where the individual is affected by Community membership: one is in the EU citizenship provisions of the TEU as modified and strengthened by the Treaty of Amsterdam, and the other concerns the rights given to citizens as consumers under the single market provisions of the SEA. To consider the first of these, it is worth remembering that, as far back as 1984, the European Council set up a committee chaired by Pietro Adonnino to consider the action required to create 'a people's Europe'. The work done by that committee prepared the ground for the citizenship provisions that make up Article Eight of the Maastricht Agreement.

Citizenship of the Union

Article Eight of the Treaty for European Union states that 'Every person holding the nationality of a Member State shall be a citizen of the Union' 4 and then goes on in a series of sub-clauses to detail the rights of citizenship that are granted within the TEU:

- the right of freedom of movement within the territory of all member states
- the right to reside in any country of the Union
- the right to work in any member state, although subject to certain national restrictions
- the right to vote and stand as a candidate in municipal and European elections, subject to the qualifications demanded of nationals of the state in question, in the country of residence
- the right to have academic and/or vocational qualifications recognised throughout the Union
- the right to parity of provision for welfare benefits

- the right, when travelling outside the Union, to diplomatic or consular assistance from the Embassy or Consulate of any member state
- the right to receive pension entitlement in whichever state the pensioner is resident, at a rate equal to that paid in the country where the entitlement was earned
- the right to petition the European Parliament, to resort to legal action in the European Court of Justice or to apply to the Ombudsman.

All these rights came into force with the ratification of the TEU and the provisions are scrutinised and guaranteed by the Commission being required to report on their application to the European Parliament, and to the Economic and Social Committee, at three-yearly intervals.

The Amsterdam Treaty reinforced the agreements that had been made at Maastricht by establishing three provisions:

1 reiterating the principles on which the Union is founded – 'liberty, democracy, respect for human rights and freedoms, and the rule of law'
2 giving powers to the European Court of Justice which ensure that these principles are observed by all EU institutions
3 providing sanctions such as suspension of member states' rights if these principles are breached.

The Amsterdam Treaty also added a clause which enables the Council of Ministers to take action against 'discrimination based on sex, racial or ethnic origin, religion or belief, disability, age or sexual orientation'.

Freedom of movement

The Single European Act of 1986 stated that 'the internal market shall comprise an area without internal frontiers in which the free movement of people is ensured'. Articles 7a and 8a of the TEU established a common EU citizenship and extended the right to study, work and live in another country within the Community to all citizens of the EU. The Amsterdam Treaty incorporated these provisions into the EC Treaty with the ultimate aim of creating an 'area of freedom, security and justice' with no controls on people at internal borders, whatever their nationality.

Freedom of movement without border controls was partially achieved by the Schengen Agreements of 1985 and 1990, integrated into the European Union by the Amsterdam Treaty in 1998. However the Schengen Agreements could not be implemented in full because the UK insisted that anti-terrorism measures meant that rudimentary passport checks must be retained for EU citizens and, with the passport union already existing between the two countries, the Republic of Ireland had to follow suit. Denmark signed the

Schengen Agreements but refused to accept provisions for free movement of people. The twelve other member states have, however, accepted the principles agreed at Schengen, which means that the EU, with the exception of Denmark, Ireland and the UK, has no internal borders for either passport or customs control.

It might be pointed out that citizens of the three countries outside Schengen, who have their freedom of movement impeded through their government's failure to implement the SEA fully, are free to appeal to the European Court over that infringement of treaty provisions. There was talk at one point during the Irish troubles that Gerry Adams, or any other Sinn Fein representative, who faced an exclusion order from the United Kingdom, might file a case against the UK government for this restriction of their movements.

Residence in any EU country is possible through 'freedom of establishment' by which EU citizens can settle in any EU country that they wish. All they need is a residence permit, which is valid for five years and is automatically renewable on request. Moreover, no EU citizen can be refused a residence permit except on the grounds of security or health. On the right to work in another country within the EU the situation differs according to the member state, as do the individual's rights to unemployment benefit and pension rights.

- **Belgium:** EU citizens working in Belgium can bring in their marriage partner and their children, all of whom also gain the right to work and all social benefits. Any unemployed have the right to reside in Belgium, if registered as a 'job-seeker'.
- **Denmark:** an EU citizen has the right to work in Denmark as the employee of a Danish employer, or to set up their own business in Denmark if they are likely to employ Danish workers. All EU citizens have automatic pensions rights and free treatment in the Danish Health Service.
- **France:** EU citizens have the right to reside and work in France but difficulties remain over the recognition of qualifications. Members of the families of registered workers have equal rights with native French citizens to welfare benefits.
- **Germany:** unrestricted access to work and benefits for EU citizens on the basis of parity with native German citizens.
- **Greece:** A work permit is not required if the police are informed within eight days of arrival in the country. Three months work qualifies the EU citizen to full national rights.
- **Ireland:** the UK and Ireland already shared full freedom of movement and the right to work before both countries joined the Community, although severely constrained at times by anti-terrorist legislation.
- **Luxembourg:** by far the most liberal of the EU countries in granting working rights, social benefits and assistance to EU immigrants since one quarter of the population are already nationals of other EU countries.

- **Netherlands:** no restrictions on EU citizens over access either to jobs or social benefits on an equal basis with Dutch nationals.
- **Portugal:** still retains limits on access to work in Portugal. Also, Portugal does not possess a social security system.
- **Spain:** a five-year work and residence permit is required but this should be automatically available to EU citizens who apply.
- **United Kingdom:** gives no guarantees on work, freedom of movement or access to welfare provision for EU citizens, although government claims that all rights are available on a reciprocal basis.[5]

Political and economic refugees

The issue of political asylum and the status of refugees from outside the borders of the EU has been of increasing importance during the 1990s with the upheavals caused not only by the break-up of the Soviet Union and the former Yugoslavia but by a series of crises and civil conflicts in Africa. The Amsterdam Treaty which came into force in 1999 attempted to deal with these emerging problems by re-defining Community procedures for examining asylum applications; the granting or withholding of refugee status, and sharing the burden of receiving refugees between the member states.

In December 1998 the Commission and Council drew up a working party to study the whole issue of immigration and asylum, with the aim of devising an overall migration strategy which was then inserted into the EC Treaty as Title IV – 'Visas, asylum, immigration and other policies related to free movements of persons'. After that, however, the situation became more serious, with several EU member states feeling threatened by what the press branded as 'floods of bogus asylum seekers'. Several states took unilateral action, as was the case with Belgium's temporary withdrawal from the Schengen Agreements. Having introduced various draconian measures to counter what it saw as a major problem, the UK was threatened with sanctions if it did not act to restore freedom of movement but, as a non-signatory of the Schengen Agreement, the UK can ignore for the moment those civil rights which relate to the internal security of the EU.

European judicial area

Until the drafting of the Single European Act the European Court of Justice and the whole body of Community Law had comparatively little to do with the rights of individual citizens, being more concerned with disputes between member states and Community institutions. There were a few high-profile cases like the sixty-year-old man who fought for equality of treatment with female pensioners, but these were essentially cases of national governments being taken to court for non-observance of Community directives, with the individual plaintiff acting as a token representative for a whole section of society. Apart from these few cases, civil rights have been more a matter of concern for the Council of Europe and the European Convention on Human Rights.

The Maastricht Treaty introduced the concept of judicial cooperation in civil and criminal law between the member countries of the EU with the aim of creating a common body of law between the member states over which the European Court might have some jurisdiction. The Amsterdam Treaty then began to create a framework for judicial cooperation in all those criminal matters that can be said to come within the third pillar of the Treaty for European Union. Amsterdam also saw the establishment of a link between judicial cooperation in civil matters and the right to freedom of movement under the EC treaties. At the same time plans were announced for the introduction of legal instruments that will rule on trans-national disputes and judicial solutions. Most of these disputes concern family matters such as divorce, ownwership of property, custody of children and rights to inheritance.

A new charter of human rights

The European Council at Cologne in June 1999 established a working party with sixty-two members drawn from the European Parliament, the Commission and the Council of Ministers and which was chaired by the former president of Germany, Roman Herzog. This working party or convention was given the difficult task of drawing up a new charter of human rights applicable to the twenty-first century. There were two main reasons for undertaking this work at this time.

- A need to reinforce existing rights, and particularly those relating to minorities, racism and prejudice, ahead of the accession of East European countries who, without having a recent history of liberal democracy, have a less than enviable human rights record. A reminder of how easily existing member states may drift away from the fundamental human rights of tolerance came in February 2000 with the rise of the Austrian neo-Nazi Freedom Party.
- A need to compensate for the concessions made to big business and the financial markets during the introduction of the single market and single currency. There was a feeling that the 'banker's Europe' which had emerged during the 1990s, giving great advantages to business and commerce, needed to be balanced by such legally constituted social and labour rights as the right to work, a minimum wage, and social security provision.

The new charter is based on the very same European Convention on Human Rights (ECHR) as was drawn up in 1950 by the Council of Europe and only recently incorporated into British law by the Blair government. The ECHR has always formed the basis of EU thinking on human rights but, although all member states are signatories of the Convention, with the decisions of the European Court of Human Rights enforced by the courts and legal systems of the individual states, the EU itself is not a signatory of the ECHR and the judgments of the Strasbourg European Court of Human Rights had never been enforceable by the Luxembourg European Court of Justice. What is more, the ECHR was drawn up in 1950 and there are a number of matters such as data protection and gender issues which did not seem to be particularly important half a century ago but which have considerable relevance today.

The idea of a new charter that might well form the basis of a constitution for the EU was regarded very critically by those opposed to European integration who saw it as a form of 'federalism by stealth'. In particular it was looked at askance by British eurosceptics, 'It is everything the tabloids cannot abide: something drafted by foreigners which smacks of central planning and sounds obscure'.[6]

Pensions and social security

From the start there has been a commitment in the Community that citizens from one member state should not be disadvantaged in receiving social or welfare benefit simply because they are resident in an EU member state that is not that of their birth, nor indeed the country in which they have spent their working lives. Basically the rule is that a welfare recipient working and living abroad in another EU country receives the benefits payable in that country. This can produce some strange anomalies, such as a British citizen working in Luxembourg who receives family benefit for his or her children, even though those children have been left behind in the family's English home. The system can also benefit some people more than others: a waiter from Portugal where there are virtually no welfare benefits will do very well if he works in a restaurant in Germany and qualifies for full German benefit.

One welfare benefit which is not paid by the country of residence is unemployment benefit, if the person concerned entered the country while unemployed. This is a necessary precaution taken by countries such as Germany or the Netherlands which pay a high rate of unemployment benefit and would otherwise be the target of hundreds of the unemployed, touring Europe in search of the best rate of pay. An unemployed EU citizen can, however, look for work in other member states and continue to receive unemployment pay from the home country, at the rate paid in that country. For the unemployed person to do so they must have the permission of their home country's equivalent of Britain's Department of Social Security, who are also able to provide useful information and advice. On arrival in their new country of residence anyone who is unemployed must register with the local authority as a 'job-seeker' within a week of arrival.

As far as retirement or disability pensions are concerned the position is clear-cut, even if a little complicated. If, after a life spent working in Britain, a couple chose to retire to a villa they had bought in Spain, they would receive their pensions in Spain, although at the British and not the Spanish rate. Complications begin when a pensioner's working life has been spent in more than one EU member state. In these cases the pension is paid *pro rata* to the pension rates in the countries concerned, according to the length of time spent in each of those countries. As an example, let us take a British citizen, a civil servant, who spent twenty years working in Whitehall but who then, for the last ten years of his working life, transferred to work for the EC Commission in Brussels. He would receive a pension two-thirds of which would be paid at the British rate and one-third at the Belgian. This, however, only applies to state pensions and there are still problems over transferring entitlement to occupational pensions from one country to another.[7]

Health

All member states of the EU have some form of health service – some offer completely free treatment, in others the patient has to make some form of payment towards the cost, and in yet others the patient has to pay in full and then claim for a full or partial refund. For some time the member states have made their health service facilities available to citizens of other member states on a reciprocal basis, whether the service is that of a doctor, dentist, hospital treatment or the issue of prescriptions. In the 1980s the EC extended this reciprocal arrangement to temporary residents of the member states, whether on holiday or on business. A special form (E111) was issued, the possession of which entitles the holder to the reciprocal medical arrangement.

In addition to this routine assistance the EU is also involved in health matters through the commitment of funds to supranational health research projects. The first such project was 'Europe against cancer', which was set up and funded with the expressed intention of reducing the number of deaths from cancer by 15 per cent by the year 2000. Similar programmes have followed that have been targeted on AIDS and drug abuse.[8] Other EU agencies that have been set up to deal with health matters include the European Agency for the Evaluation of Medicinal Products (EMEA), the European Monitoring Centre for Drugs and Drug Addiction (EMCDDA) and the European Agency for Safety and Health at Work (see Appendix 7).

Young people and Europe

Over the years the Community has set up a number of initiatives intended to foster a sense of belonging to a European Community among young people; particularly students and young workers.

- The Youth for Europe scheme is a simple exchange programme whereby young people between the ages of fifteen and twenty-five can extend their knowledge of the EU by going to live in another member country for a time.
- The European Exchange Programme for Young Workers is, as the name suggests, intended to allow young workers in the first ten years of their working lives to gain work experience or to follow a course of training in another EU member state.
- Erasmus is the established project for encouraging exchange and mobility among EU member states for students in the university sector. The programme is also intended to encourage the provision of courses in European studies on the part of colleges and universities as well as encouraging a pan-European perspective in existing disciplines.
- Comett is a project intended to improve technical training, especially in the new technologies, by placing students and young workers in firms and research establishments in other member countries.
- There are a number of schemes to promote education and training in specific fields such as science and economics, including the Lingua Programme intended to improve the teaching of languages and the Petra Programme for improving vocational training.

The Commission also funds a body concerned with research and development into the field of training and vocational education. The European Centre for the Development of Vocational Training (CEDEFOP) was founded in Berlin in 1975 but is now based in Thessaloniki in Greece, and offers academic and technical support for vocational training throughout Europe. There is also the European Training Foundation, which helps to provide vocational training in Central and Eastern Europe, the former Soviet Union and countries on the Mediterranean Basin (see Appendix 7).

For postgraduate university students interested in studying the processes of European integration there is a College of Europe which offers one-year courses in economics, law and political science from a European perspective and which receives around 250 students each year. The College is a bi-lingual institution and students must be fluent in either English or French. Based in Bruges, the College gained some notoriety for being the body to which Lady Thatcher was speaking when she made her infamous Bruges Speech.

The individual as consumer

The Community's policy towards the consumer has already been dealt with in Chapter Six, but it should be repeated that EC policy since the establishment of the single market has been to allow the sale throughout the Community of goods lawfully produced in any one country of the Union, subject to regulation by the Community of standards affecting safety, hygiene and quality. Over the years since 1993 consumer action plans have been set up to improve standards of consumer protection. Areas that have been affected include:

- food safety, with legislation controlling the safety, quantity and technical necessity of food additives, preservatives, colourings and ingredients in general
- product safety in general, but with specific directives on children's toys, furniture, fireworks, prams and pushchairs
- pharmaceuticals, medicines and cosmetics, with especially rigorous requirements for adequate testing before use and the clear labelling of constituents; as from 1998 the testing of such products on animals was forbidden
- packaging and labelling: specific regulations deal with misleading statements about the nutritional value of foods, with the clear marking of perishable goods with 'best before' statements, and with which languages should be used in the labelling of goods
- protection from unfair trading practices, including misleading advertisements, doorstep selling, excessive rates of interest on credit sales, distance selling and package holidays that do not match brochure descriptions.

In tandem with these action programmes the Commission is setting up a consumer guide to cross-border shopping, a practice which has increased considerably since the single market enabled EU citizens to import unlimited quantities of goods bought in another Community country, as long as duty and VAT had been paid at the local rate. The Commission has also set up consumer information centres located near national borders which give advice on prices and availability of goods on both sides of the border, pointing out any special offers that might be available in one country rather than another. These centres work best, of course, with land frontiers and there are, as yet, none within the UK.

The interests of consumers in the UK as regards the Community are looked after by an umbrella interest group known as Consumers in the European Community (CECG). They in turn have contact with EC institutions through the Consumers' Consultative Council (CCC), which acts as an advisory body to the Commission and which helps to organise the pan-European Consumers Forum, meeting once or twice each year.[9]

The BSE scare as it affected the sales of British beef created an atmosphere of public concern about food safety issues. In 1997 the European Commission issued two documents, *Consumer Health and Food Safety* and *The General Principles of Food Law in the European Union*, which laid down the basic principles for an EU approach to food safety issues. In Britain this initiative has led to the funding by the EU of a food hygiene programme in UK schools, developed and run by the Health Education Authority.[10]

In December 1998 the Commission initiated a new consumer action plan which set four new targets for consumer policy in the period 1999–2001.

- It is important that the views of consumers should weigh more heavily in the consultation process. The aim is to improve coordination between local and national consumer organisations and to provide a hotline to the Commission for these consumer groups.
- Improvements need to be made in the field of food and product safety and special attention paid to the labelling, hygiene and inspection of food.
- A more critical approach is needed to safeguard the consumer against misleading claims for products – especially health products promising 'miracle cures' – and other dubious practices such as pyramid selling.
- A closer look at the area of e-finance which includes closer examination of automatic cash dispensers, electronic payment means, secure payments over the internet and a consumer-friendly market in financial services.

The right to protest

As was said in Chapter Six about the role of pressure and interest groups in the Community, the access to decision-making bodies by the individual is possibly far more open in the EU than in the UK. Complaints from the individual are actually welcomed by the Commission since it is only on the receipt of specific complaints that the Commission can begin to take action against national governments for non-compliance with Commission directives. Britain has at least learned this lesson well and, since 1990, something in excess of a hundred complaints have been received each year from individuals or groups resident in the UK. It has proved one way to circumvent the closed nature of British government.[11]

An individual who joins a pressure group and uses it, or sometimes is used by it, to pursue a cause that has run into a brick wall when faced with British bureaucratic obduracy, often find success in Europe where they failed in the UK. Specific causes where this is particularly true include issues concerning women's rights, the environment or consumerism.[12]

As well as the Commission the individual is entitled to approach the European Parliament. The EP is obliged to receive any written request or complaint submitted to it, the submission being known as a petition even if there is only one signatory. Such petitions are screened, of course, to weed out the frivolous or malicious, but if there seems to be good cause behind the communication the petition will be discussed and considered by a parliamentary committee which will make any decision or take any action it deems to be appropriate, communicating the outcome to the petitioner. Under the same article (138) of the TEU which granted the right of petition, an Ombudsman was appointed to consider any examples of bad management or maladministration by Community institutions or bodies. Any individual can take action by communicating directly with the Parliament or the Ombudsman but, naturally enough, such approaches are much more effective when conducted through an MEP who can represent the petitioner's interests.

The other main channel through which the individual EU citizen can seek redress is through the European Court. There are sufficient examples quoted in Chapter Six to show the efficacy of this approach in certain matters, particularly over matters such as women's or workers' rights. Nevertheless, it has to be said that progress through the European Court suffers from the same disadvantage for the individual as do the national courts. The process is exceedingly slow – four years being the normal delay between claim and settlement – and extremely expensive, since legal aid is not readily available. Generally speaking an individual will only find legal redress a viable possibility if they have the backing and financial support of some interest group.

Summary

For much of the European Community's life the individual was often neglected, to the benefit of Community institutions. This has changed somewhat since 1993 as the Single European Act has reinforced the status of the individual as consumer and the Treaties for European Union, as formulated at Maastricht and further developed at Amsterdam, have codified the rights of individuals under the provisions of EU citizenship.

Notes

1 European Commission, *A People's Europe*, European File Series, Luxembourg, 1992.
2 Survey in *The Economist*, 5 November 1999.
3 Simon Bulmer, 'Britain and European integration', in Bill Jones *et al* (eds), *Politics UK*, 2nd edition, Harvester Wheatsheaf, Hemel Hempstead, 1994.
4 General Secretariat of the Council and of the Commission of the European Communities, *Treaty on European Union* (full text), Office for Official Publications of the European Communities, Brussels – Luxembourg, 1992. (Articles 8 – 8e, pp. 15/16).
5 Julie Wolf, 'The single market and you', in Victor Keegan and Martin Kettle, *The New Europe*, Fourth Estate, London 1993.
6 Ian Black, *Guardian*, 5 April 2000.

7 Julie Wolf, 'The single market and you'.
8 European Commission, *A People's Europe*.
9 European Commission in the United Kingdom, *Fact Sheet 7 – My Benefits as a European Consumer*, HMSO, London, 1994.
10 European Commission in the United Kingdom, *Background briefing no. 32 – consumer policy/food safety*, European Commission, London, 2000.
11 Stephen C. Young, 'Environmental politics and the EC', *Politics Review*, February 1993, p. 8.
12 Sonia Mazey and Jeremy Richardson, 'Pressure groups and the EC', *Politics Review*, September 1993, p. 22.

10

Conclusion: the future of the European Union – enlargement and constitutional reform

In 1993 the EU reached what should have been a plateau in its development, following the rapid changes of the late 1980s and early 1990s. The reform of the Common Agricultural Policy, the passing of the Single European Act and agreement on the Treaty for European Union at Maastricht had all made radical changes to the nature of the Community and it might have been thought that the Council and Commission could afford to rest on their laurels and relax. Instead, however, the Maastricht Treaty was followed immediately by an intergovernmental conference, convened in 1996, whose report to the European Council at Amsterdam in 1998 resulted in the Amsterdam Treaty which came into force in 1999. In addition, in June 1999 the Cologne summit convened another IGC which it was intended should report its findings at the European Council due to be held in Nice during December 2000.

The main concern of both these post-Maastricht IGCs, as well as the programme known as Agenda 2000 which arose from them, was to address the question of enlarging the European Union up to and including the point at which the EU could well coincide with the continent of Europe through the potential inclusion of all nation-states west of the Russian border. Enlargement brings with it, of necessity, a whole sequence of questions about how the institutions of the EU, originally designed for the needs of six countries but made to stretch with difficulty to cope with fifteen, is going to cope with a total grouping of anything between twenty and thirty countries as the EU expands eastwards.

The intergovernmental conference of 2000[1]

The immediate task of the IGC convened at Cologne was to consider the so-called 'Amsterdam leftovers': issues which need to be addressed as a matter of some urgency but which were not incorporated into the Amsterdam Treaty. These include three major constitutional issues.

1 **The size and composition of the Commission.** The original constitutional framework of the European Commission decreed that larger member states should have two commissioners each while smaller states have just one. As the number of member states has increased over the years it has been recognised that this arrangement means that the Commission has gradually become increasingly large and unwieldy. Lord Jenkins complained of the size of the Commission as long ago as 1980 when there were only nine member states. If the new applicants were to continue to receive commissioners under the same dispensation the EU could be facing the prospect of having more than thirty commissioners by the end of the next decade. Current thinking is that no member state should have more than one commissioner each and that ideally the Commission should have a maximum membership of twenty commissioners. The figure of twenty that has been suggested poses a problem in that the next round of enlargement looks set to take EU membership over the twenty mark and this in turn would mean that no member country would be assured of permanently having its own commissioner. Commission membership would have to rotate between countries.

2 **The issues covered by qualified majority voting (QMV).** Pro-integrationists like Romano Prodi believe that excessive use of unanimous voting to provide the opportunity by which member states can exercise the national veto has been the factor which has held back the progress of the EU in the past and which will have the potential ability to create paralysis in an enlarged EU. Commenting on the matter at the launch of IGC 2000 Prodi described the national veto as a 'ball and chain shackling EU progress and integration'. Areas into which it is felt that QMV might advantageously be introduced include general transport policies, the siting of EU institutions, appointments and decisions on rules and procedures.

3 **The weighting of votes under QMV.** As the EU has grown, and the number of smaller states has also grown as a proportion of the total, one unfortunate side effect is that the share of the votes given to larger countries has gone down as a proportion of the whole and this affects the whole proportionality of the voting process. The implications of this for democratic fairness were outlined by Britain's foreign secretary, Robin Cook, 'Germany, France and Britain contain the majority of the population of the the the EU, but they do not have the majority of votes in the Council of Ministers. After the next enlargement those three countries will not even have sufficient votes for a blocking majority'.[2]

Apart from these three priority areas, the IGC was also briefed to look at three further points.

• Reform of the drawn-out and expensive procedures of the European Court of Justice. The trouble experienced in bringing pressure to bear on France, in order to get the French to accept the lifting of the ban on British beef, pointed out very clearly just how slow and cumbersome the European Court can be. If the single market is going to work in an enlarged EU the legal procedures need urgent streamlining action.

- A study to evaluate a form of variable geometry known as *coopération renforcée*, allowing different member states to progress at different rates in different policy areas.
- A study to evaluate the practical effects of the decision made at Amsterdam, under which it is recommended that membership of the European Parliament should be restricted to a maximum of 700 members.

The British response to the proposals being studied by the IGC was clarified in a White Paper issued in February 2000. This showed that the Blair government was more inclined to look favourably upon the proposed reforms than the previous Conservative administrations had been and, moreover, was more inclined to play the European game of making concessions in return for a reciprocal compromise by the other negotiators. It was made clear that Britain would accept curbs on the national veto and a reduction in the number of commissioners in return for an improved weighting of votes to give the larger member countries a greater say. In some areas, however, it was felt that the national veto needed to be defended. In the White Paper it was made clear that there would be 'red lines' which would define the limits of how far Britain would be prepared to give up its veto. Under these guidelines QMV was ruled out by Britain as being unacceptable in the areas of tax, defence, border controls and EU finance.[3]

Community initiatives

Alongside the IGC due to report in 2000, the Commission also announced a programme of four initiatives in the field of financial and policy reform which would be to the forefront in the period 2000–06. These initiatives are:

1 INTERREG, a programme of cross-border, trans-national and inter-regional co-operation to encourage the balanced development of all member countries
2 LEADER, an initiative to assist rural development which would concentrate resources on small local areas not already in receipt of structural funds
3 EQUAL, an attempt to eliminate all forms of discrimination and inequalities in the labour market
4 URBAN, which, as the name suggests, is a programme of urban regeneration involving partnerships between communities at local, national and EU levels.[4]

The real debate – stay or go?

During all the debates on the future of the EU – debates on federalism versus pragmatism or on the cost of British membership and the iniquities of the CAP – there has been one constant. Even the most eurosceptical of critics seemed to accept that withdrawal was not an option and that Britain had to remain a member. There were reasons for this, as follows.

- With the single market in operation British trade and industry is part of a very large internal market. Very few members of Britain's commercial and industrial community are ready to retreat from that, with the possible threat of European tariff barriers being raised against British goods and services.
- Britain has received a great deal of inward investment from the United States and elsewhere by firms who wished to set up a manufacturing base within the Community so as to avoid the external trade tariff. Withdrawal from the Community would mean the loss of these companies, with a consequent loss of investment, tax revenue and jobs.
- If Britain rejected her trading partners in Europe it is hard to see who would replace them. Commonwealth countries like Australia and New Zealand have found new markets and the USA has made it clear that their interest in Britain is solely as a link with Europe.

Nevertheless, there are and always have been europhobes who talk openly about the possibility of withdrawal. At first this attitude was an emotive one among those whose thinking was largely guided by the tabloid press but, after the 1997 election and the influence of hostile groupings such as the Referendum Party and the UK Independence Party, the most sceptical deepened their distrust of Europe. Their view is that they would like to get rid of the EU altogether but would be reasonably content if they could reduce the EC into being little more than a free-trade area, with Britain having associate membership like Norway. The arguments that can be marshalled against membership can be described as follows.

- European regulations such as the Common Agricultural Policy have caused immeasurable damage to the British farming industry. The demands on the CAP represented by the addition of peasant economies such as Poland and other Eastern European countries would stretch the situation beyond breaking point and could well bankrupt the Community.
- European countries such as Norway or Switzerland do very nicely through membership of EFTA, having only associate status with the EU, and there is every reason to believe that Britain could flourish similarly. Breaking with the EU would allow Britain to resurrect old trading alliances within the Commonwealth and elsewhere.

- Social and employment policies imposed by Europe can harm Britain's economic competitiveness and hinder the country's recovery from recession. Membership of the EU is a retrograde step for industry that militates against efficiency, competitiveness, progress and development.
- In its growing inability to legislate without external regulation, or in the loss of freedom to make independent decisions over the direction of the economy, the sovereign rights of the British government are steadily being eroded and lost to direction from Brussels.[5]

The possibility of leaving the EU is by now so typical of Conservative right-wing opinion that it seems likely to become the entrenched position of the party for the foreseeable future. As the former chancellor, Norman Lamont, pointed out as long ago as 1994, there are various alternatives to federalism but, if all these failed, the British government should not be afraid to accept the alternative. 'One day it may mean contemplating withdrawal. It has recently been said that the option of leaving the Community was "unthinkable". I believe this attitude is rather simplistic.'[6]

Variable geometry

In order to overcome the many problems associated with progress for the European Union, compounded on one side by the economic weakness of certain applicant states, and on the other by the larger states such as Britain who are reluctant to surrender that part of their sovereignty represented by the national veto or determination of economic policy free of the European Central Bank, the vision of variable geometry has re-emerged, although it is now known by the term 'enhanced cooperation' (*coopération renforcée*). This involves a tiered system whereby groups of countries at different levels of development would be enabled to move at different speeds within certain policy objectives.

The first reasoned argument for the variable approach was produced by the then French prime minister, Edouard Balladur, in August 1994. Balladur called for a three-tier Europe which he preferred to describe as three concentric circles:

1 a strong central core of France, Germany and perhaps the Benelux countries, united politically, economically and militarily
2 a middle tier made up of the other EU countries, unable or unwilling to join the political and economic union at the centre
3 an outer circle containing the other European countries which are not part of the EU but which have economic and security links.

Only such an arrangement, it was claimed, could prevent paralysis of the Union by the problems inherent in enlargement.[7]

Two days later, the German Christian Democratic Union published a policy document which wished, 'to strengthen the EU's capacity to act and to make its structures and procedures more democratic and federal'.[8] At the heart of this aim was the need to establish a form of constitution for the EU which would create a federal structure according to the principle of subsidiarity. Reform of Community institutions would mean that the EP became a genuine legislature, the Council evolved into a second chamber on the pattern of the US Senate to safeguard member-states' interests, and the Commission would assume the functions of a European executive. However, recognising that movement towards union would be impossible if all countries progressed at the speed of the slowest, the Germans repeated the Balladur suggestion that there should be a fast-track central core of countries, which they proposed should be France, Germany and the Benelux countries, since 'they (together with Denmark and Ireland) are the ones which come closest to meeting the covergence criteria stipulated in the Maastricht treaty'.

Ironically enough, it was the British prime minister, John Major, who had made great play of a 'multi-speed and multi-layered European Union' during the European elections of 1994. Now that the mechanism for creating such a layered institution had been suggested, however, he seemed to be protesting because such a solution would relegate Britain to some second-class outer circle. In September 1994, Major made a speech in which he reiterated British adherence to the European ideal. 'Britain is irrevocably part of Europe', he said, 'but it must be the right sort of Europe'. And the right sort did not include an inner and outer core of member states. There was a wide range of policies within the EU and member states should be allowed to adopt differentiated approaches to these policies, as Denmark and the UK had adopted a different approach to monetary union. The key word was flexibility, which was 'essential to get the best out of Europe'.[9] Major concluded by attacking the idea of federalism and re-asserting Britain's belief in the nation state, seeing the European Union as an association of nation states, co-operating but each at their own speed and in their own interest.

The variable geometry option seemed to fade after the 1997 election because the Labour government adopted a more amenable approach towards the European idea, while the Conservatives under William Hague have retreated ever further from having anything to do with Europe. However, the debate over variable geometry has typified the Tory dilemma of not wanting to have anything to do with Europe but nevertheless wanting to influence the direction of European thinking. As Hugo Young said, 'It is well set to become the reality we do not want but may have to adjust to ... It would confront us with the choice we have so far avoided. Shall we be at the centre, or on the margin?'[10]

Summary

Any enlargement of the EU that takes place after the year 2000 is going to be far more difficult than any previous enlargements. Until now the countries that have entered the European Union have been typical of the West, sharing the norms and values of liberal democracy, supporters of free enterprise and market forces and the majority of them having been very securely within the Atlantic Alliance during the Cold War. Most of the applicant members on the other hand formed part of Comecon, the Soviet bloc and the Warsaw Pact during those years and do not share the values or experiences of the West. So far everyone seems to believe that expansion to the East is inevitable and a good thing for everyone concerned, both applicants and existing members. Yet the question that has to be asked is not only whether the countries of Eastern Europe will benefit from membership but, 'how far are the rich, secure and democratic states [of the West] prepared to compromise what they have achieved in order to share what they value with their neighbours [to the East]?'[11]

Notes

1   The European Commission Representation in the UK, *Background Briefing no. 37 – Inter-Governmental Conference (IGC)*, London, 20 April 2000.
2   George Jones and Ambrose Evans-Pritchard, 'Britain to set limit on Euro reforms', *Guardian*, 15 February 2000.
3   Jones and Evans-Pritchard, 'Britain to set limit on Euro reforms'.
4   The European Commission Representation in the UK, *Background Briefing no. 33 – Community Initiatives 2000-2006*, London, 26 July 1999.
5   Colin Pilkington, 'A people's Europe: federal or pragmatic?', in Lynton Robins and Bill Jones (eds), *Debates in British Politics Today*, Manchester University Press, Manchester, 2000.
6   Norman Lamont, address to the Selsdon Group of the Conservative Party, Bournemouth, 11 October 1994.
7   Edouard Balladur, prime minister of France, in an interview with *Le Figaro*, 30 August 1994.
8   The policy paper of the CDU/CSU was presented by Wolfgang Schäuble, leader of the CDU/CSU parliamentary party, and Karl Lamers, CDU foreign affairs spokesman, on 1 September 1994, but was not approved by the CDU/CSU government, as was made clear by Chancellor Kohl.
9   John Major, address to the University of Leiden, Netherlands, 6 September 1994.
10 Hugo Young, 'Major takes the soft approach to a hard core Europe', *Guardian*, 8 September 1994.
11 Stuart Croft, John Redmond, G. Wyn Rees and Mark Webber, *The Enlargement of Europe*, Manchester University Press, Manchester, 1999.

Appendix 1

Composition of the European Parliament after the elections of June 1999

1. PSE – 180
B – 5
DK – 3
D – 33
GR – 9
E – 24
F – 22
IRL – 1
I – 17
L – 2
NL – 6
A – 7
P – 12
FIN – 3
S – 6
UK – 30

2. PPE-ED– 233
B – 6
DK – 1
D – 53
GR – 9
E – 28
F – 21
IRL – 5
I – 34
L – 2
NL – 9
A – 7
P – 9
FIN – 5
S – 7
UK – 37

3. ELDR – 51
B – 5
DK -6
E – 3
IRL – 1
I – 8
L – 1
NL – 8
FIN – 5
S – 4
UK – 10

4. GUE/NGL – 42
DK – 1
D – 6
GR – 7
E – 4
F – 11
I – 6
NL –1
P – 2
FIN – 1
S – 3

5. VERTS-ALE – 48
B – 7
D – 7
E – 4
F – 9
IRL – 2
I – 2
L – 1
NL – 4
A – 2
FIN – 2
S – 2
UK – 6

6. UEdN – 30
DK – 1
F – 12
IRL – 6
I – 9
P – 2

7. EDD – 16	**8. TGI – 18**	**9. Unattached**
DK – 4	B – 2	**independents – 8**
F – 6	F – 5	(mostly far right)
NL – 3	I – 11	E – 1
UK – 3		F – 1
		A – 5
		UK – 1

Total

Belgium (B)	25
Denmark (DK)	16
Germany (D)	99
Greece (GR)	25
Spain (E)	64
France (F)	87
Ireland (IRL)	15
Italy (I)	87
Luxembourg (L)	6
Netherlands (NL)	31
Austria (A)	21
Portugal (P)	25
Finland (FIN)	16
Sweden (S)	22
United Kingdom (UK)	87
Parliament	*626*

Key to party groups
PSE – European Socialists
PPE-ED – European People's Party
ELDR – European Liberal, Democratic Reform
GUE/NGL – United Left/Nordic Green
VERTS-ALE – Greens and Radicals
UEdN – Europe of the Nations
EDD – Europe of Democracies and Diversities
TGI – Technical Group of Independents

Note
Figures based on statistical information provided on the website of the European Parliament as amended 17 January 2000: http://www.europarl.eu.int

Appendix 2

European elections

Percentage turnout in the fifteen members states 1979–99

Country	1979	1984	1989	1994	1999
Austria	–	–	–	67.7[1]	49.0
Belgium	91.4	92.2	90.7	90.7	90.0
Denmark	47.8	52.4	46.2	52.9	50.4
Finland	–	–	–	60.3[1]	30.1
France	60.7	56.7	48.7	52.7	47.0
Germany	65.7	56.8	62.3	60.0	45.2
Greece	78.6[2]	77.2	79.9	71.2	70.2
Ireland	63.6	47.6	68.3	44.0	50.5
Italy	84.9	83.4	81.5	74.8	70.8
Luxembourg	88.9	88.8	81.5	88.5	85.8
Netherlands	57.8	50.6	47.2	35.6	29.9
Portugal	–	72.4[3]	51.2	35.5	40.4
Spain	–	68.9[3]	54.6	59.6	64.4
Sweden	–	–	–	41.6[1]	38.3
United Kingdom	32.3	32.6	36.2	36.4	24.0
TOTAL	62.5	59.0	57.2	56.8	49.4

Notes:

Voting is compulsory in Belgium, Greece and Luxembourg

[1] First European elections for Austria, Finland and Sweden after accession, 1996

[2] First European election for Greece after accession, 1981

[3] First European elections for Spain and Portugal after accession, 1987

Source: European Parliament UK Office website:
http://www.europarl.eu.int/uk/elections/main.html

The status of areas of the British Isles not part of the United Kingdom

There are certain anomalous areas within the geographical boundaries of the European Union. Some of these are independent or autonomous enclaves within, or attached to, the national territory of a member state, such as the miniature states of San Marino and Vatican City within Italy. Other anomalous bodies are outlying or dependent parts of the member state which are often culturally or historically part of that state but which are not politically part of it: examples of this are the island of Greenland as an autonomous dependency of Denmark, or the Aaland Islands which are part of Finland but, as a tax-free zone, remain independent of the mother country.

Within the geographical area of the British Isles there are two full members of the European Union – the United Kingdom and the Republic of Ireland. There is also the Isle of Man which is subject to the British Crown but which is not part of the United Kingdom. It has its own administration in Tynwald, it has its own taxation system and indeed acts as a tax haven for individuals and companies, issuing its own bank notes and postage stamps. Not part of the British Isles but subject to the British Crown, with much the same characteristics of autonomous sovereignty as the Isle of Man, are the Channel Islands.

The position of Crown Dependencies of the Isle of Man and the Channel Islands as regards the European Community was dealt with in Articles 25/27 and Protocol Three of the UK Act of Accession. It was also detailed, along with the other anomalous areas, in a report paper of the Commission issued in 1993 (No. 20/93). Basically the situation is that neither the Isle of Man nor the Channel Islands are members of the EU politically and therefore are not eligible for any benefits of membership such as payments under the CAP, structural funds or regional aid. However, they do have Associated Territory status meaning that for customs purposes the territories concerned are regarded as being part of the single market and reap the benefits therefrom.

The position of Gibraltar vis-à-vis the EU has been clouded and hampered for many years by the dispute with Spain over the sovereignty of the Rock. In theory Gibraltar joined the EEC in 1973, at the same time as the UK joined. However, the hostility of Spain denied Gibraltar the full benefits of membership, resulting in the colony having what a spokesperson for the FCO called 'two-thirds membership of the EU'. Despite both Spain and the UK being full members of the EU with normally friendly relations, the issue of Gibraltar remained a bone of contention between them. On the side of Spain there were accusations that Gibraltar was used as a base by rings of criminals smuggling illegal immigrants, drugs and tobacco, as well as laundering the criminals' money. Gibraltar's complaint was about Spain's refusal to recognise passports, identity cards and driving licences issued by Gibraltar. As a weapon in the dispute Spain chose to block a whole series of EU directives, including extensive rules regulating cross-border company takeovers.

On 19 April 2000 the British and Spanish governments finally agreed a settlement after eight months of negotiations spurred on by Spanish fears of Gibraltar going it alone and aiming for independence of both Britain and Spain. Some terms of the agreement include:

- Gibraltar cannot have autonomous sovereignty; all legal and financial decisions and documents involving external relations must be endorsed by the UK government as an authority recognised by Spain as an effective financial regulator
- Spain will recognise passports, identity cards and driving licences issued by the local authority in Gibraltar as long as the Rock is identified as a British overseas territory
- Gibraltar police will cooperate fully with the Spanish police in the fight against crime
- banks and other financial institutions based in Gibraltar will be able to offer their services anywhere within the EU.

The next step is that Gibraltar will seek representation with the European Parliament and in Brussels. The UK can also use this slackening of border restriction to lead to a change in attitude towards the Schengen Agreement by the British government.

Note

Sources of information include: Colin Pilkington, *The Politics Today Companion to the British Constitution*, Manchester University Press, Manchester, 1999 and the Gibraltar Internet website: www.gibraltar.gi/

Appendix 4

Allocation of portfolios to EC commissioners

The appointment of commissioners to the Commission due to take office in January 2000 under president-designate Romano Prodi represented a major change in the Commission's way of working. The commissioners were very aware of the fact that their predecessors under Jacques Santer had been forced out of office by the European Parliament, accused of fraud, corruption and mismanagement. The Parliament had acquired new powers during that crisis, including the right to interrogate nominees to the Commission in a series of hearings modelled on the procedures of the United States Congress. During September 1999 the twenty nominees to Prodi's Commission faced intense questioning from MEPs over their financial and political pasts – not only in face to face interviews but also in a long series of written questions that were sent to each nominee, to which the proposed commissioner had to reply at equal length, also in writing. The questions asked and the responses made by each individual commissioner were published in full, both as printed matter and as part of the European Commission's website.

Prodi made it clear that he would not tolerate incompetence or sleaze in his team of commissioners and repeated that anyone offending his standards of conduct would be dismissed from office. He also promised a series of reforms in the Commission that would revolutionise the unwieldy structures of the Brussels bureaucracy, preparing it for the demands it is expected will be made by the forthcoming enlargement of the Community. In nominating his team in July 1999 he said, 'Faith in the commission is falling. What is required now is a revolution in the way it operates. I promised to launch a new era of change in the commission. This is what I intend to deliver, starting today. This is what the citizens, the people of Europe, expect of us.'

The list of twenty names submitted by Romano Prodi and duly approved by the European Parliament represented, as far as possible, a clean break with the past. Only four members survived from the Santer Commission. One of these was the British commissioner, Neil Kinnock, who was given the task of reforming not only the structures of the Commission but also the code of conduct expected of both commissioners and secretariat.

The Prodi Commission, members and their portfolios

Romano Prodi (Italy) – president
Neil Kinnock[†] (UK) – vice-president in charge of administrative reforms
Loyola de Palacio (Spain) – vice-president in charge of relations with the EP, Transport and Energy
Mario Monti[†] (Italy) – Competition
Franz Fischler[†] (Austria) – Agriculture
Erkki Liikanen[†] (Finland) – Enterprise and Information Society
Frits Bolkestein (Netherlands) – Internal Market
Philippe Busquin (Belgium) – Research
Pedro Solbes Mira (Spain) – Economic and Monetary Affairs
Poul Nielson (Denmark) – Development and Humanitarian Aid
Günter Verheaugen (Germany) – Enlargement
Chris Patten (UK) – External Relations
Pascal Lamy (France) – Trade
David Byrne (Ireland) – Health and Consumer Protection
Michel Barnier (France) – Regional Policy[*]
Viviane Reding (Luxembourg) – Education and Culture
Michaele Schreyer (Germany) – Budget
Margot Wallström (Sweden) – Environment
Antonio Vitorino (Portugal) – Justice and Home Affairs
Anna Diamantopoulou (Greece) – Employment and Social Affairs

Notes:
[†] Member of the Santer Commission which resigned in 1999.
[*] Also responsible for the Inter-Governmental Conference.
Note that this Commission will serve for five years, coincident with the term of the EP elected in 1999.

Source: Website of the European Commission: http://europa.eu.int; *Observer*, 11 July 1999.

Appendix 5

Rotation of the European presidency

The Presidency of the European Union rotates among member states, each of which in turn holds the responsibility for a period of six months. During their tenure ministers of the country holding the presidency will call Council meetings, decide the agenda, introduce initiatives and take the chair for all Council meetings. The presidency changes hands in the same order as members are seated in Council meetings, and this was originally by alphabetical order, according to how the country's name is spelt in its own language: the rota therefore beginning Belgie/Belgique, Danmark, Deutschland, Ellas, Espana and so on. It was intended that the rota should change after each complete cycle, each pair of countries which shared a year's presidencies reversing their alphabetical order. Thus the round which ended in 1992, with Portugal having the presidency in the first half of the year and the United Kingdom in the second half, began 1993 not with Belgium again but with Denmark, Belgium taking over in July.

However, the accession of three new members in January 1995, taking the number of members to fifteen, necessitated a revamping of the rota. This is still approximately alphabetical but some adjustments have been made. What will happen after the new cycle is completed is not known but that is not due to happen until the year 2003, by which time the enlargement by yet more new members will require a complete re-ordering of the system.

Year	January–June	July–December
1995		Spain
1996	Italy	Ireland
1997	Netherlands	Luxembourg
1998	United Kingdom	Austria
1999	Germany	Finland
2000	Portugal	France
2001	Sweden	Belgium
2002	Spain	Denmark
2003	Greece	(Source: http://europa.eu.int)

Appendix 6

British criteria for joining the euro

Soon after the Labour victory of 1997 it was made clear that the Blair government would follow very approximately the line on the single currency that had been adopted by the Major government. Britain had an opt-out from joining the single currency but reserved the right to join later if it seemed desirable to do so. There was a slight difference of emphasis between the Conservative and Labour positions. Even before the more hostile stance of William Hague the Conservative view was that Britain was best outside the single currency and it would take a great deal to convince the party of the benefits in joining. The position adopted by Gordon Brown and others in the Labour government is more that Britain will no doubt join the single currency at some point and it only remains to choose the most suitable moment.

On the British Treasury's website is a section devoted to the situation concerning the single currency. Included are the five questions drawn up by the Treasury to represent the pre-conditions for the UK to go ahead and join EMU and the euro. The questions are worded in a deliberately vague manner and are so vague as to allow partisans of both the pro and anti camps to use the questions to their own advantage. However, the questions are:

1 Would joining EMU create better working conditions for firms making long-term decisions to invest in the UK?
2 How would adopting the single currency affect our financial services?
3 Are business cycles and economic structures compatible so that we and others in Europe could live comfortably with euro interest rates on a permanent basis?
4 If problems do emerge, is there sufficient flexibility to deal with them?
5 Will joining EMU help to promote higher growth, stability and a lasting increase in jobs?

Appendix 7

Agencies established by the European Commission or the Council of Ministers

Like many other modern administrations the European Union has transferred some of its powers and functions to a number of executive agencies, all of which operate as autonomous bodies. New agencies are being formed all the time but the list which follows was the situation obtaining at January 2000.

European Agency for the Evaluation of Medicinal Products (EMEA): Based in London, the agency evaluates the pharmaceutical market on behalf of both the consumer and the industry. Operational as of 1 January 1995.

European Environment Agency (EEA): Based in Copenhagen, established in 1994 to gather information on the environment from all member countries and provide the necessary information base for the formulation of the Community's environmental policy.

European Training Foundation: Helps to provide vocational training in Central and Eastern Europe, the former Soviet Union and countries on the Mediter-ranean Basin. Provides technical assistance for the EU Tempus programme.

European Centre for the Development of Vocational Training (CEDEFOP): Founded in Berlin in 1975 but now based in Thessaloniki in Greece. Academic and technical support for vocational training throughout Europe.

European Monitoring Centre for Drugs and Drug Addiction (EMCDDA): Estab-lished 1994 and based in Lisbon. Exists to provide 'objective, reliable and comparable infor-mation at European level concerning drugs, drug addiction and their consequences'.

European Foundation for the Improvement of Living and Working Conditions: An autonomous body set up by the Council of Ministers in 1975. Located in Dublin. Aims to 'plan and establish better working and living conditions'.

Community Plant Variety Rights Office: Based in Angers, France, grants 'patents' to new varieties and strains of plants.

Office for Harmonisation in the Internal Market (OHIM): Established 1 September 1994 and based in Alicante. OHIM (Trade Marks and Designs) has the responsibility for the Community-wide registration and administration of trade marks and patented designs.

European Agency for Safety and Health at Work: Founded 27 October 1995 and located at Bilbao.

European Monitoring Centre on Racism and Xenophoblia: Established in 1998 and based in Vienna. Collects and collates data on racism, xenophobia and anti-Semitism, Europe-wide.

Translation Centre for Bodies in the European Union: Set up in 1994 and based in Luxembourg, the Centre provides translation services for all the bodies listed above.

Further reading and sources of information

This book has no bibliography, partly because texts referred to are fully listed after each chapter, and partly because the reason for writing the first edition of this book was the lack of authoritative texts at this level dealing with Britain's place in the European Union. And it remained true until fairly recently that it was difficult to find books about the Europe Union that were not highly academic. The last few years have, however, seen an increase in the number of books intended for the school and college market. Three such texts are:

Bainbridge, T. and Teasdale, A., *The Penguin Companion to the European Union*, Penguin, Harmondsworth, 1995.
Rose, R., *What is Europe? A Dynamic Perspective*. HarperCollins, London, 1996.
Watts, D., *The European Union*. Sheffield Hallam University Press for the Politics Association, Sheffield, 1996.

There is also a growing recognition of the European perspective in general politics text-books. For example, in the latest edition of the book edited by Bill Jones, *Politics UK* (Longman), published in summer 2000, all contributors to the book were instructed to include discussion of the European dimension as it relates to their own specialised political structure or process.

For a full academic analysis of EC institutions and policy-making processes, the best technical account remains the fundamental work by Neill Nugent, *The Government and Politics of the European Community* (Macmillan), the current version of which is the 4th edition, published in 1999. Nugent himself has also edited a number of annual reviews of EC matters, an early example being, *The European Community 1992: The Annual Review of Activities* (Blackwell, 1993).

There is a number of more general texts which has proved particularly useful in writing this revised edition. As a wonderful historical overview of Britain's relationship with Europe there is Hugo Young's monumental work, *This Blessed Plot*, published by Macmillan in 1998. For a fascinating view of the treatment of European issues by the British press, and the tabloid press in particular, the study by Anderson and Weymouth, *Insulting the Public?*, (Longman, 1999), is to be recommended. And, looking to the future, *The Enlargement of Europe* by Croft, Redmond, Rees and Webber was published in the Political Analyses series by Manchester University Press in 1999.

There are several academic and highly specialised journals related to European studies which concentrate on the EC, of which the *Journal of Common Market Studies* is probably the most prominent, but two journals which are specifically aimed at A-level and first-year undergraduate students (and their teachers) are *Politics Review*, published by Philip Allan Publishers of Deddington, Oxfordshire, and *Talking Politics*, the journal of the Politics Association. Both journals deal with politics as a whole but regularly feature studies of European issues, as can be seen by the frequency of references to the journals in the footnotes of this book. Among non-academic journals, the *Economist* has regular features dealing with European economics, industry and trade while both the *New Statesman* and the *Spectator* cover the field from time to time.

With the speed at which change takes place in the political world, the serious student cannot ignore the importance of the press in keeping up to date on developments in Europe. But it is not easy because, although the four 'quality' broadsheets – *Daily Telegraph*, *Guardian*, *Independent* and *The Times* – and their Sunday counterparts, together with the *Financial Times*, all pay some attention to European issues in both their news and feature pages, that coverage is not always as extensive as it may be, and the tabloid press often ignore European news stories entirely unless they are critical in a negative sense. It so happens that the newspaper most quoted in this book is the *Guardian* simply because it was one of the first newspapers to base a special correspondent in Brussels to cover developments in the EC and the newspaper has a reputation for reporting on Europe, albeit from the point of view of the eurorophiles.

The most prolific and most obvious source of information concerning the European Community is the European Commission itself. In Luxembourg the Commission produces a vast range of books and booklets covering all aspects of the constitution and workings of the European Union as well as a monthly journal, the *Bulletin of the European Communities*. All these are published in the various official languages of the Community. An idea of what is available can be gained from the publication *The European Community as a Publisher*, obtainable from the Commission's UK offices at Jean Monnet House, 8 Storey's Gate, London SW1P 3AT; Windsor House, 9/15 Beford Street, Belfast BT2 7EG; 4 Cathedral Road, PO Box 15, Cardiff CF1 9SG; 9 Alva Street, Edinburgh EH2 4PH. The UK Office of the Commission occasionally undertakes publication of literature aimed at Britain only, often in association with British government departments, and issued through the HMSO.

The Commission also maintains a network of information centres throughout the United Kingdom to serve the interests of small and medium-sized businesses, students and academics. There are twenty-four Euro Info Centres (EICs) for business information to be found within existing organisations in most major towns or cities. European Documentation Centres (EDCs) for students are found in academic institutions in forty towns or cities throughout the UK, some cities such as Birmingham, Coventry, Leeds and London having more than one EDC in different universities or colleges. Finally, to complement the above information centres, the EC maintains three depository libraries in Britain which receive copies of all EC documentation. Their telephone numbers are: London – 020 7798 2034; Liverpool – 0151 207 2147; Wetherby – 01937 546044.

As well as the Commission, the European Parliament also produces literature which can be obtained from The European Parliament UK Office, 2 Queen Anne's Gate, London SW1H 9AA. A mass of statistics about the EC, including an annual survey of statistical information, is produced by Eurostat, the Statistical Office of the EC. Eurostat publications should be available through the Commission but, if there is any difficulty, you can try the Office for Official Publications of the European Communities, 2 rue Mercier, 2985 Luxembourg.

A truly vast amount of information is available to anyone who has access to the Internet. The UK office of the Commission is at:

http://www.cec.org.uk

The UK office of the European Parliament is at:

http://www.europarl.en.int/uk/

Access through the UK offices provides links with home pages of the institutions themselves but the server for the whole European Union is at:

http://europa.eu.int

This server offers direct access to the home pages of all community institutions, basic information on the EU, official documents, databases, two years' worth of EU press releases, the Euro exchange rate and so on. This is a truly massive site which is available in all eleven languages of the Community and you should select English on the homepage before beginning any search of the site's web pages.

Another massive site, which is a little simpler since it merely offers two languages – English and German – is a directory-cum-search engine which can connect you with any institution or public body within the EU. This is:

http://www.gksoft.com/govt/en/eu.html

This same server also provides a similar directory service for most countries in the world. The pages for Great Britain and Northern Ireland are at:

http://www.gksoft.com/govt/en/gb.html

Index